STEPHANIE MAY WILSON

THE
Lipstick Gospel
DEVOTIONAL

Days of Saying Yes
to a God Who is
Anything But Boring

Stephanie May Wilson

©2017 Stephanie May Wilson
StephanieMayWilson.com

PUBLISHED BY ANTHEM WORKSHOP
ANTHEMWORKSHOP.COM

All Scripture quotations are taken from the Holy Bible, New International Version®, NIV®, Copyright © 1973, 1978, 1984, by International Bible Society.

To Gramie,

who taught me to always be the last one off the
dance floor, that making the trip to see your people
is always worth it, that a rainstorm is the perfect
time to go for a swim, and that a pinch of silliness
makes everything better.

Also by Stephanie May Wilson

THE LIPSTICK GOSPEL

THE LIPSTICK GOSPEL PRAYER JOURNAL

THE REAL GIRLS' GUIDE TO TAKING IT ALL OFF

DEAR BEST FRIENDS, WHERE ARE YOU?

MAKE THE MOST OF YOUR SINGLE LIFE

"Every day God invites us on the same kind of adventure. It's not a trip where He sends us a rigid itinerary, He simply invites us. God asks what it is He's made us to love, what it is that captures our attention, what feeds that deep indescribable need of our souls to experience the richness of the world He made. And then, leaning over us, He whispers, *Let's go do that together.*"

Bob Goff

Introduction

Hey sweet friend,

Welcome to *The Lipstick Gospel Devotional*! I am so happy to have you here.

Right this second, I wish I was inviting you into my living room and putting a steaming cup of coffee in your hands. I wish we could hang out for a while, sinking back into the couch together to talk about life—the hard parts, the best parts, and every part in between.

To me, this book is the next best thing. It's a safe place to rest, a place to be filled up with what you need for the day, a place to sort out the things you're going through, and to find out that no matter what those things are, you don't have to walk through them alone.

I am so excited for what's ahead!

Just a few years ago, I wrote a book called *The Lipstick Gospel*.

In the years leading up to the book, God transformed my world completely. I was totally lost in my life, deeply insecure, and I had just gone through a breakup that left me so heartbroken, I could feel it in my fingertips. But that's when God swooped in. He showed up in my life, surprising me completely with the depth of His love, the power of His healing, and a plan for my life that was better than anything I could have dreamt up on my own.

That's the story of *The Lipstick Gospel*, and I just knew I had to share it. I wanted to tell girls just like me what God had done in my life so they would know what He's capable of in theirs too!

(If you haven't read *The Lipstick Gospel* yet, let's get you a copy! The stories in this devotional will make way more sense once you've read it. You can pick up a copy at SMayWilsonShop.com!)

The response to the book has truly blown me away, but there's this question I'm often asked after people read it. It happened most recently at a sorority event where I was speaking.

When I got off the stage, one of the girls came up to me with a question. "I want this," she told me, "I've been a Christian all my life, but my relationship with God just isn't as rich and colorful as the one you described. I want to know God better, to trust Him, and to see Him do amazing things in my life. But I have no idea how to get there. What do I do next?"

That was the night I began writing this devotional—this book is my very best answer to her question.

It's an invitation to see God in a whole new way, to step into the story He has for you—perfectly fit for you, and full of love and life, and it's a practical guide for how to do that, one day at a time.

For years, I thought Christianity would take me away from the kind of life I wanted to live, but actually, it plopped me directly in the center of it. I've learned that God is a God of champagne, and best friends, and laughing so hard you cry (or pee your pants). He's trips to the mountains, and your toes in the sand, and love beyond anything you even knew your heart could hold. He's healing, and redemption, and the best friend you could ever have. And that's what we'll find the more we get to know Him.

Over the next 90 days, we're going on a journey toward a fuller relationship with God, with our lives, and with ourselves. I cannot wait to get started!

You with me? If so, go ahead and turn the page! Let's start walking together.

a New Beginning

"Satisfy us in the morning with your unfailing love,
that we may sing for joy and be glad all our days."

Psalm 90:14

There's something magical about new beginnings. We look forward to New Year's Day with hopeful resolutions—ringing in a fresh start with a toast of champagne and a kiss. School years are the same, brought in with new clothes and perfectly sharpened pencils—the summer and a new haircut giving us a chance to redefine ourselves.

Sometimes in life, we just need a clean slate. Have you ever felt this way? I know I have.

Some seasons are full of hurt and sadness and loss, leaving us wanting to close that chapter so we can begin a new one. Sometimes our years, and weeks, and moments start to feel a bit wild and out of control. We need a second to collect ourselves so we can start again. Sometimes we find ourselves in the rubble of more mistakes than we can count. We need to draw a line between who we were, and who we want to be. And sometimes I think we just need a do-over. Yesterday was okay, but we think today can be even better, we just need a fresh start.

I think this is why we love makeovers—whether it's our home, our hair, or our heart. We desire renewal, a clean slate, a new beginning, and this is why I love mornings.

Mornings are the new beginnings that come every single day. They're a chance to start over—our slate cleansed with a hot shower and warm coffee and, for me, by spending some time with God.

I began what I call "Quiet times" several years ago. They're not complicated, not fancy; it's just some time I carve out to spend with God each morning.

The day starts slowly, the morning cool. The house is quiet as I pad to the kitchen to start the coffee, the rich aroma warming the sleepy air. I settle in with my journal and my Bible, ready to connect with God before the day officially begins. I read a section out of a devotional, and then a passage out of the Bible. Sometimes I'm guided by a study, and sometimes I do it on my own. Then I pray, I always pray—the truth of my heart and my life that day captured in a scribbly, messy journal just between me and God.

You can tell if I haven't done this because I tend to fall apart somewhere around lunchtime. I get frazzled, insecure, short-tempered, and stressed out. I need this time—time with God each morning to pray through things that are on my mind.

Sometimes it feels like going to a gas station and filling up with the things that I need for the day: God's truth, His presence, His Spirit, yes please! Sometimes it feels more like cleaning out my closet—gathering up the mess, the things I don't know what to do with, and bringing them to someone who does.

God and I sort through the things that are weighing on my mind and my heart each morning, "Can you help me with this? What about this? I'm worried about this, can you carry that?" And to each question, His answer is the same, "Of course, sweet girl. Give it to me; I can take care of it. I've got this under control." (My interpretation of 1st Peter 5:7).

My quiet times each morning are a fresh start, a deep breath. They're a time of lifting weights off of my shoulders and handing them over to God, admitting with a bit of a blush and TONS of relief, that He is God and I am not, and thank God, right? We were never meant to do this on our own.

During this time over the last several years, God has become my very best friend. He's been the first one to hear about my triumphs and my total failures. He's been the one to listen as I've talked endlessly about jobs, and boys, and friends, and decisions. We really are walking through this life together—the big things, the little things, the scary things, and the funny things. We're in this together, God and I, and I've found there's nothing sweeter in the whole entire world.

That's what I want to invite you into over the next few months. I want to invite you into a relationship with God that is sweet, and close, and honest, and silly. I want to invite you to curl up with Him and get to know Him—telling Him about your life, your hopes, your dreams, and your fears.

I want you to know the God who created the heavens and the earth, the God who is big and sweeping and powerful and majestic. But I also want you to know the God who's become my very best friend, who I know wants to become yours too.

That's what we're doing in this quiet time we're carving out over the next several months. I can't wait for the friendship, the intimacy, and the adventure that's about to begin.

Over the next 90 days, what if you committed to starting your day with God? Use this devotional to get the conversation started. Then spend some time journaling and writing to Him, or praying out loud, or in your head. I promise you by the end of these 90 days God will feel closer than you can even imagine. He really can become your best bud and your very closest friend.

Life With God is Anything but Boring

"Look at the nations and watch—and be utterly
amazed. For I am going to do something in your days
that you would not believe, even if you were told."

Habakkuk 1:5

I had a girls night at my house a few weeks ago. It's one of my
favorite things to do. The pizza arrived just after my friends did.
We opened the boxes and popped open a bottle of wine. Then,
we each found a place to perch on the kitchen counter—hopping
down every so often to grab another slice. I don't know why conversations are so much better when they happen on kitchen count-
ers, but I've always found that they are.

We talked about all kinds of things that night—our relationships,
our friendships and, after awhile, our faith. That's when a friend
said something I haven't been able to stop thinking about since.
She said, "People need to stop talking about God like He's boring."
I couldn't agree more.

Christianity wasn't a part of my life growing up—it was just never
something I was interested in.

That only got worse somewhere around middle school when I
joined up with a youth group to go to camp. On our first night
there, my friends and I were curled up together on the top bunk
long after lights out. We were giggling, and talking about nail
polish, or something of equally grave importance when, all of a
sudden, one of the other youth group girls walked in. She was the
goodie-goodie of the youth group, the tattle-tale type so, up until
that moment, I'd kept my distance.

She walked in, surveyed the room, and then, seeing that our light was still on, she shook her head in disapproval. Then in the most motherly tone I've ever heard, she said, "It's time to go to bed girls."

Girls? I'm sorry, what?!

Then, having noticed our stunned expressions, and the fact that we weren't immediately hustling into our jammies, she said words I will never forget. Out of her 12-year-old mouth came the words, "Early to bed, early to rise, makes a person healthy, wealthy and wise."

Can I just remind you again that we were 12?

Now, I get that we shouldn't judge a book by its cover, or an entire belief system based off of one goodie-goodie in our youth group but, in that moment, I did.

I didn't really know any Christians—I had no idea what faith looked like in real life. So I figured this must be it! Christianity must be all about following the rules and being tattled on when you don't. It must be early to bed, and early to rise and, to be honest, that sounded terrible! It sounded like such a vanilla way to live! It sounded boring which made me think that God might be the very same way.

It sounded like signing up for a life with God meant signing yourself up for a lifetime of Friday night Bible studies, boring shoes, turtlenecks and absolutely zero fun. And that's not the life I wanted to live at all. I wanted a life full of best friends, and weekends at the beach, a life that sparkled and popped, a life that was full of life! And I was pretty sure God didn't know much about that, so I kept my distance for a long time.

But, just because I was keeping my distance from God didn't mean He was keeping His distance from me. He spent a long time pursuing me, loving me, and showing me what life could look like if I let Him have a say. So finally, I decided to give Him a chance.

The more I got to know Him, the more I found out that I'd been wrong about God. He isn't boring at all. In fact, He's the total opposite! And that's why I love the phrase my friend said that day. "People have to stop talking about God like He's boring," because, all too often, I think that we do.

We talk about God like He's a hall monitor with a clipboard—keeping us in line. "No running!" "Keep your voices down!" "Do that one more time, and you'll have detention!" But that isn't who God is!

God absolutely has ideas for how to best live our lives, and of course, that includes things He says not to do, but I just don't think that's the whole story. When we talk about God like this, we forget about all the other things He is: How powerful God is, how deeply good He is, how loving He is—He's also so much fun!

God is a God of champagne, and best friends, and laughing so hard you cry (or pee your pants). He's trips to the mountains, and your toes in the sand, and love beyond anything you even knew your heart could hold. He's healing, and redemption, and the best friend you could ever have. And that's what I started to see the more I got to know Him.

I thought that God would restrict my life, keep it small, keep it tucked away, but the opposite has been true.

Since getting to know God, I've gone on a safari in Tanzania, sipped cappuccinos in Rome, ridden elephants in Nepal, and skinny-dipped in Malaysia. I've fallen in love, and made amazing friends, and pursued my dreams, and started feeling beautiful in my own skin. Best of all, I've gotten to wake up every single day knowing that I'm on an adventure with the greatest storyteller of all time. I've gotten to know that, as I continue to give Him my love and my trust and, as I keep saying yes, my life will continue to be a story that's better than anything I could have ever asked for or imagined—so amazing, I wouldn't believe it even if I were told.

And you know what? This is true for you too. God has big plans for you, a beautiful life. They may look exactly like the ones He's had for me, or nothing like the ones He's had for me. And either will be amazing.

We serve an incredible, gigantic, mighty, adventurous God. And He's issuing you an invitation right now, today, to get to know Him better, to walk through life with Him, and to trust Him with your future. When we start walking with God and letting Him guide the way, there are such good things ahead, better than anything we could come up with on our own. All we have to do is say yes.

My friend was right. People have to stop talking about God like He's boring because nothing could be further from the truth.

Over the next few months, we're going to talk more in depth about how to invite God into specific areas of our lives, how to get to know Him better, how to start trusting Him more, how to see His goodness in the best and even the most broken parts of our lives. But, for today, take just a few minutes to reflect.

What does your life look like these days? What does your relationship with God look like? What things are going well, and what would you like to see change? Take a minute to journal about it, to write it down. That way, when we reach the end of our time together, you can go back and remember where you were when we started and truly see how much God has done. I can't wait for the journey that's ahead. See you back here tomorrow!

God Isn't One-Size-Fits-All

"Within your temple, O God, we meditate on your
unfailing love."

Psalm 48:9

The thing that kept me away from Christianity for so long is that, from what I could see from the outside, it just didn't look like me. From the small bit I knew, and with the clichés, stereotypes, and assumptions I used to fill in the rest of the picture, the practice of the Christian faith just didn't resonate with me.

It seemed to me that if you wanted to hang out with God, the only place to find Him would be at a boring Friday night Bible Study. You could find Him there or at church much too early on Sunday morning—complete with music you'd never listen to any other time, and a sermon you, quite frankly, couldn't relate to or even understand.

I'd only been to a few churches, and I'd never been to a Bible Study, so I didn't have much to go off of. But my cobbled together picture of the practice of Christianity was enough to convince me that I didn't want any part of it, something I believed for a really long time.

That all began to change, slowly of course, when I read the book *Eat, Pray, Love* by Elizabeth Gilbert. I read it during the worst breakup of my life, and it was all about the worst breakup of her life. So I decided that whatever my new friend Liz (I call her Liz because while we're not friends yet, I think we should be) did to get over her broken heart, I wanted to do too.

However, one of the things my friend Liz did to heal from her broken heart was to begin a relationship with God, which I found to be very confusing.

That was one escape route I'd never considered. Rebound relationship? Sure. Drinking too much? I'd considered that too. Traveling around the world on a journey of self-discovery? I was in, 1000%. But getting to know God? That was a route I hadn't considered—not since I rejected it years before.

But as I read her story carefully, my curiosity piqued. She was experiencing God through silence, through yoga, through meditation. I loved that. Those things seemed to be physical and spiritual all at once. They sounded holy, grounded, centered, otherworldly. They seemed like the antithesis of the dry practice of faith I'd always pictured in my mind.

I wanted that, exactly that! And that's why I didn't want to be a Christian, I told my best friends, Kelsey and Michelle, because Christians don't seek God that way. They protested, trying to show me that there are a million different ways of seeking God in Christianity—that it's not the one-size-fits-all situation I seemed to have assumed—but I just couldn't hear it.

One day when we were studying abroad in Spain, Kelsey and I went on a class field trip. We weren't going far, our teacher told us; we were going to a convent just down the street from our school. She wanted us to meet the nuns who live there.

We arrived a few minutes later at a big stone building with heavy wooden doors. There was a small window next to the doors, and our teacher gave it a little knock. The window swung open, and a nun with the kindest, warmest face poked her head out. "Magdalenas?" she inquired, and our teacher nodded. She handed out a basket of warm muffins that the nuns were famous for baking before she came around and opened the doors, ushering us inside.

The rooms were quiet and dark, candlelight flickered on the walls, and the air was thick with what I could only attribute to God's presence. God must live here with them, I thought. I just couldn't explain the deeply holy and spiritual feeling of the place any other way. I had goosebumps up and down my arms.

Our teacher asked them questions about the way they live and the way they worship, and they told us about their days in Spanish that seemed to dance right off their tongue.

"We wake up early," they told us, "and we spend a few hours each morning in quiet meditation with God."

Kelsey poked me in the ribs.

I couldn't believe what I'd just heard. This quiet holiness, this deeply spiritual place, it housed a way of interacting with God that felt holy, grounded, centered, physical and spiritual all at once—and they were Christians. I'd never seen Christianity look like this before.

We passed through a tiny gift shop as we left the convent, and I wandered through it lost in thought. They had candles, and a few Bibles, and a rosary with bright beads that were my favorite shade of pink. I ran my fingers over them for a moment, thinking about the nuns and the way they meet with God. Then I followed my teacher back out into the sunshine on the street.

A moment later, Kelsey emerged, pulling her hand out from behind her back. It was the pink rosary. She'd bought it for me, a little reminder of the fact that God isn't one-size-fits-all the way I thought He was.

The way I think about God began to transform that day. I started to see that God meets and speaks to each of us in different ways because we are all different. We can connect with Him and worship Him in all kinds of ways too.

You can find Him in Bible studies and on Sunday mornings in church, but you can also find Him in silence, in meditation, while eating magdalenas, or at the beach.

God got my attention in Europe over cappuccinos, through the words of best friends, and as I wandered the cobblestone streets in Spain. He speaks to me in fresh ways every time I'm near the ocean, as well as first thing in the morning over coffee as I pray in my journal. I learn the best, most transformative things from Him when we're traveling, and when God and I really need to talk something through together, we go for a long walk.

That's how I worship and connect best with God, but your way may be totally different.

Maybe meditation really is your thing, or yoga, or diving deep into heady theology. Maybe you're a big hiker, a painter, a singer, or a guitar player. Maybe you hear from God when you're on a long run or an even longer drive.

How you and God connect is unique and special to you; that's one of my favorite things about Him. So allow your way of seeking God to break out of any box you might have it in. Let yourself worship Him and connect with Him in new and different ways. He's waiting for you—arms wide open to invite you into a relationship that fits you and Him perfectly.

God isn't one-size-fits-all, and your worship doesn't have to be either. Spend some time today considering: How do you connect best with God? Where do you hear from Him most clearly? How do you learn from Him? If you aren't sure, try some different things this week. Take a long walk and listen to a sermon along the way, or go on a hike without your earbuds and let your mind wander. Take a yoga class, or a dance class, or buy some watercolors and paint. Your way of connecting to God will shift and change over time, of course, but it's a journey you can take a big step forward in today!

"Hello God, it's Nice to Meet You."

"Then you will call on me and come and pray to
me, and I will listen to you."

Jeremiah 29:12

When was the last time you talked to God? I mean really talked
to Him. I'm not talking about praying before a meal, or going to
church, or talking about Him, or listening to Christian radio.

When was the last time you had a conversation with Him—telling Him about your hopes, your dreams, the things you're worried
about, the things you could use some help with if He wouldn't mind?

Prayer is a tricky, confusing thing. It's like hope, or joy, or folding a
fitted sheet. It's one of those things that's hard to master; it's hard
to know if you're doing it right.

Prayer is particularly tough when you haven't done it in a while,
especially if your silence was on purpose—not just because you
were busy or thinking about other things. How do you pray when
you're mad at God, or when you've spent your entire life being
mad at Him? How do you break a silence like that? What on earth
do you say?

I've been through lots of seasons with God. Sometimes we're so
close, I feel like I can reach out and touch Him, and sometimes
He feels so far away from me that I'm sure He's left for good.
Sometimes I'm so distracted, so busy, and so focused on other
things I forget to talk to Him altogether. Then, when I realize how
long it's been, it's really hard to begin again.

When I'm at a stuck place in my prayers—whatever the reason—

there's one thing I come back to: one story that reminds me just how simple and wonderful prayer can be.

Like I mentioned yesterday, a large part of my journey toward becoming a Christian happened because of the book *Eat, Pray, Love* by Liz Gilbert.

I came to the book with a deeply broken heart, and it melted a part of myself I hadn't realized was frozen over. Liz's words opened up a whole new world for me that I had never even considered. I could have a relationship with God? Really? I never thought I wanted one, but suddenly I wasn't so sure.

It opened up the idea for me that God might be a pretty decent guy, that He might be a friend I could talk to, and that maybe it didn't take "thees" or "thous" or a perfect knowledge of the Bible to be close to Him. It made me wonder if maybe I could talk to Him, and maybe, just maybe, He'd listen.

It was in Eat Pray Love that I came across the story that changed my thoughts about prayer forever. From her position sobbing on the bathroom floor, a broken hearted Liz prays her very first prayer. She looks up at the ceiling and says, "Hello God. How are you? I'm Liz. It's nice to meet you." She stops herself before she says, "I've always been a big fan of your work," having nothing more than cocktail party etiquette to guide her in her very first prayer.

I love this. I love this down to my toes, and, when I'm at my best, this is exactly how I pray. I pray honestly, humbly, and with normal-person words: the kind I use when I'm talking to my best friend.

This story reminds me that our prayers don't have to be impressive. Really, how could we impress someone who hears all our thoughts (not just the good ones)? Our prayers can be honest and raw. I think that's how God likes them best because, at least in my life, He does His best work in me when I'm opened up to Him like that.

So, if you haven't prayed yet today, or if you haven't prayed ever, or if something's pulled you away from God and you're not sure how to begin again, try starting the way Liz Gilbert started, the way I start when I'm not sure what to say.

"Hi God. How are you? It's me, Stephanie. It's been a while." It's simple and honest, and He can take it from there.

> Carve out just a few minutes today to talk to God. It doesn't have to be perfect. Don't worry about having the right words, or anything fancy or profound to say. Spend just five or ten minutes, and tell God something honest and true today.

Gifts & Gratitude

"Rejoice always, pray continually, give thanks in all circumstances; for this is God's will for you in Christ Jesus."

1 Thessalonians 5:16-18

I don't know if you're allowed to say you love a whole continent, but I'm going to go ahead and say it. I love the continent of Africa. The places I've been have been beautiful, and captivating, and the people I've met there have completely rewired my heart, showing me love and sides of God's character beyond my wildest dreams.

But not every day there is easy (which, of course, is true at home, too) and, during one month when I was in Tanzania, I was having a really hard time. I found myself exhausted, uncomfortable, at the end of my rope, and really ready to come home. I needed a lifeline.

And that's when I met Ann Voskamp. Well, I didn't exactly meet her as much as I was introduced to her book, *One Thousand Gifts: A Dare to Live Fully Right Where You Are*—a book that has dramatically changed the way I will see God forever.

The concept of the book is simple, really. You make a list of things you're grateful for. Ann was trying to count to 1,000. It's simple, but the implications are profound.

As Ann counted gifts, as she took the time to zoom in and notice God's goodness and how He was taking care of her and so present in her days, she found herself experiencing so much joy and contentment getting to know Him in a whole new way.

Noticing His fingerprints on her life showed her so much about the God behind them, and before she even explained the concept fully, I was in.

I bought a tiny little notebook that was made by beautiful Tanzanian children with special needs and began to count. Sometimes the gifts were teeny—a cup of coffee or twenty extra minutes to sleep. Sometimes they were grand and sweeping—watching someone meet Jesus for the very first time, a relationship mended, a sick friend getting better.

The days we spent in Tanzania were hard sometimes, just like our days are here. They were long, hot, and required more of us than we thought we had to give. But the days we spent in Tanzania were good, also just like our days are here. God was in them, working through them, and providing for us in ways we would never have imagined. He was sprinkling reminders of His love in obvious places like hiding Easter eggs for children—delighted at our delight when we found them… just like He is here.

This way of living—looking for God, and the ways He's showing up in my life and taking care of me—changed my life completely. That season was hard for a million reasons (only a few of which were the lack of running water and cockroaches in more places than I even want to describe), but I've never been more joyful.

And so I continue the practice here today. "God thank you for this great cup of coffee. Thank you for time to talk on the phone with my best friend. Thank you for this Chipotle burrito (an item you'll find sprinkled all the way through my gratitude list!)." With each "Thank you" I see God more clearly, I feel Him more closely, and joy washes over me like a cool bucket shower on a hot Tanzanian day.

So let's do that together today. Let's intentionally look for God's fingerprints on our lives. They can be small, or sweeping, but each is a reminder of God's presence, God's provision for you, and how much God loves you.

Let's notice God and His creation and let's delight in it—snuggling up to Him and whispering "Thank you" in His ear.

Today, keep a piece of paper with you, or open a new note in your phone. Count 15 things you're grateful for throughout the day and, if you want to, you can do it tomorrow, and the next day too! Gratitude changes things. I can't wait for you to experience it!

Planting Seeds

> "I pray that out of His glorious riches He may
> strengthen you with power through His Spirit in
> your inner being."
>
> Ephesians 3:16

I think every single one of us has things in our lives that don't look the way we want them to. We don't have the community we wish we had, we're unhealthier physically than we ever thought we'd be, our relationship with God isn't as close as we wish it was, our relationships never seem to work out the way we hope they will. (Please tell me I'm not the only one who's found themselves in one (or all!) of these places.)

Not long ago I was walking around my favorite park in Nashville, taking a sort of inventory of my life: how's it going, what's going well, what would I like to see change? As I did, some flowers next to the trail caught my eye.

Now—I have to stop here and tell you that the analogy I'm about to share would be WAY better if I were one of those girls who has a really beautiful garden. Unfortunately, I am totally not that girl. I've killed everything I've ever tried to grow.

But seeing those flowers reminded me of basically the only thing I know to be true about gardening: if you want a particular thing to grow, you need to plant that kind of seed. The kind of seed you plant dictates what kind of plant is going to grow—and that's true every time! You wouldn't plant a tomato seed and find cucumbers growing out of the ground. That would never happen. It's impossible. If you plant tomato seeds, you get tomatoes. That's just how it works. This is such an obvious reality of gardening, right? (And trust me—if it's obvious to this plant-killer, it's obvious!)

But this principle is also true in our lives. The seeds we plant in our lives turn into something. If we want something specific to exist in our lives, those are the kinds of seeds we have to plant. There's a direct correlation, but if you're anything like me, you don't always think about it that way.

One of the things I want in my life more than anything else is a deep, connected, intimate relationship with God; and for years, I've known that one of the best ways for me to connect with Him is to spend time with Him each morning.

Well, to tell you the truth, there have been seasons in my life where I honestly haven't made that a priority. My alarm would go off, and I'd lay there for an hour, scrolling through my email, or worse, scrolling through social media. After a while, I found myself frustrated that I was not only feeling totally distant from God but also feeling totally overwhelmed by comparison.

I wanted to see my relationship with God grow and thrive, but those aren't the seeds I was planting each morning. Instead, I was spending tons of time looking at other people's lives on social media, and comparison shot up like a weed.

I let that go on for far longer than I should have before I realized that there was a correlation going on there. I wanted a close relationship with God, but I'd been planting seeds of comparison, so I decided to make a change. For one week, I committed to not checking my phone until after I'd spent time with God. I would wake up and start the day curled up in my favorite chair with my Bible, my journal, and a really great cup of coffee. No more than two days in, I started to feel closer to God again. It was amazing! Comparison had quieted down, and God's voice and presence in my life had turned back up.

There is such a direct connection between the decisions we make and the things that develop in our lives. It happens with how we take care of our bodies, in our relationships with friends, with our career, in the goals we want to achieve, in how we spend our money. If we're always putting things on our credit card without thinking, we're not going to get out of debt. If we're constantly eating cheeseburgers and never working out, we're probably not going to have a 6-pack (says a girl who knows from experience).

But the opposite is true as well. If we're honest with ourselves about where we want to be a year from now, and start planting those seeds in our lives, each day taking a small step in that direction, our goals and our dreams and the lives we want to live are absolutely possible! We'll get to reap the fruit of the great seeds we've sown.

When we make small intentional changes today, it can change our whole lives down the road. It has for me, and I know it can for you too!

Take some time to reflect today. What seeds are you planting today and what are they going to look like a year from now? Are there seeds you're planting today that are going to grow into things you don't want in your life? What do you want to be true about your life a year from now, and what seeds do you need to be planting today in order to make that a reality?

The Bible Is a Chocolate Book

> "Keep this Book of the Law always on your lips;
> meditate on it day and night, so that you may be
> careful to do everything written in it. Then you will
> be prosperous and successful."
>
> Joshua 1:8

When I first became a Christian, I was totally intimidated by the Bible. I picked up a free one at church, and it sat on my nightstand making me feel a little extra holy, but I never quite opened it to start to read.

The first time I ever actually read it was on my first mission trip to Costa Rica. They told us to bring one, so I did, and that first morning they gave us an hour to read and spend time with God. I had no idea where to start.

I whispered to my best friend, Michelle, who was sitting across the room, "Where do I start? I have no idea what I'm doing!"

"Start in Matthew," she whispered back. "There's a table of contents. You'll find it there." I fumbled until I found it, but the words read like gibberish. I closed it and took a deep breath, opting to journal instead.

The Bible is intimidating for a lot of reasons, but one of the main ones is its size. It's a massive book (technically, 66 books). If you were assigned that book in school you'd groan, and whine, and reach immediately for the CliffsNotes version—is that just me?

It's full of names we don't know how to pronounce and details too hard to remember. Its stories and lessons aren't just difficult to make sense of or relate to; they're even harder to put into practice.

Not only that, but at least to me, reading the Bible didn't sound fun. It sounded like the opposite actually. It sounded like the kind of thing you know you have to do but dread: like going to the gym, or getting an oil change, or eating a salad. But just a few months into my life as a Christian, I read a book, a passage specifically, that changed everything for me.

I don't know if you have ever read the book *Blue Like Jazz* by Donald Miller but, if you haven't, you should! There's a section in which Don is talking to a friend of his who is telling him about when she first became a Christian. This is how she describes it:

"We would eat chocolates and smoke cigarettes and read the Bible, which is the only way to do it, if you ask me. Don, the Bible is so good with chocolate. I always thought the Bible was more of a salad thing, you know, but it isn't. It is a chocolate thing."

I read that paragraph, and read it again. I skipped right over the cigarettes part, but my eyes stopped at the last sentence. "I always thought the Bible was more of a salad thing, you know, but it isn't. It's a chocolate thing."

She had me. That's exactly what I had always thought about the Bible. It was a salad thing, a "have to" instead of a "get to" —like folding your laundry or eating your vegetables. But she suggested that I might have gotten it all wrong, that there might be another side to the Bible I'd never experienced before.

All along, I'd known that the Bible was full of things I should know. When people explained things to me from it, they were helpful, and relevant, and insightful, and I wanted to be able to find those things for myself. Not only that, but I knew that if you wanted to get to know someone better, and that someone had written a book, you should probably read it. I wanted to get to know God better, and so I knew I should probably read His book.

I decided I wanted to give this Bible thing another try—this time looking for the chocolate in it—so that's exactly what I did.

Later that night, I put on my favorite album, turned on the twinkle lights above my bed, found the golden bar of Toblerone I'd been saving for such a time as this, and put on my favorite over-sized yoga pants. I climbed into my bed, opened my Bible, and began to read, popping a triangle of Toblerone in my mouth every few pages.

"The Bible isn't a salad book; it's a chocolate book." She was right!

I started in Matthew again, and read right through. I looked for the richness, the relationship, the lessons I could apply to my life, for places where God shows us who He is, for times when He shows us how much He loves us. And as I did, the Bible started to open up to me, to come alive beginning that day, and more and more the more I read.

Reading and understanding the Bible is a lifelong process. It's an almost magical book where it never gets old; every time you open it, it teaches you something new. I didn't just magically understand it overnight, but I did start to discover that it's so much more than first meets the eye.

It's a love story, an epic adventure, an eternal battle of good versus evil. It's a guide to life that makes way more sense than anything I've ever found in a magazine or the self-help aisle. It's full of stories of people just like you and me—messy people, imperfect people—and how God used them (and wants to use us!) to do miraculous, beautiful, life-changing things in His world. And that day, with the twinkle lights sparkling overhead and the Toblerone melting in my mouth, I started to see that for the very first time.

Later that year, I started the very first small group I've ever led. It was a small group of 27 (not small at all, now that I think about it) sorority girls—messy, honest, amazing women. We would gather in this cozy room above the church on oversized couches every

Sunday afternoon. We'd talk about God, and life, and where the two meet, and how to connect with God in real, authentic, and helpful ways.

But on our first day, before we got started with anything else, I wanted to set the tone for where we were going. I wanted them to know what was in store for them. So they walked in to find a stack of Bibles and a huge bowl of chocolates.

"The Bible isn't a salad book," I told them, "It's a chocolate book." Then, we began to read.

Carve out some time today (even if it's just a few minutes) to read the Bible in a whole new way. Curl up in something cozy, turn on something twinkly and bright, get your favorite chocolate, and read a passage of the Bible. If you need a place to start, begin by reading the book of Mark, and don't forget to look for the chocolate in it as you do. I promise you it's there.

If you're looking for a great Bible Study, check out *Seamless* by Angie Smith, or anything by Beth Moore. They've helped me understand the Bible so much better, and I know they will for you too!

God is Good; God is Faithful

"One thing God has spoken, two things have I
heard: that you, O God, are strong, and that you, O
Lord, are loving."

Psalm 62:11-12a

Fading on my palm in blue, ballpoint pen was this: "God is good;
God is faithful."

God's character is deeper and wider than the sea, but that day, I
just didn't care. That day, that's all I needed to know.

"God is good; God is faithful."

My room was a mess. It looked like I'd been robbed—the thieves
looking for anything valuable, finding nothing, and leaving heaps
of unfolded laundry behind.

The space by the front door looked like a mountain range. A mountain of books, a mountain of clothes, a mountain of shoes, and a
growing mountain of kitchen-wear that my mom kept adding to
every time she'd walk by.

I never thought I'd move away from Colorado. And I never imagined moving away would be so hard.

This wasn't my first time leaving Colorado by any means. I'd been
away from home more times than I could count. I'd pack up and
leave for a while, go on an adventure, study abroad, leave for camp,
and then wander home again. I thought I'd always wander home.

But this time, I knew something was different. This time I was leaving. Actually leaving.

This time I wasn't packing a bathing suit or two, some sunscreen, or a tent. This wasn't that kind of adventure.

This was the kind of adventure where you need to buy things like brooms and mops and dish towels. I had to buy mugs, and plates, and spoons, and things to clean my shower. I was moving away—22 hours away if we want to be exact.

22 hours is not a quick drive home. I can't swing by for lunch or to pick up a sweater I've forgotten. I can't go to church on Sunday with my parents or be there for every birthday party or baby shower. There's no deadline to my gone-ness. No day when I know for sure I'll be coming back.

I was moving away, and my heart ached under the possible permanence of it.

We all come to these moments in our lives: the moment when it's time to leave. Maybe it's a relationship, or a job, or a way of life, or maybe you're leaving for college, or to study abroad, or maybe like me, you're moving away from your hometown.

You know it's what you're supposed to do. You've thought it over a hundred times, prayed about it until you were totally out of words, asked for advice, insight, input, and this is the conclusion you came to. This is what you have to do.

It's going to be better, best, amazing. God is going to be there and do incredible things in this next season of your life. But when you're actually doing the leaving, hearing that doesn't really help. We're too busy aching from the loss of what we already know, and the fear and unfamiliarity of what's ahead.

There was no doubt in my mind that this was where I was supposed to go. I had been offered the perfect job in Georgia, and I knew I was supposed to take it. But that didn't make it any easier.

This was a lot of things—blessed, right, good, beautiful—but it was certainly not easy.

I knew that the next day I would be getting into my car, and driving away from my house, my home, my family, my friends, my life, for the last time for a long time. And the thought of it made me suck in a deep breath, hoping that if I filled my lungs with enough air, I wouldn't feel the deep pain in my chest.

This was an adventure, a new one, a great one. I knew God had amazing things in store. But, in that moment, I didn't need to be reminded of those things. In that moment, as I put one foot in front of the other into the next step of my life, I didn't need to know much of anything.

I just needed to know that God is good, and that God is faithful.

And He is.

Whatever you're facing today, that's what I want you to know too. God is good; God is faithful. Maybe you need to find a blue ballpoint pen and write it on your hand too. God is good; God is faithful. I promise He is and the best part is, He promises that too.

Enemies & Instant Coffee

"Love your enemies, do good to those who hate
you, bless those who curse you, pray for those
who mistreat you."

Luke 6:27-28

Have you ever had a person in your life you just couldn't like, no matter how hard you tried? Have you ever had a person in your life you were constantly comparing yourself to, and always coming up short?

I have. Her name is Kacie.

Kacie and I went on a long mission trip together, and in the beginning, everything was fine. But by the end of our first month, we despised each other. I wanted to be a writer, and so did Kacie. Kacie led worship and played the guitar, and I wanted to also. We both wanted to be leaders, wanted to be the smart one, both wanted to have our ideas heard, and our opinions respected. We were growing and changing and figuring out who we were, and the more time we spent together, the more who we wanted to be seemed the same.

We slid easily into roles of being fierce competitors and, after a few short weeks, enemies. We infuriated each other—the smallest things were enough to set us off. Our arguments were broken up by our teammates, our dislike for the other growing exponentially by the day. We watched in horror as ugly versions of ourselves rose to the surface—versions of ourselves we didn't even know existed.

Finally, in a swirl of anger, frustration, and downright dislike, we did what any normal person would do: we went to our leaders and asked to be separated. But they said no.

They said no because they recognized that Kacie and I were making each other better—drawing out insecurities, fears, and doubts that we had never seen in ourselves before. They knew that if Kacie and I could work through our issues with each other and ourselves, we would grow so much, and we could even be great friends. I wasn't convinced.

So there we were, stuck in a small group of people on the other side of the world. We shared everything—meals, bedrooms, free time, friends. Nothing was mine that wasn't also hers. There was no escaping her. So one day we decided to call a truce.

We'd read Jesus' command to His disciples, "Love your enemies, do good to those who hate you, bless those who curse you, pray for those who mistreat you." So we decided to give it a shot. We wanted to see if maybe, just maybe, He could fix what felt so irreparable.

"I'm not sure I'm ever going to like you," I said to her, and she agreed, "I honestly don't think this is going to work." But with no other options, we gave it a try anyway.

Every morning we prayed for each other and wrote each other a note of encouragement. We also brought each other a little gift. We were in Moldova at the time—a small country on the edge of Eastern Europe—living in a town where coffee was impossible to find. Desperate, we went to a small shop in the town's center and bought the family-sized box of 3-in-1 instant coffee packets. Powdered coffee, creamer, and sugar all in one. It sounds awful now but, for that month, it was a delicacy.

So we each bought a box and each morning we'd come into breakfast bringing a note, and coffee for ourselves and for the other. We'd trade off. I'd bring us coffee one day, and she'd bring it the next. Each day began with a prayer, a note, and a small gift either for or from someone I saw as my enemy.

I'm sure you can guess what happened, but I sure wouldn't have.

We discovered during that month just why Jesus tells us to love and pray for our enemies. It's not so we can be holy, or be better people—maybe a little bit, but that's not the full reason. As we prayed for each other, Kacie and I discovered that when you're praying for your enemy, at some point, they're not really your enemy anymore.

Love and prayer soften anger, hate, and comparison. It is the water that tends to the tiny shoot of compassion we often don't know is there.

My eyes for Kacie changed that month. I stopped seeing her as my enemy, as the source of my insecurity, or the roadblock keeping me from becoming the person I wanted to be. Despite my best efforts, and my desire to stay mad, distant, and cold, I started seeing her as a friend.

That month changed everything for our friendship. We went into that month as enemies and walked out as friends. Kacie was one of my closest friends for the rest of the year, and when the year was over, we moved down to Georgia together. Kacie was my partner in crime, my best bud, and still is.

Today, Kacie feels more like my sister than a friend. She's the one who knows me like the back of her hand—the best parts, and the very worst parts. She's had a major impact on who I've become and has been a constant thread of love tying together the last several years of my life.

There are people in the world we don't get along with. There are even people in the world we hate and, while not all of them will become our roommate, our best friend, or our sister, they just might.

Jesus tells us to love our enemies and pray for those who mistreat us. In the moment, nothing feels harder, or more unnatural, but

He tells us to do it anyway because you can't hate someone when you're praying for them. Prayer and love change everything.

Who came to mind as you read through that story? Is it someone you're angry at, or someone you compare yourself to, or someone you're constantly competing with? Maybe it's someone who truly is your enemy or even someone you hate. Pray for them today. Nothing feels more unnatural, I totally understand. But prayer really does change things. Maybe they won't become your best friend—if it's someone who's really hurt you, maybe they shouldn't. But anger and resentment are heavy things to carry, and praying for them will help set you free.

To the Girl with the Broken Heart...

"He has sent me to bind up the brokenhearted, to
proclaim freedom for the captives and release from
darkness for the prisoners, to proclaim the year
of the Lord's favor and the day of vengeance of
our God, to comfort all who mourn, and provide
for those who grieve in Zion—to bestow on them
a crown of beauty instead of ashes, the oil of joy
instead of mourning, and a garment of praise
instead of a spirit of despair."

Isaiah 61:1b-3a

About a year ago, I was talking to a girlfriend of mine when she
asked me a question I just haven't been able to get out of my head.
We were talking about *The Lipstick Gospel*, about the terrible heartbreak that turned my life around completely, and she asked me,
"If you could go back and tell yourself something when your heart
was so broken, what would you say to her?"

It took me about three seconds to know what I would want to
say—what I needed to hear when my heart was shattered like a
puzzle, into a thousand mixed-up pieces.

If you're going through something hard today, if you've lost something (or someone) important or if your heart is broken or bruised,
I thought you might need to hear this too. Here's what I'd say:

Sweet girl,

I am so sorry you're hurting right now. I know that right now it feels like darkness is everywhere—like everything you knew, were excited for, were counting on, and could rely on has crumbled.

I know your heart hurts in a way that is so tangible it's surprising—like you didn't know heartbreak actually hurt in your chest—but now you know it definitely does.

I want you to know that this is one of the hardest things you're ever going to go through. Broken hearts always are. They hurt in a way that's deeper than almost anything else we experience; it's just more personal somehow, more gut-wrenching. And so I want you to know that it's okay to be sad. It's okay to grieve. It's okay to cry. You've lost something really important, and the only way around this pain is through it.

But as you grieve, I want you to know, this darkness won't last forever. You don't have to see it today, and you don't even have to believe me, but it's true. Light is coming!

In the meantime, I'm not going to tell you to get over it or to pick yourself up and dust yourself off. You don't have to do any of that. All I am going to ask you to do is just cling to Jesus.

Spend as much time with Him as you can, tell Him everything you're thinking and feeling, invite Him into the places that hurt the most. Believe me when I tell you that He's right there with you, loving you, and taking care of you. He'll never leave you, never forsake you; He's right there with you and will always be. You can trust Him.

In this moment, sweet girl, that's my biggest piece of advice for you. Just stick close to Jesus, because He's the one who's going to heal this broken heart of yours. Not only that, He's the one who's going to redeem this.

I know this feels like the worst thing that's ever happened to you, and you might be right. But I want you to know, if you stick close to Jesus, He's going to use this heartbreak in your life in ways that are seriously beyond anything you could ever ask for or imagine.

God does His best work in us when we need Him the most, and that's absolutely what He's going to do in you through this. He's going to use this to transform you into the woman He created you to be. He's going to create things in you and through you that you actually wouldn't believe, even if you were told.

And I know it doesn't feel like it today—it couldn't possibly—but there will be a day when you're glad this happened. There will be a day when you look back on this dark time in your life with actual gratitude because the beauty God will bring up out of these ashes will be just that amazing.

So keep feeling the feelings, and journaling, and praying through this. Keep your heart tender and open for how God is working in your life. I promise you this pain won't last forever, and the way God will use this in your life is going to blow you away. You can trust Him.

You will make it through this, and joy beyond your wildest dreams will be waiting for you on the other side.

All my love,

Stephanie

Whatever hard thing you're navigating today, know that I'm praying for you. I'm praying for comfort, and peace, and hope, and redemption. Stick close to Jesus. He's going to bring beauty up from these ashes in your life too. I just know it!

Cathedrals

"The grass withers and the flowers fall, but the word
of our God endures forever."

Isaiah 40:8

There are so many places in the world where I love to meet with God, but one of my very favorites is inside a big, stone cathedral.

I've never gone to church in a cathedral, at least not regularly, not as my usual place of worship. My churches usually meet in slightly less grand locations. My favorite church back home meets in a revamped grocery store and, before that, it was an old feed store. Yes, certainly more humble.

But cathedrals are my favorite place to go when I need a quiet moment with God, when I don't want to be disturbed or greeted or asked questions. I go when I just need to sit there and be reminded of the fact that, while God is intimate and tender and loving, He's also grand and steadfast and holy.

My love for cathedrals began when I was really young, long before I ever got to know Jesus, before I became a Christian on my own.

My parents were married at the Washington National Cathedral in Washington, D.C. Every May, we would visit my grandparents who lived nearby as an early birthday celebration for me—the whole city celebrating as the cherry blossoms peeked out in all of their bright pink glory.

There's a festival right around that time on the grounds of the cathedral called The Flower Mart—complete with funnel cakes, rides, performances, and flowers everywhere. So we'd go for the festival, for my birthday, and for the cherry blossoms, too.

Every year, after we'd been on the rides, and before the stickiness of the funnel cake, we'd venture into the cathedral. We'd wander down the aisle of the nave, soaking in the majesty of the stone arches, with the red and blue and green light filtering down from the stained glass windows. Every time we visit, from when I was very young to just a few months ago, I always wander away from my family for a few minutes, taking a quiet moment to soak it all in.

Cathedrals, that one, in particular, remind me of something important about God, something I tend to forget in the course of my daily faith.

We live in a world full of advice. If you go to a bookstore, the advice and self-help section is enormous, taking up more than one row. Everyone seems to have a different idea of the best way to live, the things we should all be eating, how we should be cleaning our houses, the way of living life that will certainly change ours.

The problem is, the advice is always changing. There's always a new idea wiping away the old. There's always a new fad, always a new promise, "No, but THIS will REALLY change your life."

And on particularly hard days, I wonder if Christianity is just another version of this very same thing. Is this just another fad, just another way of living life, just another category of advice? I start to wonder: is this really something I can lean my life against, something that will hold my weight, something that will really change me?

Can I trust Christianity? Can I trust God? That's what I'm really asking. Then I step into a cathedral, and with quiet grandeur, it gives me my answer.

Cathedrals are massive, sturdy, and built to last. Many of them are centuries old pillars of a faith and a God that has been saving and transforming the lives of his people for thousands of years.

Construction of the Washington National Cathedral began in 1907. More than a hundred years ago, there was a group of people who loved God so much, who had been so changed by Jesus, by the Gospel, by the God of Christianity, that they wanted to build a pillar—a marker, a lasting holy place where people could go to spend time with Him, to get to know Him.

So much has changed since 1907. We've had two world wars since then; the first successful air flight was just four years before. We've gone through 20 presidents right there in Washington, DC., but the cathedral has not changed. That holy ground hasn't changed, and neither has the God it's dedicated to.

Notre Dame in Paris, one of my other favorite cathedrals, was built starting in the year 1163. I can't even begin to imagine what's changed since 1163. But it's amazing to think that there was a group of people almost a thousand years ago who loved God so much, and were so transformed by the Gospel, that they wanted to create a holy place dedicated to Him. They created a place where over 1000 years of people have come to spend time with Him, to get to know Him—the very same God they built the cathedral for in 1163, the very same God I worship today.

On particularly hard days, I start to lump Christianity together with so many other ways of living life. I start to think of the Bible as another self-help book instead of a love letter from the God of the universe.

Every so often I wonder if I can really trust this faith, if it can really change me, if it's sturdy, if it can hold me up in the midst of my sorrow, in the midst of my hardship. I start to wonder if I'm going to crash through the temporary wall if I lean on it too hard.

But walking into a cathedral reminds me of what's true. I lean against immovable stone pillars and stare up at the altar, and it reminds me that people have been worshipping the very same God for thousands of years. It reminds me that He's been transforming people all over the world, who speak all different languages, in all different time periods, for more years than I can count.

The God we love is bigger than culture, bigger than a fad, bigger than a changing philosophy.

He's immovable, holy, grand, timeless—He's been saving and transforming lives since long before I was born, and He will continue to long after I'm gone.

It makes me feel small but in the very best way. I feel small compared to a big God, and a big faith that's held up so many lives before mine. It reminds me that God's word, and God Himself, are pillars we can lean our lives against. Sometimes, we just need a quiet and majestic place like a cathedral to remind us.

> The Bible is a love letter from this eternal God. It's the same book that's been connecting people to Him and transforming their lives for thousands of years. Read Romans 8:28-39 today, and as you do, read it through this lens. Remember how many people have read those words and been changed by them throughout the years. Then, pray that God helps you see how sturdy of a pillar He is, that He's more than strong enough to hold up your life.

DAY TWELVE

Name Tags & Sticky Notes

"He has taken me to the banquet hall, and His
banner over me is love."

Song of Songs 2:4

There's a verse from Song of Solomon in the Bible that has gotten
stuck in my head and I swear will never leave. It says, "His banner
over me is love," and I love everything about that.

Can you picture what that would look like? I picture God holding
a gorgeous, hand-lettered banner high over our heads that follows
us everywhere we go. I picture it like one of those "Hi, my name is
_____" name tags, but totally over the top in the very best way.

"His banner over me is love." Love is my name tag. Love is how
I'm recognized, the umbrella that stretches over my head. I want
that to be my story, and I want that to be yours, too. Unfortunately,
more often than not, I think we're standing under banners that say
drastically different things.

When you think of the banner over your head, what does it say?
What words do you carry as you walk through your life? What
words define you? I have a feeling that "love" might not be at the
top of that list.

I began thinking about this a few years ago and was mulling it over
with a friend when she suggested I make a list of the name tags I
was wearing in place of "love." "What do you believe to be true
about yourself?" she asked me. I realized I didn't know, but I wanted
to find out. I grabbed my journal and began to make a list. What
words actually define me? What words am I wearing around like a
name tag? What words do I actually believe to be true about myself?

The list looked something like this:

I am...

A lot of work

Not worth the effort

Unlovable

Annoying

Somebody's last choice

Awkward

Insecure

These words, these horrible, devastating words, were the things I honestly believed about myself—I had just never said them out loud.

I read down the list again and again. I could remember with painful clarity all the times those words had made me feel small, all the times those words held me back from taking chances, or believing in myself, or believing other people when they told me I was loved or good enough.

Those words felt so true about me, but they stood in stark contrast to that verse. "His banner over me is love." Does that mean God sees me differently than I see me? I wanted to know!

I spent hours combing through the Bible looking for the words God uses to define us. And when I was finished, I took a deep breath. God and I disagreed about me, it turns out. We disagreed quite a lot. I didn't think I was good enough, but God did. In fact, God says I'm chosen, that I'm enough, perfectly and wonderfully made, that there is no flaw in me.

His words felt too good to be true, but I wasn't about to argue with Him. Instead, I simply wanted to believe Him. This whisper had begun to echo in my heart. "What could life look like if I actually believed these things to be true?"

It wasn't going to be easy, and it wasn't going to be instant. But I wanted to believe God when He said those things, and I couldn't think of a better way to start than by creating some new name tags. I grabbed a Sharpie and a stack of sticky notes and got to work.

"Chosen, Loved, Enough, Daughter, Beautiful..."

I made one, then two, and then went crazy and made about 20. I stuck God's words about me all over my room, surrounding my bed with them to make sure they'd be the first and last thing I saw every day. I began sleeping under a sticky note that quite literally said "Love," letting that banner remind me of the truth until I really started to believe it.

Over the next several months, things began to change. I began to stand taller, somehow. I felt new, different, and confident in a way I never had before.

Every so often, when I'm tired, or overwhelmed, or extra emotional, those old name tags creep back in. But these days, when they do, I chase them back out with God's truth—knowing that what He says about me is stronger and truer than they can ever be.

And today, more than ever, I can see that banner over my head, and the banner says "love."

What banner are you living under? Who does God say you are? Is it time to rewrite some name tags of your own? Turn to the next page to see a list of the things God says about you (and that list is just the beginning!) Grab a stack of sticky notes, and a Sharpie, and try it yourself! I truly believe you'll start to stand a little taller, just like I did.

God's Truth About Me

God loves me and has chosen me.

1 Thessalonians 1:4

I have nothing to worry about; God is taking care of me.

Matthew 6:25-34

The peace of God guards my heart and mind.

Philippians 4:7

I don't have to be afraid of God, or of talking to God.
I can approach Him with freedom and confidence.

Ephesians 3:12

I was created by God to do good, beautiful things.

Ephesians 2:10

I am FREE!

Galatians 5:1

I am a child of God.

John 1:12

I am fearfully and wonderfully made.

Psalm 139:14

No matter where I go, God will be there with me,
guiding me and taking care of me.

Psalm 139:7-12

God's Truth About Me

I am chosen by God.

1 Peter 2:9

I don't have to live in darkness. I have been called
by God into His wonderful light!

1 Peter 2:9

I can trust that God's plans for me are good.

Jeremiah 29:11

God delights in me.

Zephaniah 3:17

God will never leave me or forsake me.

Hebrews 13:5

God has not given me a spirit of fear, but of power,
love, and a sound mind.

2 Timothy 1:7

In all things, God is working for my good.

Romans 8:28

His banner over me is love.

Song of Songs 1:4b

I'm beautiful. There is no flaw in me.

Song of Songs 4:7

God Is Still Here

> "Be strong and courageous. Do not be afraid or terrified because of them, for the Lord your God goes with you; He will never leave you nor forsake you."
>
> Deuteronomy 31:6

I have this fear that sneaks up on me in every life transition. Every time I move to a new place, I always feel like God may have been left behind. It's not that I got ahead of Him. I don't think I can outrun God. But he was so close to me in the place where I was before; I worry that maybe He didn't come with me to the place where I am now.

In some ways the fear makes sense. When we meet God profoundly somewhere—on a mission trip, or at our old church, or in our college ministry, or when we live in a particular city—it's really hard to move on from that place, because suddenly our relationship with God feels different. If we found Him to be so close in this one chapel, we're at a loss when that chapel isn't available to us anymore. Where do we go to meet with Him now?

I've always experienced this when I've gone somewhere new, but the first time it happened was just after my first mission trip to Costa Rica.

When I arrived back in Colorado after the trip, my parents brought me home for a night before I headed back up to college. Showered, and fed, my clothes safely in the washing machine, I climbed into bed and took a long, deep breath. So much had happened in the last ten days. It almost seemed like a lifetime had passed since I'd packed my bags just a week and a half before.

My mind flipped through a slideshow of my time in Costa Rica, and as I remembered, I started to cry—one tear and then another, and then big gasping sobs. I couldn't identify why I was crying at first, but then it hit me. I missed God. I missed Him desperately, and I was afraid that the God I'd gotten to know in Costa Rica hadn't come home with me to Colorado.

This happens to me every time I go somewhere new. You'd think I'd have learned by now, but my heart still worries.

When I left Colorado for Ghana, and then Ghana for Colorado; when I left Colorado for LA, and then LA to travel around the world; when I moved to Georgia I had to remember that the God of Colorado lives there, too. Then, most recently, when I left Georgia for Nashville, I had to remind myself that God didn't stay behind.

One of my favorite verses is in Deuteronomy 31:6. It says, "Be strong and courageous. Do not be afraid or terrified because of them, for the Lord your God goes with you; he will never leave you nor forsake you."

God goes with me. He will never leave me or forsake me. I need that reminder all the time. Don't you?

Life feels big and scary sometimes, especially when we're attempting new things, or going through a transition. When we're starting a job, or buying a house, or getting married, or ending a relationship; when we're beginning a new year of school or graduating from college life feels big and scary, and we need to know that God is with us!

It's like a kid's first day of school. He's ready; He has his new shoes and his shiny new lunchbox. It's a moment he's been preparing for all summer but, as he steps into his new classroom, he reaches back, just to make sure his dad came with him. I do that all the time—reaching back, looking up and around, just to make sure God's still there.

That's what I do when I start to worry that God isn't with me. Every once in awhile, I'll look up and just say, "Hey God, you still there?" And I feel like He smiles. It's not a profound prayer, but it's just my way of reminding myself that I'm not alone. God will never leave me or forsake me, not now, not ever. And He'll never leave you either.

I love the way Psalm 139:7-10 says it. It says, "Where can I go from your Spirit? Where can I flee from your presence? If I go up to the heavens, you are there; if I make my bed in the depths, you are there. If I rise on the wings of the dawn, if I settle on the far side of the sea, even there your hand will guide me, your right hand will hold me fast."

God will never leave us. There's nowhere we can go where He isn't there too. You can trust that. Take some time to reflect on that today, and write yourself a reminder. Write it on a sticky note and put it on your bathroom mirror, above your bed, or behind your steering wheel. Keep it somewhere you'll be able to see it easily when those shaky moments come, and you need a reminder that God is right there beside you.

Reclaiming Delight

"Give thanks to the Lord, for He is good; His love
endures forever."

Psalm 107:1

Something really sad happens to us as we grow up. We lose not only our baby fat but also our whimsy, our delight, our ability to dream.

Kids don't need to be told to dream. They don't need to be told that life is fun or that the world is lovely or that blanket forts are the best. They run after those things, birthday cake smeared in their hair, with shoes an inconvenient afterthought.

But all of that seems to fade as we get older. Somewhere along the line, I think we decide we're a bit too old for fun, that there's no time for whimsy, and that there's no room for dreaming in between meetings, and mortgages, and finding an investment adviser. I think a lot of people feel that way.

I'm a full-fledged adult these days, although my dad who's in his 60s says no matter how old you get, you never really feel like it. In a lot of ways, my life is full of responsibility. I own a house and a car. I'm in charge of making sure we have trash bags and that our water bill is paid. I keep (and even stick to) a budget. I even own a business! I'm saving for retirement, and I pay my taxes on time, and I even floss on a regular basis (I can't believe it either.)

But, even though I'm not a kiddo anymore, I decided a long time ago that there were parts of being a kid I wasn't willing to give up. Yes, we have to grow up, and I'm glad we do—being a grown up is great in so many ways. But grown up things don't always have to lie heavily like an x-ray smock on our chests, weighing down every moment and squashing out every spark of joy. But sometimes we act that way. So I feel like I need to stand on a soap box and yell, or sing as I jump on the bed, that being an adult doesn't have to be boring. Responsibility isn't the death of delight!

Life is still fun and funny and silly and weird. The world is so full of lovely things—things just waiting to be played in, tested out, and explored. There's not an age limit to playing with Play-Doh or flying a kite or singing extra loud in the car. Sleepovers with best friends should happen at every age, along with late-night runs to the store for ice cream, and trips to the zoo. We can blow bubbles, and do cannonballs into the water, and wear bows in our hair just because it's Tuesday.

Let's be responsible and save money and buy a house if we want to. Let's floss, and stick to a budget, and pursue our goals and be wise. Those things are good and right—let's do them! Let's do them all.

But let's also keep our joy, our whimsy, and our ability to dance when the moment is right—and especially when it's not. Let's laugh, and play, and drink orange juice straight out of the carton. Let's remember that blanket forts are the best, and that footie pajamas are the very definition of cozy (Let's get a pair or two—they come in adult sizes now!).

No matter how old we get, or how responsible we become, let's remember that life is beautiful and fun and ridiculously funny. Let's hold onto our dreams and our ability to laugh so hard it hurts. Let's leave our shoes behind every so often, and maybe get a bit of birthday cake in our hair.

What's one way that you can add a spark of joy and whimsy back into your life today? You may have a big day at work, but what about stopping by the store on your way home and buying some bubbles? What about pinning a bow in your hair on the day of a big test? What if you took a break from a big project and ate ice cream for lunch? Let's add some whimsy into our day today. Shall we?

Don't Wash My Blanket

"Now to Him who is able to do immeasurably more than all we ask or imagine, according to His power that is at work within us."

Ephesians 3:20

One of my favorite books when I was little was called *Don't Wash My Blanket*. It was a small book, square, with thick cardboard pages, and it depicted a little boy and his very favorite blanket. The blanket was a cape, and a fort, and his very best friend. More than anything, the little boy didn't want his mom to take the blanket away, never mind the fact that she was taking it to wash it and would, of course, bring it back.

I love this story even now because it reminds me of one of the hardest things about being a Christian: Trusting God with something we love.

When I was in college, there was one thing I wanted for my life above anything else: I wanted to be a journalist. I thought about it constantly, remaking my five-year plan every few weeks just so I could think it through again. I wanted to be a network anchor on CNN or NBC or the Today Show—I didn't care which. I wanted to change the world with my stories, and I couldn't wait for my career to begin.

Five months before graduation, I gave up my dream completely.

I was sitting in a damp chapel in Costa Rica on the last day of my first mission trip. I'd experienced God that week, had come face to face with Him, had begun a relationship with Him, and it had changed everything.

As I was sitting there in the glow of this transformative experience, I knew I wanted to give my life to God fully. I knew I wanted to know Him better, to go on an adventure with Him and find out what He was capable of doing with my life. But in order to dive in fully, I knew I had to let go of the things I'd been holding onto so tightly.

If I wanted God to do something amazing with my life, I was going to need to give Him some room. I had to trust Him with my blanket. So, there in that chapel, I gave God my dream of being a journalist.

When I graduated from college, I took a job in a church, taking myself out of the journalism ring for good. Then, someone told me about a year-long mission trip that goes all around the world, and I felt like that's where God was leading me next. Then when I I got home from that trip, I felt God leading me to move to Georgia—a region of the country I'd never considered nor visited, and one I had no interest in calling home.

The road I walked with God took me all over the world, and through decisions I never thought I'd make, and experiences I never would have chosen on my own. But with each decision, God gave me something I would never have had if I'd been following my own map.

Working at the church, I got to lead a small group of sorority women, girls who stole my heart and taught me the power of walking through life together.

In going on that mission trip we were asked to keep a blog and, as I blogged my way around the globe, I was knocked over by a passion I never knew existed within me. It was on that trip that I became a writer.

Then, in moving to Georgia, I got to pursue my dreams of writing and speaking, and on my first day, I met a guy named Carl—a coworker of mine who ended up becoming my husband.

There's nothing we hold onto in our lives quite like our plans and our dreams. We grip them, keeping a constant eye on them, warding off anyone who's going to change them or mess them up, including God.

It's hard—gut-wrenching even—to trust God with the things that matter to us most. In handing them over, there's always the chance He'll change them. But when we trust God with our blankets, with our most prized dreams and plans, He does things with them we never could have done on our own.

He washes them and makes them better, transforming our blankets into a real life capes, or forts, or best friends. And we find ourselves living a life and a story that's more thrilling, more beautiful, and more magical than anything we could have dreamt up on our own.

What would it look like to trust God with your dreams? What do you stand to lose and, even more importantly, what do you stand to gain? Take some time to talk with God about it today. What if you invited Him into one of those dreams today? I can't wait to see what He does with it.

Grace Jeans

"Grace and peace be yours in abundance through
the knowledge of God and of Jesus our Lord."

2 Peter 1:2

I'm not sure how it happened exactly. It didn't happen overnight, or even quickly, and I certainly didn't realize it, but somehow in the six or so months after my husband and I got married, I got bigger.

Maybe it was the date nights or the fact that he was teaching me how to cook. Maybe it was the fact that my wedding dress had fit and the photos were taken—done and done. Maybe it was the fact that I couldn't peel myself out of bed in the morning, couldn't bring myself to trade in the world's greatest cuddler for a treadmill. Or maybe it was all the life transition we were going through— newlyweds in a new city with new jobs. New everything! It was probably a combination of all of the above.

I really started noticing it sometime in the fall. I traded my sun-dresses for skinny jeans, and I realized I wasn't quite so skinny anymore. They didn't fit like the glove they used to be. Instead, they were miserable to wiggle into. They took a fight to get up and over my hips, and an army to close, and once I was finally in them (which was still possible, although barely), I began counting the minutes until I could take them off again.

I felt gross. I felt uncomfortable. But worst of all, I was furious with myself.

How could you have let this happen? I berated myself. I'd glare at my fleshy body every time it had the nerve to pass a mirror. I thought that if I was mean enough to myself about it, or disgusted enough, that something in that would make me change.

Have you ever thought that?

I catch myself doing this with lots of things—trying to motivate myself through criticism, or intimidation, or by being just plain mean. I think I've always figured that if I was my toughest critic, nobody could be tougher on me. I found comfort in that somehow, although I'm not sure exactly how.

So I continued to wear my skinny jeans. I continued to force myself to put them on and tried to squeeze myself into healthy submission. *You have to eat a salad today. Have you seen yourself?* I'd ask myself with disdain. And when I'd inevitably fall off the wagon and order a cheeseburger, my inner critic was relentless.

Life went on like this for months, until I'd finally just had enough. I desperately need some grace, I found myself thinking one day. So against everything I'd done before, that's exactly what I decided to give myself.

My mom and I were going shopping a few days later, and I made it my mission to buy the softest things I could find. Soft, flowy tanks, loose fitting shirts, and oversized sweaters that made me feel small and tucked in—cozy instead of squeezed.

For the first time, I shopped like I loved myself, like I wanted to do something nice for myself instead of punishing myself until my body got its act together. And then I arrived in the jean section.

I wavered. I've always been the same jean size. Buying a size up felt like admitting defeat. *If I buy a bigger size, what will ever make me lose weight?* But then I remembered grace. I remembered how those squeezy, awful jeans made me feel, and I remembered that I had decided to love myself, so I marched straight in and asked for the next size up.

The saleswoman knocked on my dressing room door and handed

me a pair of jeans. "They're the size you asked for," she said. "They're high-rise, and they're stretchy. I think you'll love them." They felt like butter in my hands.

Slipping them on was one of the best feelings I'd ever felt. It was like slipping down between cool sheets at the end of a long day or taking a shower for the first time after a long camping trip. They felt delicious. They were soft and forgiving, and buttoned up perfectly over my hips, hemming me in just enough, but not too much.

I could move in them, breathe in them, be in them without counting the seconds until I could take them off again. Best of all, I felt beautiful in them, and with grace wrapped around my slightly bigger body, I felt like maybe, just maybe, I was okay after all.

The thing is, we're not perfect. Sometimes life happens, and we end up in situations that we never intended. We make a mistake, lose our way, or get distracted for a bit too long and end up lost. We find ourselves being someone we never intended to be, making bad decisions, or even just lazy ones. And, in response, it's easy to berate ourselves. It's easy to become our own worst critic, shoving ourselves back into line as though that will help.

But what I learned that fall is that criticism really doesn't help. We don't need to be berated or shown again and again all that we've done wrong. Being mean to ourselves doesn't make us hustle more, and it didn't make me lose the weight faster to punish myself for putting it on in the first place.

What we really need is grace.

A few months later, I was getting ready for work. I grabbed my favorite jeans, about to slip them on, when I realized all that had changed in the last few months. I'd been able to get dressed for work without feeling awful about myself. I'd been able to concentrate while sitting at my desk because I didn't have denim squeezing my middle too tight. I'd felt comfortable in my own skin for the first time in a long time and, much to my amazement I'd even shed a few pounds.

"Thank you, Jesus," I began to pray. "Thank you for loving me, and accepting me, and giving me heaping amounts of grace, and thank you for helping me give grace to myself too... " Just as I said that, I looked down at the pair of jeans in my hand. Stitched into the label was a word, plain as day, that I'd never noticed before:

"Grace."

Are there any areas of your life today where you feel like you've fallen short? Maybe you made a mistake, or dropped the ball, or let things slide, or even messed up big. In situations like these, it's easy to be hard on ourselves, to punish ourselves even, but treating ourselves that way never gets us where we want to go. So today, think of a way you can show yourself grace. Maybe it's doing something kind for yourself, maybe it's saying once and for all, "I forgive you." Maybe it's letting yourself rest, or talking to yourself more kindly. God has infinite grace for you in this situation and in all of them. So today, let's follow His lead and have some grace for ourselves too.

Tears & Strength

> "Therefore, as God's chosen people, holy and dearly
> loved, clothe yourselves with compassion, kindness,
> humility, gentleness and patience. And over all these
> virtues put on love, which binds them all together in
> perfect unity."
>
> Colossians 3:12,14

I have a mentor who I just love to pieces. Her name is Jackie, and she's beautiful and wise and really, really funny. But one of my favorite parts about Jackie is how much she cries. When it comes to something beautiful, or something hard, something switches in her heart and tears begin to pool in her ocean-blue eyes. She's not weeping, or even crying really—just continuing on as tears release peacefully one by one.

Her tears speak of love, of her resolve to overcome, and of sorrow for those who have been wronged. They speak of a deep connection to the world, and to the people she loves in it. They speak to the fact that she's paying attention. She's brave with her heart, wide open in the moment with you, present for the joy and present for the pain too. Her tears remind me of Jesus. They mourn, they fight, and they're not afraid of the depth and ferocity that it takes to truly love.

Jackie's tears aren't weak. They're a picture of strength. They're holy. And Jackie's tears have helped me embrace, and finally admit out loud that I am a major, major crier. It's a big deal that I can say it out loud like that because that hasn't always been the case.

I've always been sensitive, don't let me fool you. But I've always hated that about myself with the fury of a thousand hurt feelings. I saw no redemptive quality in having a heart that bruised like a peach. I envied my tougher friends—the way life would bounce off their thick skin while piercing me to my core. So, for years, I did everything I could to be different, to toughen up, or at least to hide my tender insides.

Sensitivity isn't something we usually embrace or value. It's something we hide, something we cover up and downplay saying, "No really, I'm fine." We throw on our sunglasses when we feel like we're about to cry because we don't want anyone to see. Tears feel weak, to hurt feels weak, emotions feel weak, at least that's always what I thought anyway. But then I met Jackie, and things started to change.

I think sometimes we just need someone to go before us, to show us how to feel our feelings, and still be strong. We need someone to show us in real life that the two are actually one and the same.

The fact that Jackie felt things, and could say she felt them, and didn't try to hide or apologize, woke something up in me. And slowly but surely, since then, I've been making friends with my emotions—embracing them as not just an okay part of me but actually one of the best.

These days, I'm a total crier. There's no hiding it, not even for a second. I cry at everything. I cry when I'm sad, when I'm frustrated, and especially when I'm angry. I cry when the world is hard, when it's confusing, or when it's really, really scary. More than any other time, I cry when things are beautiful. Any display of kindness, or compassion, or strength, or love is enough to wring out my tear ducts completely. My emotions escape my eyes and slip down my cheeks before my brain has the chance to intervene.

And I've learned to love that about myself, because now it actually feels like a strength. I'm connected to the world around me; I'm really paying attention. I'm seeing the pain, and noticing the joy, and I'm allowing myself to bravely feel both. I'm secure enough and confident enough to stand in the world with my heart open, and to do it without my sunglasses on, just like Jackie. And this is exactly who I want to be.

It's easy for us to believe that tears are a sign of weakness, but I just don't believe it anymore. Our tears allow us to enter into life with the people around us. They say, "You're not alone," and "I hear you," and "Me too." Each time we cry it takes down that wall that we build around ourselves and, as we allow emotions to flow in and flow out, we're opening ourselves up to truly live and to truly love.

Sometimes we just need a friend to show us how.

Are there parts of you that you've always considered a weakness? Maybe it's your tender heart, or how often you cry, or maybe it's something else! What would happen though if you started to embrace them? What would happen if you gave yourself the permission to see them as a strength?

Learning to Surf

> "He got up, rebuked the wind and said to the waves,
> "Quiet! Be still!" Then the wind died down and it
> was completely calm."
>
> Mark 4:39

There's no place in the world I love quite as much as I love the ocean. I don't care where I am, which ocean or which part of the world. If I can stand in the place where the sand meets the water, my feet digging in deeper and deeper as the water washes up and washes away, my heart sighs with happiness.

A few years ago, I spent the summer living in Southern California. I've always thought California was my place. You know how people have that place that just looks and feels like them? Southern California has always been that for me. So, during my time there that summer, I thought it would only be right to take my love for the ocean one step further, another step closer to clinching my place as a bonafide California girl. I wanted to learn to surf.

Surfing looks peaceful and exhilarating all at once from the shore. It seems like such a good idea. The waves are gorgeous to watch, and the sound of them crashing unwinds my heart in an instant. But when you're out in the middle of them, it's a whole other story.

I'd have my feet firmly planted on the ocean floor, and then, without warning, a mountain of water, huge and unpredictable, would come and sweep me away, tossing me around like a rag doll. I'd scramble to the surface, disoriented, gasping for air. My eyes would be wide with fear, stinging with salt, as my heart raced triple-time. It took all of my courage to face the next wave instead of swimming as fast as I could for dry land and a warm towel.

That is how I feel in life sometimes.

A few years ago, my husband Carl and I got let go from our jobs. We, along with most of our department, got called into the office on a random Thursday morning and were handed severance checks. The company was in debt, they needed to make cuts, so we were to clean out our desks and go home right away. It was that quick. One moment we had jobs, a community, a steady paycheck, and a place to belong for the next several years at least; and, the next, all of that was gone. It was a transition I never asked for, one I never saw coming, and it came right smack in the middle of a transition I very much asked for—this happened just three months before our wedding.

Over the next three months, we applied for jobs and addressed wedding invitations, looking for apartments in cities all over the country while we confirmed details with our florist. We were elated about the coming change and heartbroken and angry about the change we were currently enduring. Life dealt us one wave after another, knocking us over again just as soon as we'd come up to take a breath. We were ragged and exhausted, with sand in our bathing suits, and our eyes burning with tears.

We knew deep down that this would all be okay, but we also weren't really sure how it could be.

I bet you've been in this place before too. You have your feet firmly planted in life; you have a plan, you've thought it through. Then, all of a sudden life crashes over you, sweeping the plan, your confidence, and your sense of security right out from under you. You're scared and confused and not entirely sure how this is all going to be okay.

The thing is, the ocean is wild and unpredictable, but it's also the greatest physical representation of God in my life. There's nowhere I see Him more clearly. But that's true about big changes and scary life transitions as well. Life can be wild and unpredictable but, in the seasons that it is, there's no other time I see God so clearly.

Through the big changes in my life, God has taught me more about Himself than I ever could have learned otherwise. In the moments when I was most afraid, most unsure, and most out of control, God was there. He was there calming the waves, providing for me in the midst of my need, and showing me that, while the waves may be entirely too big for me to handle, they'll never be too big for Him.

Through the big changes in my life, God has swept me away to a place I would never have found on my own, a place that was painful to get to, but worth it x10,000. If I could go back and do it again, I wouldn't have stayed safe and warm on my towel. I would have jumped into the waves because otherwise, I never would have learned to surf.

Think back to a time when you were hit by a wave, when something unexpected happened, when you lost something you thought was a sure-bet. Now take some time this morning to look for God in it—how was He there, how did He bring you through it, how did He make that season beautiful? If you're in the midst of one of those seasons now and can't see God in it yet, I promise you He's there. He's there and, while the waves are certainly too big for us, they'll never be too big for Him.

A Team of Best Friends on Our Side

"A new command I give you: Love one another. As
I have loved you, so you must love one another. By
this everyone will know that you are my disciples, if
you love one another."

John 13:34-35

A few years ago, I had the privilege of speaking at a middle school camp in Wisconsin.

The week was a bright and silly blur of 600 giggling middle school girls and hilarious middle school boys. I showed up armed with what I thought they needed to hear. But you know what we talked about most? How we see ourselves.

You see, we all—middle schoolers and adults alike—wrestle with insecurity, with our body image, with fitting in, with measuring up. We look in the mirror, frustrated and disappointed with the image looking back. We compare ourselves to the women around us, coming up short in a bazillion different ways. We all have thoughts that play in our heads like a scratched CD telling us we are too much, not enough, not as good as her, which causes us to see the women around us with skepticism and competition instead of community.

This has been a struggle for most of my adult life, and I bet I'm not the only one. And if you remember back to middle school, this was such a thing back then too. It certainly was for the girls at the camp.

I walked into a particular youth group's debrief time after the day was over. They had invited me to come and spend time with them, and I had no idea what I was going to find when I arrived. What I found was a group of 12 and 13-year-old girls who felt like they weren't good enough. They all reported not fitting in, being made fun of, feeling left out. They all felt like they didn't measure up, all felt insecure about something (usually a whole pile of things), and most of them felt alone in their struggles.

I answered questions for a while, sharing my stories and experiences. But then I had an idea. There's an activity we do in my friendship small group guide, and it's my favorite thing to do with a group of girls. We take turns going around the circle, and each girl gets a turn in the hot seat. As she sits there, (usually blushing), each person in the room tells her all the great things they see in her, so that's what we did that night. One by one, we went around the circle. They each offered themselves up bravely, allowing themselves to be really seen, and they glowed in the light of the words that came back to them.

Girls who had felt small and insecure, left out and unloved, began to be showered with love and praise, and affirmation. "You're so brave!" the group told one girl, "You're a great friend, and I've always admired how smart you are," they told another. It was a scavenger hunt of the very best kind—the group looking for the beautiful things God had placed in each and every girl, and pointing them out, holding them high so she could see them in herself too.

When we left, there wasn't a dry eye in the place. The girls were bowled over by the depth of the love they felt for their sisters in the circle, and even more so by the love they felt in return.

That group changed before my eyes. Each girl stood taller, smiled brighter, carried herself differently — as if she had just found out how wonderful she is (which in so many ways is what had just happened!). They transformed from a group of middle school girls to a group of sisters—fiercely loyal teammates, hugging each other and wiping each other's tears.

We have tender places in our lives and our hearts. Women of all ages do. We have lies we've believed about ourselves for years, doubts we've had, insecurities, and, most of the time we wrestle alone. We wrestle with our thoughts and our worth, trying to figure it out on our own, but we don't have to.

One of the most impactful, life-changing things I've ever had were girlfriends to speak into my life, best friends to bring me to the mirror and help me see the truth about who I am when I can't see it for myself. We need that! Best friends change our lives—they make them easier and certainly more fun. But they also have the power to change the way we see ourselves—helping us see the truth of who God created us to be, and how stunningly beautiful we are.

We need community in our lives, we all do. We need truth-tellers, backup, reinforcement, a team of best friends on our side. If you already have this group of friends, reach out to them this week. If you don't, take a step in that direction. Invite someone to coffee, join a small group, make a phone call, volunteer. All it takes is one small step of bravery. You can do this!

Love Your Girlfriend As Yourself

"For the entire law is fulfilled in keeping this one command: "Love your neighbor as yourself.""

Galatians 5:14

On a random morning a few months ago, I had a spa day in my bathroom.

It was one of those mornings when you don't want to get out of bed, when every movement seems to require 10X the effort, and when getting yourself ready for the day feels all but impossible. It was one of those mornings when you're over the day before your eyes are even open, when you feel like you've failed before your feet even hit the floor.

I had a spa day that morning because I needed one. I needed a quiet moment alone, a tangible way of proving to myself that I still care, that I haven't forgotten about myself, that I'm still on my own team.

One of the things I pride myself on is being a really good friend. It's one of the most important things to me, one of my favorite things to be. But the thing is, while I try to be a great friend to the women in my life, sometimes I forget to be a good friend to myself. That's where I was that day. I'd been running myself ragged for as long as I could remember. I wanted to be the perfect friend, never needing anything but always having an extra measure to pour out. I want to take care of everyone around me, never asking for anything in return. And those expectations had begun draining me like a slow, steady leak.

I was packing things into my schedule, determined to be everywhere and there for everyone: "Yes, I can bring cookies." "Of course, I'd love to come to dinner." "Yes, call me now, I can talk, I'm not busy!" "Please come and stay." "Let me take care of that for you. Do you need anything else? How can I help?"

I had all the grace and care and tenderness for everyone else. "You do not have to do that today, give yourself a rest!" "Let me bring you some soup; you shouldn't be lifting a finger." "You don't have to say yes to that; you already have too much on your plate."

I had grace for everyone else, care for everyone else, but in the meantime, I had none leftover for me.

"Hurry! You're going to be late! I can't believe you forgot the gift! You need to get your act together! You're disappointing everyone!" Those were the things I was saying to myself. Not only that but, in the process, I'd turned on my poor body. I was speaking to it with disdain when it got tired and couldn't keep up. I was so wrapped up in being a good friend to everyone else; I forgot to take care of myself along the way.

So that morning, I decided I needed to make a change. It didn't happen overnight, or all at once. But that morning I took a step in the right direction. I carved out a few minutes to be a good friend, not to anyone else—but this time to myself.

I climbed into the shower and stayed there a little longer than usual. I breathed in the steam, and let the hot water wash over my skin. I scrubbed down with the best smelling sugar scrub: eucalyptus spearmint (my very favorite scent). When I got out, I used my fanciest lotion. I normally reserve it for special occasions, but I don't know what a special occasion for lotion really is, so I decided that day was as good as any.

As I put the finishing touches on my morning and prepared to walk out the door, I caught myself feeling a bit fuller, happier, more awake, more joyful. Tenderness and care on the outside had seeped into my heart just a little bit.

Later that day, I met up with a girlfriend for lunch. I laughed more than I had in awhile, had more energy, more encouragement for her, more patience, more to give. I realized that my spa day really had shifted something in me. Designer Emily Ley has this quote that says, "You can't draw out of an empty well." and that's what I realized I'd been doing for so long. I'd been drawing up anything I could find, never taking the time to put more back in.

Galatians 5:14 says, "For the entire law is fulfilled in keeping this one command: 'Love your neighbor as yourself.'" What it doesn't say is to love your neighbor and forsake yourself, or love your neighbor as yourself—meaning running your neighbor ragged, never giving her a chance to rest. It says to love your neighbor as yourself, which I think means that if we're going to love our neighbors well, we have to love ourselves well too.

So that's what I started to do that morning.

I'm still not great at it. I still let myself fall by the wayside far too often, but I'm learning. I'm learning to be a better friend to myself so that I can be a better friend to the women in my life too.

Take some time to be a good friend to yourself this week. Take yourself out for coffee, give yourself a spa day, let yourself sleep in, or pour yourself a glass of wine and read a book. If you carve out some time to love yourself this week, you'll be able to love others better too.

If God Were Holding My Hand...

> "Be strong and courageous. Do not be afraid; do not
> be discouraged, for the Lord your God will be with
> you wherever you go."
>
> Joshua 1:9

Have you ever tried to make a big decision and found yourself hopelessly stuck? I have. Sometimes in life we're faced with big decisions, huge decisions, and more than anything we don't want to make the wrong one.

Do I go to college here or there? Do I take this job or that one? Do I move or do I stay? Do I have kids? Do I get married? Do I buy this house? Do I sell this one?

A few years ago, I had a big, life-changing decision to make, and I didn't know what to do. Everyone in my life had a different opinion. There was no consensus. Neither option would take me far away from God, or be against who I know Him to be and what I know He wants for our lives. The decision was entirely up to me.

There was the safe, sensible option, and I really liked that option. But there was also the riskier, scarier option. I wanted to want to take the riskier option, but it absolutely terrified me.

I was lying in bed one night, going back and forth for the thousandth time on which path I was going to choose when an idea popped into my mind. It was a simple idea, as all the best ones are. It was a question to ask myself, a way of filtering past all the fear and "what ifs" that were clouding up my mind. It's a filter I've used ever since.

The question is this: "What would you do if you knew God would be holding your hand every step of the way?"

At first, the question seems hypothetical; kind of like, "What would you do if someone gave you a billion dollars?"

It seemed hypothetical until I ran through all the things I know about God and realized that it's true. God promises us He'll never leave us and never forsake us, which is a fancy way of saying, "I'm right there with you kiddo; you can do this. We can do this together!"

Okay, I thought, *if God's going to be holding my hand every step of the way...* I took a deep breath, and my heart said definitively, I'd pick the scarier option. It's the thing I wanted to do in the deepest part of my heart where all the bravery lives. The rest of me had just been too afraid to admit it, but with God holding my hand the entire time, I knew I could do it. So I did!

God promises us that He'll never leave us or forsake us. And with that kind of promise under our belt, we have the freedom, permission, and safety to make courageous, bold choices—the ones we know are right and best, the ones we actually want to make when we listen to the deepest part of our heart where all the bravery lives.

We can paint a life full of adventures that are bigger than anything we could do on our own because we're not on our own. That's the best part. We don't have to be afraid. God will be with us every step of the way.

Whether you're making a huge decision these days, or one of the small ones we're each faced with on a regular basis, try using this question as a filter. What would you do if you knew you didn't have to be afraid, if you knew God would be with you every step of the way? Because the best news is: He will be.

You Are Never Too Broken for God to Use You

"Therefore, if anyone is in Christ, he is a new
creation; the old has gone, the new has come!"

2 Corinthians 5:17

I wasn't sure why God brought me to Guatemala. I knew why I was there, logistically speaking. I was there to film the four-day mission trip, to create a promotional video to invite future groups to come. But I didn't know why God specifically wanted me there. I had a feeling He had a plan; I just wasn't sure what it was quite yet.

I showed up in Guatemala in a pretty messy state.

The thing is, I have a past. I do. I've made more mistakes in my life than I can count, some of them by accident, a great many of them on purpose. And for the most part, since I've become a Christian, I've accepted God's forgiveness with wide-open hands.

That's the truth of the Gospel after all. Jesus died on the cross to pay for our sins so we can be free, redeemed, forgiven, and whole. So I don't feel shame about my past very often. If anything, it reminds me of how much God has done in my life. I see His redemption in it, His forgiveness; I see His healing. Not only that, but I see Him using my past for good every time I get to help someone through something I've been through too.

But all of that had changed just a week before that trip.

I was on Facebook when I got a message from a guy I went to college with. We hadn't talked in years, so we caught up about where were living, and what we were up to. It was great to hear from him.

"I noticed that you went on a long mission trip," he told me, "and that now you work for a missions organization. I have to tell you Steph... I never would have seen that coming for you."

He meant it as a good thing. I knew he did. But as he said it, I could suddenly see what I must look like from his perspective.

The thing is, I liked him in college, I really did, he was a great guy. But for some reason, every time we were together, I was a mess. I was crying, doing something stupid, drinking too much, even getting sick. He was the sole witness to some of my most humiliating behavior, and I'd forgotten until that very moment.

I'd forgotten there were witnesses, people who would still see me as I used to be. And it hadn't occurred to me until that moment what they might think of the "changes" in my life they saw glimpses of on Facebook.

That's what happened in that moment, "changes" all of a sudden had quotes around it, because, with my past peering over my shoulder, it suddenly felt like those "changes" might not be so real after all.

I don't often feel shame when it comes to my past, but it showed up in that moment, and it showed up big.

"Who do you think you're fooling to be living as you are right now?" the shame whispered in my ear. "Did you think your past would disappear? Not likely. You were that girl, and whether you are her now or not, there are people in the world who still see you that way. There are people who think you're a fraud."

And that's how I'd been feeling ever since. I knew the truth of the Gospel—that Jesus paid for our sins, that God has redeemed us and made us whole. But, with my past peering over my shoulder, the Gospel was feeling more like a nice idea than actually true. I was "forgiven," I guess; I was "redeemed." But mostly, I just felt like a fraud. I felt like a disaster with a shiny façade, like a run down shack with some curb appeal. "Maybe I still am her; maybe I haven't changed. I thought God was using my broken-down past, but maybe I really am too broken after all."

That shame tucked itself into my carry-on and followed me all the way to Guatemala.

On our first day there, I spent the afternoon wandering around Antigua with my new friend Carolina. We walked in silence, taking in the sites and the sounds when suddenly, we both froze. There was a building to our right that literally stopped us in our tracks. It was an old church, a cathedral really, that must have fallen down years before. It looked ancient, like an untouched ruin, which I guess is exactly what it was. We were transfixed, taking in every eroded detail, tears slipping quietly down our cheeks. It was the most beautiful church I'd ever seen. You couldn't go in because the doors were chained up, but you could easily see past them to the giant boulders that had tumbled down when the building fell apart.

I don't know what made me do it, but despite how I'd been feeling lately, my first thought was a prayer. "This is a mess Lord," I told him as if He couldn't see it. "It's a mess, but it's so unbelievably beautiful. It's amazing to me that something so messy and broken could be so beautiful, and so full of your spirit."

"Exactly," I felt like He replied, and all of a sudden I knew we were no longer talking about the church.

My heart began to beat faster as it all clicked into place. The power of God and the ability to be part of His story doesn't require perfection; it doesn't require having it all together. And that church was a perfect example. I've never seen something more broken in my life, but I've also never seen something more beautiful. Staring at the brokenness through those locked up gates felt like staring God straight in the face. It felt holier than most churches I've attended.

In the same way, our broken-down pasts don't keep us from God, or keep God from us. They do not discount us from being used by God in beautiful stop-you-in-your-tracks ways. Our God is the God who brings life from death, beauty from ashes, and who uses the most messed up, ragamuffin misfits to do the most world-changing things.

That church didn't have to be clean, or perfect, or entirely pulled together for God's Spirit to be in it, and with it, and exploding out of it like fireworks. And we don't have to be clean, or perfect, or have squeaky-clean pasts for God to be in us, with us, and working through us in ways that positively light up the sky.

I was beginning to understand why God brought me there.

It doesn't matter where you've been, or what you've done, there is nothing in your past that could ever disqualify you from God's love. There's nothing in your life that's broken beyond God's ability to repair. And no matter where you've been, no matter what you've been through, no matter what you've done, God can and will still use you to do beautiful, miraculous things in this world.

Finding the Divine in Art

"Then the Lord God formed a man from the dust
of the ground and breathed into his nostrils the
breath of life, and the man became a living being."

Genesis 2:7

When I walked into the Sistine Chapel, I never imagined I'd walk
out believing in God. I could never have imagined it because I had
never really wanted to believe in God. Christianity and the people
who practiced it had always seemed so boring to me, so vanilla, like
they wore orthopedic shoes and followed all the rules. (Granted, I
didn't know many Christians, but I stood by my beliefs). I wanted
a life of kaleidoscope color, and I was certain (or was until this
moment) that God had nothing to offer me.

However, doing my part as a student studying abroad, I walked
into the chapel quietly and with reverence. I may have had as
much faith as the cappuccino I drank that morning, but I had
enough sense to know when I was standing on holy ground.

The ceiling, as you'd expect, was gorgeous. A vast expanse of
colors and scenes, every crevice overflowing with detail and story.
It rewarded the viewer for taking another look and then another,
revealing more and more the longer you stayed to notice.

After fully taking in the ceiling, I turned around and caught sight
of Michelangelo's fresco, *The Last Judgment*. I almost looked away,
but then something intangible compelled me to stop. There, in
the middle of the Sistine Chapel, my eyes locked on the fresco,
I was overwhelmed by a sudden and inexplicable desire to know
God. I've tried a thousand times to explain what happened that

day—how a piece of art changed my life so entirely, and I can't be sure why it did. All I know is that I walked into the chapel with a thousand doubts about Christianity and Jesus, and I walked out a Christian—certain that whatever Jesus had for me, I wanted it. I wanted in.

I know that lots of people have stood in front of that fresco. I'm sure they've had all kinds of reactions. Some people may have felt nothing at all. But, for some reason, that day Michelangelo's art slammed right into a desire for a relationship with God I never knew I'd had. Michelangelo's art cleared a space—a perfect, quiet space—for something to change in me, to shift entirely. Art does that. It invites us to be different.

I've thought about Michelangelo a lot since that day. I wonder what he was thinking about when he painted that fresco. I wonder what he was trying to say. But mostly, I wonder if he had any idea while he was painting it—covered up to his elbows in paint, I'm sure—that people's lives would be changed because of it.

When we create something, whether we're painting a fresco, or writing a book, or designing a bookcase, we're bringing something beautiful and holy up and out of ourselves to share with the world, and the world is better for it. The creation is a process in itself. It's a terrifying, beautiful thing. The process of creating changes us. I'm sure it changed Michelangelo. Creation requires something of us. It requires us to dig deep within ourselves, to face the things we'd rather ignore, to confront our inner brokenness as well as the beauty stored up within. The process of creating makes us braver, makes us bolder, and makes us freer as the divide between ourselves and the world around us seems to grow thinner.

But, while the process of creating is intimidating, the process of sharing our creation is even scarier. Sharing our creations is like the culmination of all your terrifying naked dreams coming true—everyone staring at you with nothing to cover up with but the blush that's somehow coloring both sets of cheeks. But when we do these things—when we create something deep within us, and when we share it with the world—what we created becomes far bigger than us.

I can be certain that Michelangelo wasn't thinking about me when he painted The Last Judgment. He surely wasn't picturing a 20-year-old sorority girl, or the life change his painting could inspire in her. But that's exactly the point. When Michelangelo breathed that beautiful thing into the world, it became bigger than him. It became a holy thing, a moving thing, something that God could use to change people and make the world better in ways beyond anything he could have ever imagined.

When we create art, we join in the divine process of creating, following in the footsteps of our Creator. We draw out the best, most beautiful parts of ourselves and share them with the world. When our creation comes out of us, it expands beyond us. It has the ability to be something bigger than what we first pictured when we sat down to create it.

There's something holy and beautiful inside of you—something uniquely yours that you're specially gifted to share with the world. It's a scary process creating that thing and then putting it on display, but the world needs what you have to offer. People need it because of what it will stir up inside them.

When I was in Nepal a few years ago, we were taught to greet each other by saying "Namaste," putting our palms together and giving a little bow. Namaste means, "The divine in me recognizes the divine in you," and that's what I think art does when we share it.

When we create, we draw what God has placed inside of us up and out, and we put it on display. And then, in the most sacred and holiest of moments, the divine in someone else—for instance, a wandering, wondering sorority girl in Rome—might lock eyes with what you created, and the divine in her might be awakened.

I believe that God created each one of us on purpose and for a purpose. What's one gift you know God has given you? Maybe you're artistic, or a beautiful singer, maybe you're a whiz at math or an amazing teacher. Maybe you're really kind, or a great listener. Maybe you have a passion for fighting the injustices of the world or a gift for making really great food. God put these things in us because He wants to use them. He wants us to use them to love His people, to take care of them right alongside Him.

So what's one thing you know God has placed in you that He wants to share with the world? Thank Him for that, and take a few minutes to think of one way you could share that gift this week.

Asking Better Questions

"God is able to bless you abundantly, so that in all
things at all times, having all that you need, you will
abound in every good work."

2 Corinthians 9:8

I don't know about you, but I'm a productivity gal. I love living
good and busy, with big dreams and a long list of to-dos for how
I'm going to get them done. I ask, "What else can I get done today?
What's next on the list? How much more can I fit in?" always convinced that I can do just one more thing, or 12. I'm the picture of
efficiency, not wasting one single moment.

The problem is, after awhile of living this way, I start to get tired. I
start to get tired, and my heart starts to harden. I'm getting things
done, absolutely, but I'm not really living the kind of life I want to
live. I'm not really being the woman I want to be.

That's where I found myself at the beginning of last summer. My
heart was hard, and I was missing it, and it wasn't until my best friend
called one afternoon that I realized just how far things had gone.

You see, I have this rule for myself. When my people call, I answer.
It doesn't matter what I'm doing, where I am, or how busy my day
is. I will never give up an opportunity to talk to my best friends. I'll
never miss a chance to talk to my parents. I'll never be too busy for
them; I've promised myself. They are #1.

But that day, when my best friend called, I saw her name flash
across my screen and rolled my eyes. "I don't have time for this
today," and my finger hovered over the "reject" button. It took me

a minute, but I did answer her call. And at the end of our conversation, I felt so full, so connected, and so aware of how hard my productive little heart had become.

I'd been so focused on the doing, I'd missed out on the being, the resting, the playing, the connecting, the savoring. My checklist was in good shape, certainly. But I was so concerned with not wasting a single moment, that I was missing so many moments, and I could see the effects all over my life. I couldn't write good words anymore, couldn't think thoughts that were full and true. The time I was spending with God felt more like a business meeting. "What do we need to get done today? Okay. Let's get to it. Ready? Break!"

My productivity was seeping into every good corner of my life, hardening it, and stealing the life, the joy, and the goodness out of everything. So, as I walked into last summer, I knew that something had to shift.

For so long I'd been asking questions like, "What's next? What else can I fit in? How much can I check off the list today?" and so I decided to try asking some different questions instead. "What do I want to do right now?" I'd try asking myself a few minutes each day. "What does my soul need? How can I love both my people and myself well today? What sounds like fun?"

At first, the questions felt foreign—the idea of answering them, and actually doing something with that answer, even more so. But with some practice, the questions began to feel rebellious and exciting. "I could get used to this," I thought.

A week later I was heading to Denver to visit my family and friends. I was there a bit early, and my flight was delayed. I debated. Hours to kill in an airport with good wifi? That's a productivity junkie's dream! My checklist beckoned.

Then a tiny thought spoke up, a whisper of an invitation: "What sounds fun?" I heard it say, and I instantly knew the answer.

I found a place at a wine bar in the airport, and I ordered a sandwich with prosciutto, brie, arugula, and a bit of fig jelly. To drink, I welcomed in the summer as I sampled a flight of Rosé. I pulled out the book I'd been reading for ages but never made enough time for, and there, at the bar, I got lost in good food, great wine, and stories of Julia Child's years in France.

For the first time in a long time, productivity scooched over a bit and gave some space for delight. Deep breath, sigh, smile. "This," I thought to myself, "Let's make more time for this."

What does your soul need today? How can you love both your people and yourself well? What sounds like fun? How can you take a few minutes today to scooch productivity over a bit and leave some space for delight?

Climbing Out of the Hole

"Praise be to the God and Father of our Lord Jesus Christ, the Father of compassion and the God of all comfort, who comforts us in all our troubles, so that we can comfort those in any trouble with the comfort we ourselves receive from God."

2 Corinthians 1:3-4

Have you ever heard something that just changed you? The words, the story, the way it was told resonated so much with you, it felt like it cracked open your ribs and re-wired everything within them?

I heard something a few years ago that did that for me. It was a simple story, a story I heard told in a TV show of all places, that gave words to a way of doing life that has transformed me.

The story went something like this:

There's a guy walking down the street one day when all of a sudden he falls into a hole. The hole is deep, and he tries everything but, no matter what he tries, he just can't get himself out.

He starts calling up for help and, after a few minutes, a doctor walks by.

"Doc!" he yells up, "I'm down in this hole, can you help me?" The doctor says, "Sure!" He writes him a prescription, tosses it into the hole and keeps on going.

Next, a priest walks by. "Father!" the guy yells up when he sees him, "I'm down in this hole! Can you help me?" The priest says,

"Of course!" He writes down a prayer, tosses it into the hole, and keeps on going.

Finally, the guy's friend walks by. He yells up when he sees him, "Joe! Hey, Joe! I'm down here in this hole. Can you help me out?"

Joe says, "Of course!" and proceeds to jump down into the hole too!

"What are you doing!?" the man exclaims, "Now we're both stuck in here!"

But Joe shakes his head. "Don't worry. I've been down here in this hole before and I know the way out."

When I first heard this story, tears sprung to my eyes before my brain could even catch up. It's such a simple story, but it captured perfectly something that has changed my life completely.

Sometimes in life, we get into holes that we just can't pull ourselves out of. We make a big mistake or a whole long string of them. We get into debt, into a bad relationship, we find ourselves stuck in a lifestyle we never thought would define our lives. We find ourselves depressed, or addicted, or the victim of something that should not have ever happened to us.

We try everything to pull ourselves out. Of course we do! But sometimes the hole is so deep that we just can't do it on our own.

When I was going through the terrible breakup I talk about in *The Lipstick Gospel*, my sadness was so deep, so dark, that I had no idea how to pull myself out. I tried everything I could think of—all of my old tricks. I went to the gym, tried to breathe deep, tried to just "get over it" (whatever that means). I tried to drink away my pain, I tried to numb it by throwing myself into my work, by throwing myself into another relationship, but none of it helped.

Finally, exhausted from fighting the pain, I laid down on the damp floor of the hole I'd found myself in, convinced I'd be down there forever. But then, I woke up with a start when I heard a familiar voice. My best friend, Michelle, had hopped in there with me. She'd been in that hole before, she knew it well, and she knew how to get me out.

Sometimes we need help to climb out of the holes we find ourselves in. We need someone who's been there before to walk with us, to show us the way.

When we link arms with each other, when we let someone else link arms with us and walk alongside us for awhile, I'm convinced there's nothing we can't get through or over or past. No hole is too deep with two of us down there together. So, if you are in a deep hole today, I pray that you find the courage to ask for help.

But once you're out of the hole, remember that your job is only just beginning. The next time you walk past that same hole and see someone else stuck down there in it, I hope you jump in there with them, and say, "It's okay, you're okay—let's get you out of here. I know the way."

Take a few minutes to reflect on where you are in life right now. Are you in a hole or have you recently learned the way out of one? If you're in it now, ask for help – you don't have to do this alone. If you're out, find someone who is in their own hole right now and jump in with them. Show them that they don't have to do this alone either.

Making Our Dreams Come True

"Do not fear, for I am with you; do not be dismayed,
for I am your God. I will strengthen you and help
you; I will uphold you with my righteous right hand."

Isaiah 41:10

What do you dream of doing in your life?

Maybe you want to open your own shop or go back to school.
Maybe you want to be a nurse, or a teacher, or get a job in mar-
keting. Maybe you want to go to law school, or be a photographer,
or steal the show on Etsy with your hand-lettered masterpieces.

I love our dreams. I also believe that we're totally capable of
achieving them. We can do hard things as women, hard things and
big things. I know because I've seen it. I've seen it in the women
around me, and I've seen it in myself. Writing my book, *The Lipstick
Gospel*, was one of the hardest things I've ever done, and every time
I hold it in my hands, I'm reminded of this: we can do hard things,
big things, good things.

We can meet our goals and achieve our dreams; we can make the
world a better and brighter place. I can and you can. But there are
two things we have to do if we want to get there—if we want our
dreams to do anything but sit in our heads, safe and warm.

We have to do these two simple and almost impossible things: we
have to start, and we have to keep going.

Starting is always the hardest part. It's the moment when your toes
are peeking out the door of the airplane, knowing you're about

to jump. The fear kicks down the door at this point, little armies in your head telling you to quit, turn back, land the plane, give up. It's the voice in your head that tells you that this is stupid, or that you'll never make it, or brings to mind all the people who are doing the same thing but better.

Sometimes the fear comes in the form of excuses: *I was going to start, but then I had to do the laundry, re-organize the pantry, deep clean the garage, and have you seen my fingernails lately?* Fear does anything it can to keep us from starting, but we have to start, and we don't have to wait until we're perfect or perfectly ready before we do.

Our dreams can't begin unless we do, so we have to get started. Not only that, but we have to keep going.

That's the second thing we have to do. We have to keep going, and this might be the hardest part—or maybe they both are; I really can't decide.

That was certainly the hardest part about writing *The Lipstick Gospel*.

I loved getting started, and as I did, I had all the energy in the world. But about halfway through I got tired. I'd run out of good ideas, gumption, confidence. My words were a jumbled mess, and I had no idea how to make sense of them. I wasn't so sure I could do this anymore—I wasn't even sure I wanted to.

I thought about quitting and I was just about to when a friend stopped me and told me this. She said, "Anything worth doing is going to be discouraging in the middle. In taking on something new, you're wandering into a dark tunnel. At first, you can still see some light. It gives you hope and direction and keeps you moving forward. But when you get deep enough into the middle, you lose the light from the beginning, and you haven't yet gotten to the point where you can see the light at the end. But you have to keep going. You have to keep shuffling forward in the dark, putting one foot in front of the other, because if you keep doing that, you'll get there. You'll make it to your destination, and it will be so worth it."

So that's what I did. I sat down at my computer again and again, even and especially when I didn't want to. I reordered the words one more time, tried saying the same thing in a different way, and moved the chapters from this place to that one. It didn't look like much for the longest time, but I kept going, kept shuffling my feet forward, kept moving toward the light.

Finishing that book was one of the best feelings in the world, and it's been such a gift to share the story of what God's done in my life. But for that to happen, I had to start, and I had to keep going. And I know that if I can do it, you can do it too.

I can't imagine what the world would look like if we all mustered up the courage to start and the courage to keep going in the pursuit of our dreams.

> We are capable of so much more than we imagine. We can do hard things, big things, good things. I can and you can. We can make the world a better and brighter place. So wherever you are in your dreams today, I dare you to start, and I dare you to keep going.

Every Woman Is Beautiful... Including You!

"Encourage one another daily, as long as it is
called "Today."

Hebrews 3:13a

I heard a question a few years ago that I absolutely can't shake.
I was sitting in the audience at a conference when the speaker
asked, "How can we intentionally make women around us feel
more beautiful?"

The question stopped me in my tracks because it's something I
hadn't thought about before. I've thought about how to help other
people, how to be a good friend, and how to love other women
well, but I've never thought about how to make other women feel
more beautiful.

It made me wonder why.

I thought about it for a long time and finally came to a conclusion: beauty, to me, feels like one of those things where it's every
woman for herself. We understand, at least cerebrally, that if
another woman is in a relationship, or gets a promotion, or signs
a book deal, it doesn't steal our ability to do the same. (I said cerebrally. Those things are much harder to understand in practice).
But beauty is another animal entirely.

When other women are beautiful, it does sometimes feel like
they're stealing something from us. It feels like if they're beautiful,
we must not be, or at least we must be less so. It feels like there's
this worldwide continuum of beauty, and someone else being

beautiful bumps us down a few rungs.

Maybe we don't say those things out loud. Maybe we don't even realize that we feel this way, but I think that beauty, more than any other area of our lives, is the area where we don't want to give anything away because it already feels like there's not enough to go around.

I think this is why we, as women, can be so cruel to each other. We're fighting each other for a place in the world, fighting each other to matter, fighting for love and attention and a spot at the table. We can be so cruel to each other, pointing out each other's flaws, picking each other apart, giving ourselves a secret high five when the mean girl in high school gains weight, or when someone says his new girlfriend isn't quite as pretty.

But the satisfaction never really lasts. Her being less doesn't actually make us feel like more. Pointing out someone else's flaws never actually makes us feel better about our own.

Matthew 7:2 says, "For in the way you judge, you will be judged; and by your standard of measure, it will be measured to you." I've found that to be so true. We're not great about being selectively critical. If we're critical of the people around us, chances are the one receiving the harshest critique from us, is us.

That's why I love that question so much. It changes the conversation completely. It's a challenge to recognize and celebrate the beauty in the women around us, believing, and putting into practice the belief that every woman is beautiful, and it really is true! Every single woman on the planet is beautiful in her own unique way. There's more than enough beauty to go around. And if we start to realize that every woman is beautiful, and we can practice believing that, then maybe we can see that we are too.

So what would happen if we put this truth into practice? If we decided to believe that we're all beautiful, none of us is replaceable, and that we don't have to compete for a place at the table?

What if we made it our mission to help the women in our lives see the truth of how beautifully and perfectly and flawlessly God made them? I think it would make the women around us stand taller, feeling confident, and good enough, and beautiful in their own skin; but I think it would actually do the same for us too.

When we're looking at the women around us with generous, kind eyes—looking for the beauty in them, celebrating it, and holding it high for the world to see, I think we're able to cultivate that same kind of generosity and kindness towards ourselves.

When we're looking for the beauty in the women around us, it's easier to find it in ourselves too.

So let's be generous today, with the women around us and with ourselves. Let's celebrate our beauty and their beauty, sprinkling compliments around, giving them away for free. Let's intentionally help the women in our lives feel more beautiful, and I truly believe we will start to feel more beautiful too.

Make it your mission today to make three women in your life feel beautiful. Maybe it's your co-worker, a woman in the bathroom, a woman at your doctor's office, or your best friend. Compliment three women today. Find something beautiful about them, recognize it, and celebrate it. Tell them how beautiful they are, that you love their outfit, that they did a great job today, or tell them something you admire about them. And next time you pass a mirror, give yourself three compliments too.

DAY TWENTY-EIGHT

Carbonated Holiness

"See what great love the Father has lavished on us,
that we should be called children of God!
And that is what we are!"

1 John 3:1a

Does Christianity ever feel complicated to you? Please tell me I'm not the only one. Every once in awhile, it can feel like this intricate maze of dos and don'ts. Do this, but only a little bit. Don't do this, because if you do, God will be mad. But He won't be mad, because of Jesus. But don't push it, because you reap what you sow. Wait a minute… is that in the Bible? How does any of this work?

Life as a Christian feels that way to me sometimes and, on days when it does, there's this one verse I always go back to. It's when the Pharisees, a group of slightly-uptight religious people, ask Jesus what the two greatest commandments are. This is what Jesus says in response:

"'Love the Lord your God with all your heart and with all your soul and with all your mind.' This is the first and greatest commandment. And the second is like it: 'Love your neighbor as yourself.'"

Deep breath, sigh. Thank you.

Make no mistake, these commandments aren't easy, but they're also not complicated. They're a place to shoot for that makes sense, that I can see, that I can wrap my mind around. They cut away all the red tape and set me free to love God and to love His people. I come back to this verse all the time.

There are also times when I feel like finding and spending time with God is really complicated. Everyone has thoughts about it: ways you should pray, formulas for prayer, how much you should read in your Bible and how often. And I totally get it! Spending time with God is this totally intangible thing. There's the small detail that we can't actually see Him, or really hear His voice. We just sort of stare up at the ceiling and hope He's up there somewhere.

It's a lot to wrap our minds around because God is big, and also small all at the same time. God is the God of gigantic cathedrals and pomp and ceremony. He's also the God of sweatpants, and tearful prayers whispered up at our ceilings in the middle of the night. So how do we spend time with a God like that?

Sometimes I get caught up thinking I have to perform, or tap dance, or show Him how spiritual I can be in order for Him to feel close. I feel like it's a formula, like there must be rules, and if I can just do X, Y, Z, turn around clockwise three times and close my eyes tight, He'll finally feel close. But it just doesn't work that way.

I was home in Denver visiting my family a few years ago when I decided to go for a walk. I only had a few minutes, so I headed over to the park right around the corner from where I grew up.

I was praying as I walked, half performing with big words and lots of theology, and half begging, "Where are you and why do you feel so far away?"

"Where do I go to find you, God?" I asked, frustrated. And in the next moment, a piece of scripture came to my mind. Jesus said, "Let the little children come to me, and do not hinder them, for the kingdom of heaven belongs to such as these."

As I wandered through the playground, the slides I've zipped down a thousand times, the bridges I've bounded over, the tunnels I've hidden in, I thought about how I've always felt like kiddos had this faith thing dialed in. They just don't make it quite as complicated as the rest of us do. They just seem to get it somehow.

And right at that moment, I caught sight of the swings. I knew exactly what to do. I knew how to seek God in that moment, where I could find Him. I didn't have to think twice.

Higher and higher I swung as my legs pumped back and forth, until all I could see ahead of me were my pink sneakers kissing the sky.

I laughed out loud, feeling freer than I had in ages, feeling like God was as close as my breath, and remembering my favorite quote from author, Anne Lamott. "Laughter is carbonated holiness."

It absolutely is.

Does spending time with God ever feel complicated to you? Next time it does, instead of trying to perform or trying to get it right, try thinking like a child. Approach him like a kid would, simply, purely, and with tons of whimsy and laughter. You'll find Him there. I promise, and so does He.

Green Grass & Contentment

"The Lord is my shepherd, I lack nothing. He
makes me lie down in green pastures, He leads me
beside quiet waters, He refreshes my soul."

Psalm 23:1-3a

We're all guilty of it. We do it all our lives. We peer over the fence
and wonder, "Is the grass greener over there? It looks like it to me!"

I distinctly remember thinking that my life was going to be so
much better when I was a mature eighth grader instead of a lowly
seventh grader. I remember thinking that I would finally be the
woman I've always wanted to be if I could just get into that one
specific sorority. I remember peering over at other people's relationships thinking that if I could JUST find a boyfriend like that,
my life would be complete.

If we lost five more pounds, or made a bit more money, or had a
slightly bigger house, or if we could just get married, THEN we'd
be satisfied.

We all have stipulations for our lives—hurdles for them to leap over
before we finally give them our stamp of satisfied approval. But, in
my experience, satisfaction never seems to come. It's not that life is
all downhill from here, not even for a second. I've discovered and
decided that life only gets better the more of it we live.

But I also have never found the satisfaction I was hoping for in
reaching the next step ahead. Because here's the trick to the whole
thing: if we're always looking a step ahead, then we're always looking a step ahead. When we finally get to that next stage, or job, or

weight-loss goal, our eyes will still be fixed ahead. The satisfaction will still evade us. We'll never feel like we've arrived.

Not only that, but I've discovered that when we spend all our time peering over the fence, longing for grass that isn't ours, there's no faster way to miss or spoil the season we're in. And that's such a tragedy, isn't it? I would hate to miss the goodness in my life because I'm always looking forward to whatever comes next.

So this is what I've been working on these last few years in my life. I've been working on being present and grateful right where I am because I think that's where we find true satisfaction.

Satisfaction comes when we decide we love our house, even before it's the perfect one. Satisfaction comes when we decide we're beautiful today—with or without those five pounds. Satisfaction comes when we decide to make the most of our single lives, living our life to the full whether we're married or not.

The truth is that the grass is green on the other side of the fence. It is. We have so much to look forward to! But the grass is also green right where we are. It's squishy and soft just like grass is supposed to be—a lush carpet under your bare feet that smells distinctly like summer. You can lay in it for days, and it will cradle your head, giving you the perfect bed to watch the clouds roll by.

The season we're in has so much to offer—so much laughter, so much connection, so much to teach us, so much great food! And, if we can be present and grateful and fully live this season of our lives, we'll know we can do the same thing when it's time to move on to the next.

We get one wild and precious life. One. It's happening right this second and, I don't know about you, but I don't want to miss a minute of it. I want to live my life today. I want to love this stage of life to pieces—to wear it out like an old pair of sweatpants I can't bring myself to get rid of.

Because when we do this, we're no longer chasing contentment, frustrated when we can never quite grasp it. We're bringing contentment with us no matter what grass we're in, like a lawn chair, and an icy lemonade, deciding to live this season and this life to the absolute full.

Let's be present on our side of the fence today. Let's practice presence and gratitude and be all here like it's the best gift we've ever been given. Then, when it's time to move to another side of the fence, we can do the same thing there. So start by thinking of five things that are great about the season you're in today.

Defeating Giants

"You intended to harm me, but God intended it for
good to accomplish what is now being done, the
saving of many lives."

Genesis 50:20

Have you ever begged God to take something away from you?
Hurt, pain, a broken heart, a situation you know isn't going to go
the way you want it to? Have you ever prayed that kind of prayer?

I have.

More times than I can count, my heart has shattered into a million
pieces, and, every single time, I prayed, "God, please take away this
pain, please don't let this happen, please change these circumstances."

I pray these prayers over and over again, hoping that maybe if I
pray hard enough, God will just vacuum the problem, the struggle, and the pain away from me. But the truth is, sometimes it
seems like God doesn't answer: my boyfriend still broke up with
me, our friendship still ended, the hard season continued, I still
didn't get the job.

A few years ago, I was in a Bible study with some pretty spectacular women. As we crowded into this perfect little apartment, we
began to talk about the giants in our lives. Giants, as our leader
Caroline named them, are the problems we beg God to take away
from us. Tey are the things we beg Him to change; the hurts we
are desperate to avoid.

We each sat quietly for a few minutes, listing out our individual giants—the circumstances we wish God would change. When we were finished, Caroline pointed out something that changed everything:

"Maybe God allows giants in our lives so that we can be filled with whatever it's going to take to defeat them."

Um… come again?

"Okay, here are some examples," she started, seeing the puzzled looks on our faces. "When David faced and defeated the giant, Goliath, he was filled with courage and total confidence in the power of his God, and it was those things that enabled him to be a great king. As Joseph faced a whole collection of difficult circumstances, God was getting Him to the right place, at the right time to save not just His family, but all of Egypt. David and Joseph wouldn't have been ready otherwise—just to name a few."

I was with her at this point; it was starting to make sense. As weird as it is to say and as hard as it is to swallow, maybe God doesn't just instantly remove those giants for a reason. I'm not saying that God wants us to hurt because He doesn't—not at all.

But she got me wondering if maybe God has a higher aim than eliminating our discomfort. Maybe He wants to draw us close to Him, walking with us through those situations, using them to make us taller, more confident, smarter, and more capable for the amazing ways He wants to use us in the future. I instantly had a pretty good idea of what that would look like played out.

In the midst of a very broken heart, I begged God to take my pain away. I wanted to stop hurting, right now, if He wouldn't mind. But, if God had just vacuumed my hurt away all at once, I never would have realized I needed Him. I'd never have met Him in the Sistine Chapel that day. I wouldn't be writing to you right now.

God works in and through our hardships, teaching us things and preparing us in beautiful ways for the road ahead. That's the story behind so many great people who are doing amazing things.

A friend of mine was abused when she was in high school, and now she's hard at work, helping girls who have gone through the very same thing. Another friend of mine found herself deep in debt after college, and now she's teaching other women how to handle their money in smart and healthy ways.

One of my closest cousins almost died of pneumonia a few years ago. She was perfectly healthy and then she got deathly ill, almost overnight, but through the experience, she decided she wanted to become a doctor. An empathy and a passion was born out of her suffering, and that's my story too.

I've walked hard roads in my friendships, in my faith, in my relationships, and with my identity. They were tough giants, not easy at all, and God didn't just vacuum them away. But He did walk me through them and teach me so much, and now I can walk other women through those things too.

We're faced with giants all throughout our lives—giants we wish would just be whisked away. And God can feel cruel, or absent sometimes, when the problem sticks around or when the pain doesn't instantly subside the moment we want it to. But I think God has a bigger plan in mind. Instead of just taking away our momentary pain, God is in the business of replacing it with much deeper healing, with newness, with growth, with transformation. He's doing so much more than a vacuum ever could.

God might be allowing these giants to stay in our lives a little longer so we can be filled with the things we need to defeat them for good. That way, we can turn around and help other people do the same with their giants too.

What are some giants in your life these days? I just love how Caroline said it, "Maybe God allows giants in our lives so that we can be filled with whatever it's going to take to defeat them." What is God teaching you as you battle these giants? What is He filling you with? If it's hard to see from where you're sitting right now, try to just imagine. How could you use the things you're learning and walking through today to help others in the future?

Messy-House Friends

"Love is patient, love is kind. It does not envy, it
does not boast, it is not proud. It does not dishonor
others, it is not self-seeking, it is not easily angered,
it keeps no record of wrongs. Love does not delight
in evil but rejoices with the truth. It always protects,
always trusts, always hopes, always perseveres."

1 Corinthians 13:4-7

There's a sweet spot in every new relationship that I wish we could stay in forever. In dating relationships, it's that perfect time when dates are no longer awkward but are actually really fun. You're both still wearing your cutest outfits, your best behavior, and you still have a full arsenal of your funniest stories. From where you stand in the midst of that sweet spot, the romantic possibilities are endless.

However, over the course of my dating relationships and eventually marriage, I learned that we can't stay in that place forever.

If a relationship is going to progress—whether it's in dating, or even in friendships—we have to let the other person see more than our best behavior. We have to let them really get to know us. We miss out on the best parts of relationships if we don't.

There's an amazing woman named Brené Brown, who you just need to know. She's an author and a researcher focused on helping us all live wholehearted lives. After years of research and thousands of interviews, she found that true connection with others is one of our soul's greatest needs. She also found that the only way to really have this kind of soul warming connection is to allow yourself to be really seen and really known.

The only way to get to this place is through vulnerability, and I wish that wasn't true.

Vulnerability is letting someone see you for the real you, not just on your best days. It's letting someone into your house, or your heart when it's not tidy and all put-together. It's crying in front of your new boyfriend or telling a friend about an insecurity. It's telling your small group the real, honest backstory, or telling your fiancé your greatest fears. It's that moment when you're left wide open to the possibility of being hurt and rejected—hands limp, defenses down. At least for me, there's nothing in the world more terrifying.

There's also nothing more counter-cultural. We live in a world that puts such a high value on perfection—a world where we are constantly working on, and filtering away our flaws, hiding beneath pants that are made to flatter and kind lighting.

We live in a world where you say, "I'm great!" when someone asks how you are, a world where you don't let people see your dirty laundry, and God forbid someone comes over when your house is a mess. But having people love us because of our flattering pants and clean house just doesn't do much for our souls, does it? We need deeper love than that.

I was heading over to my friend Kacie's house a few months ago when she sent me a text that said this:

"I'm so glad you're a messy-house friend and not a new, need-to-impress friend. Because my house is messy and I just can't do much about it right now, and I'm happy to invite you into it anyway."

We're messy-house friends, absolutely. But it took some vulnerability to get there. Kacie and I have seen each other at our worst: angry, insecure, even a bit mean. We've heard each other's stories—the messiest parts, the heartbreaking parts, the parts where we made our biggest mistakes.

We let the other one see us for who we really are, on our best days and our worst. And, while it was scary at times, the result couldn't be more worth it. It led to the kind of friendship that makes your heart bigger and your life warmer as you know that in the deepest way you don't have to walk through any of it alone.

That's the good stuff of a relationship. That's true connection.

We cannot be fully loved if we are not fully known, which leaves us with a decision to make. We can either hide and protect ourselves, ensuring that, although we won't feel truly connected, we definitely won't be hurt; or we can go with something a bit more daring.

We can choose another way to live—a way to live and breathe and love that's wild and audacious. We can choose to let people see us, who we really are, at our core. We can be bravely imperfect, knowing that the person across from us isn't perfect either—we can take us both off the hook. We can choose to gather up the courage to tell the whole truth of who we are with our whole heart. We can let someone in, knowing that while they can hurt us, they can also deeply love us, and it's a risk that's worth taking.

Vulnerability is the daring proclamation that we're worthy of love, and open to being loved—not only in good lighting, and while wearing our most flattering pants—but because of who we really are. There's just nothing more courageous or soul-filling than that.

Maybe you're comfortable with being vulnerable, or maybe the thought of it makes your skin crawl. But, either way, that's my challenge for you today. Open up to someone in your life. It doesn't have to be all at once. You don't have to tell them everything, but open up to them a bit more today. I promise you that they won't think less of you once they know you're imperfect. They'll be relieved because neither are they. And once you can sit there together, perfectly imperfect, that's when the best friendships and relationships really begin.

Turn On a Flashlight

"For I know the plans I have for you," declares the
Lord, "plans to prosper you and not to harm you,
plans to give you hope and a future."

Jeremiah 29:11

This boyfriend was the one; I was positive. I could picture our life together perfectly. We would have three kids and live in a small house with a great porch. I couldn't picture my life with anyone else, couldn't imagine anyone else in my future, and then over the course of one fight, that future disappeared.

I knew which college I wanted to go to. It was my dream school, the one I'd been planning to attend since 7th grade. I had a t-shirt from that school, and I slept in it for a week straight, waiting for my acceptance letter to come in the mail. But when responses came back, I got the small envelope. They thanked me for my application, but they didn't see me as clearly in their future as I'd seen them in mine.

I walked into work one day, confident, settled, sure that this place, this company, and my position within it was secure. Then, 20 minutes later, I walked out of the office with a severance check. They were downsizing; there wasn't room for me anymore. The future I had planned for myself had once again gone up in smoke.

Have you ever been in this place? You can picture your future perfectly. You're planning for it, preparing for it, envisioning it, walking toward it and then, in an instant, there's a hard yank on the rug beneath your feet, and it's gone. You're on your back. You can't decide which is more bruised, your pride or your tailbone.

The life you've been walking toward is gone in a flash, and your heart feels unfixably broken.

When we find ourselves in one of those moments, it feels like the world slows down and speeds up all at once. We're there in the center of the cyclone of humiliation, loss, and hurt looking around wondering, "How the heck did I get here?" And even more, "How am I ever going to move forward?"

It's these moments, when even the best-laid plans have fallen to pieces, when we realize that no matter how far in advance we plan or how tightly we try to control over our lives, we may not get to where we thought we were going.

It's humbling more than anything else. These moments remind us just how small we are, just how little we're able to do on our own. They break the "can-do" attitude in each of us, reminding us that life is much bigger and more unpredictable than we'd like to believe. These are the moments in our lives that stand out like towers, markers of where something important fell apart.

But, if we let them, these excruciating endings can also mark the beginning of something new. When life cracks us open, breaking our hearts, our determination, and our plans, that's the moment we finally ask for help, hoping that even on the darkest of nights, some-one can turn on a flashlight and lead us to somewhere beautiful.

And the good news? There is. God is with us in these moments. He's busy, active, moving, and at work in the midst of the rubble. It's between these cracks—in our chest, our confidence, our plans—when God can begin a rebuilding process and take us somewhere more beautiful than we've ever dared to imagine.

Is there something in your life that feels cracked these days? Is there something that has recently fallen apart? Maybe it's something small, or maybe it's something that towers over you in its bigness and its pain. But, whatever it is, whether a small crack in your life, or whether you're standing in the rubble—nothing is ever too broken for God. Hold that reminder close to whatever part of your heart needs it today. Nothing is ever too broken for God! Not only that, but there's nothing in the future that could break beyond God's ability to repair it. There are never ashes too burned for God to bring beauty up and out of them.

Thin Places

"Ask and it will be given to you; seek and you will
find; knock and the door will be opened to you."

Matthew 7:7

In one of my favorite books, the author explains a concept called
"thin places." Thin places, as she describes them, are the Celtic
idea that there are places where the distance between the human
and the divine is extra thin. In other words, they're places where
God feels extra close.

I love that idea. I've had lots of thin places in my life. The ocean
is always a thin place for me. Something about the vast beauty, the
power of it, the twinkle and the sparkle, my feet digging further
down into soft wet sand with every brush of the tide. Staring into
the ocean always makes me feel like I'm looking God right in the
face—close enough to see the kind wrinkles around His eyes and
the way He's smiling at me like I'm His favorite daughter.

I've spoken some of my best prayers into the ocean. There's
something amazing about standing on the edge of something so
big and either whispering or shouting your deepest hopes, pain,
dreams, and passions into the void. It's like the water sweeps up
your prayers and carries them out to sea—a message in a bottle
that's sure to get where it's going.

Sevilla, the beautiful Spanish city, is a thin place for me. It's the
place where I learned that God doesn't just exist in cathedrals and
speak through the Bible, but that He's dancing and swirling to Las
Sevillanas (the flamenco-like dance we could never quite master).
It's the place where my desire to know Him ignited like the enormous candles that drip wax onto the streets during the Semana

Santa parade. It's a city that romanced me with food and wine and the smell of orange trees lining the streets.

Thin places are all around us. They really are, and I think they're different in each season.

One of my thin places near our house in Nashville is a loop I walk around as often as I can. It's 3.8 miles of winding trail with several wooden bridges zig-zagging across a wooded stream. Every time I cross one of these bridges I pause, just for an instant, while I close my eyes, put the world and my life on hold, and I breathe God in. It is here my soul unwinds because it is here God feels especially close. These bridges are some of my favorite thin places.

The truth is God is everywhere. He's no closer when we're near the ocean, or at the top of a mountain, or on a walk by a beautiful stream than he is anywhere else. God is in our breath, and in our hearts, and riding shotgun with the windows down, singing with us to the new Zac Brown Band album (at least I always like to think so!).

So thin places aren't for God's sake. They're not a shrine where we go to visit Him because that's the only place He can be found.

Thin places are gifts to us. They're places where we can shed the busyness of our days, and our minds, a place where we can get away, where the scenery, and the change, and the beauty of the landscape reminds us that God is near, ready to talk whenever we are.

What are some of your thin places? Where do you go to have your best moments with God? If you don't have a thin place, maybe it's time to find one! Find a quiet place, a beautiful place, and look up. God's right there with you, with kind wrinkles around His eyes, smiling down at you—His favorite daughter.

P.S. That book is *Bittersweet* by Shauna Niequist. If you haven't read it, I can't recommend it enough!

Little Traditions

"I commend the enjoyment of life, because nothing
is better for a man under the sun than to eat and
drink and be glad. Then joy will accompany him in
his work all the days of the life God has given him
under the sun."

Ecclesiastes 8:15

One of my favorite things to do when I travel is to create a new tradition. It's my favorite way of adding a new beat to the rhythm you create when you're far away from home.

When Carl and I were on our honeymoon in the Dominican Republic, our tradition was wine and cheese. We were staying at an all-inclusive resort, so we decided to live it up. As we'd head back from the beach each day, we'd call and order room service and, by the time we were showered and in hotel bathrobes, there would be a knock at the door. We'd take our cheese plate and our bottle of wine out onto the patio, eating and sipping as we soaked in the beauty of the evening. It was one of my favorite things about our honeymoon.

When we were studying abroad in Spain, my best friend Kelsey and I started meeting our Spanish friends for lunch on Wednesdays. We'd meet at a little sandwich shop called 100 Montaditos. It was always packed with locals. The shop featured tiny sandwiches called montaditos, we learned, and there were 100 different varieties, all just a Euro each.

We'd all squeeze around a small high-top, laughing, and speaking in Spanish, and we made it our mission to try as many different montaditos as possible. It was one of the best parts of our week, and it was a tradition Kelsey and I carried on for awhile once we got back home to college. Sandwiches after class at Half Fast on The Hill? Yes and amen to that.

Not long ago I went to Cancun with a few of my girlfriends—a business retreat, technically—mostly a time for friendship and sun. Each day, as the sun was about to set, we sprinted up to the 12th floor of the hotel, asked for a glass of champagne on the way, and jumped into the pool that overlooked the ocean. We sipped our champagne as we paddled around on pool floats, telling stories and laughing so hard our stomachs hurt, as we watched the sun go down.

I just love these different traditions.

But travel and the traditions we create along the way, aren't always possible in every season of life. There's not always time to leave; there's not always the money. Since Carl and I have gotten married, we've had lots of transitions, expenses, and life changes. So we haven't been able to travel much. That's how life is sometimes, but that doesn't mean we can't still make these little traditions. In fact, recently, I realized we can!

I was feeling particularly wanderlust-y a few months ago. I was itching to travel somewhere new, wishing I could go to 100 Montaditos, or back to the Dominican Republic, when I suddenly remembered this scene from one of my favorite movies, *Under The Tuscan Sun*. Halfway through a massive renovation of a very old Italian villa, the movie shows Diane Lane sitting at a table in her backyard with a bottle of wine. She says, "These days I mostly like hanging out at a little bar I know, conveniently located in my backyard!" She tilts her face up to the sun and then takes a sip of her wine.

I realized that I could do the same thing. I didn't have to go far away, not that day at least. I could create an escape, a mini-travel destination, a little tradition right here at home. So that's what I did! I rifled through our pantry, pulling out crackers and cheese and olives and jam. I poured deep, red Cabernet into my favorite wine glass, and put on my favorite traveling playlist, the best of Bossa Nova. I pulled a stool up to our breakfast bar, and there I sat—at a new little bar I know, conveniently located between my kitchen and my living room.

So, these days, that's my favorite new tradition. Whenever I'm looking to end a day well, to transition into the weekend, to satisfy my wanderlust, or just to infuse a day with extra whimsy and delight, I visit this little bar.

We can't always go to the Dominican Republic, or Spain, or Cancun. But we can start new traditions right where we are—bringing a little bit of whimsy into the middle of an ordinary Wednesday.

Try creating a new little tradition this week. Maybe you decide to start your Saturdays with a latte and a long walk. Or maybe you decide to end your work week with a bubble bath as you watch your favorite show. Maybe you decide to meet your girlfriends for Happy Hour on Thursdays. Or maybe you sidle up to a little bar of your own, right there in your kitchen. These traditions don't have to be elaborate or expensive. They're just ways of adding a new rhythm and some fun into our weeks. So give it a try!

One Stone at a Time

"Let us not become weary in doing good, for at the
proper time we will reap a harvest if we do not give up."

Galatians 6:9

A few years ago, over the course of just about six months, I put on
quite a bit of weight. I didn't mean to. There was no reason or excuse
or medical change that caused it. We just had a lot of life transitions,
and I ate way too many cheeseburgers. It just sort of happened.

For a long time I pretended that nothing had changed, but finally,
my clothes stopped fitting completely, and I had to face facts. I
didn't want to be secretly unbuttoning my pants at my desk at
work; I didn't want to feel squished or squeezed or disappointed
in myself for being so lazy. I wanted to be diligent and faithful in
taking care of myself. I wanted to feel healthy, strong, and confident in my skin.

I decided I needed to make a change.

I got to work immediately. I started taking long walks, and listening to podcasts as I peddled away on the elliptical. I started doing
Pilates videos from the floor of my living room. I paid a bit more
attention to my cheeseburger intake.

At first, it was going well. I was feeling better already, proud of
myself for my diligence. But then, after about a week, I stepped
in front of a mirror to check out my progress. I know it's hard to
believe it, but I hadn't changed one bit.

Now, I know better than to think that health and fitness show up
in full after a few days of mild exercise. But still, I was discour-

aged and frustrated. Fitness started to feel like an impossibly tall mountain looming over me. I had no idea how I'd ever make progress—if I would ever reach the goal that I had set for myself.

Then I remembered a lesson I learned awhile back while I was working on creating a course all about making the most of your single life.

Creating a course like this is a MASSIVE undertaking that takes years of planning, prep, and research, and then solid months upon months to write, create, film, and edit.

I was in the midst of creating the course when I had a similar thought, *I'm working and working, but am I making any progress? Am I ever going to make it to the top of this mountain? Am I ever going to get this done?* It felt entirely impossible from where I was sitting that day. I was totally discouraged. But, in that moment, an image popped into my mind, and I haven't been able to shake it since.

I pictured the beautiful buildings I've seen around the world— holy, iconic buildings like Notre Dame in Paris, and Angkor Wat in Cambodia—and tried to imagine how in the world they were made.

I realize that buildings are, of course, made possible by architects and engineers and lots of math and science. But really, what built those buildings was a dedicated team working diligently every day, stacking up one stone at a time.

As I peddled away on the elliptical a few hours later, I remembered that image, and I realized that's how my goal was going to be achieved as well. Fitness doesn't happen overnight. In fact, nothing good really does. The biggest, best things in life happen when we show up faithfully day after day, stacking just one more stone on the pile. Businesses, communities, getting out of debt, friendship, marriages—all the best things in the world are built that way.

That's what I had to remind myself that day.

No, I couldn't visibly see progress in just one week. We rarely can, no matter what we're working on. But if we keep showing up, and keep putting one stone on the pile each and every day, after awhile we'll be able to look back and see that we've built something spectacular.

I don't know what big things you're attempting today, but I'll bet you have something in mind. Maybe you're applying for a new job, or for colleges or grad school. Maybe you're in the process of packing up and moving or trying to finish a course. Maybe you're writing a book or starting a blog or opening up your own business. Maybe you're trying to get healthy like I am—trying to take care of your body (and maybe shed a few extra cheeseburger pounds. Or maybe that's just me).

Whatever your thing is, whatever you're trying to create or do or build, that's how it'll get accomplished: one stone at a time. So let's stack one more on the pile today together. We can do this!

Our relationship with God is built the same way. We get to know Him better with every minute we spend with Him: every time we open our Bible, pray, learn something new in church, or decide to trust Him. Our faith gets stronger one day at a time, one moment at a time, one stone at a time. So put a few stones on the stack today. And also—don't forget that you can invite God into whatever else you're building. You get to have the Creator of the universe on your side.

In The Face of Darkness, I Choose Beauty

"The thief comes only to steal and kill and destroy; I have
come that they may have life, and have it to the full."

John 10:10

It happens more often than I really want to think about. Tragedy
strikes, and we're left in its wake, checking news feeds and waiting
for updates. A shooting, an earthquake, a terrorist attack, the list
goes on. We call friends to make sure they weren't there and pray,
having no idea what to say other than, "God, please help!"

There have been so many of these days, so many headlines and,
throughout all of these instances, I've never figured out how to
handle them.

To be honest, part of me wants to just ignore it. I want to cover my
eyes, look away, and pretend it's not happening, because I don't
know how to handle the fact that it really, truly is.

These instances remind us of just how dark and scary and dan-
gerous the world can be. So part of me wants to hide, or build a
panic room all the way around my house. I want to hunker down
and buy 20 years of canned food, trying anything I can think of to
make myself feel safe again.

Every part of me wants to fix the problem, to make it better, to
take all of the pain away, but I just don't know how. I feel helpless
in the face of the destruction. I donate, I re-Tweet, I support the
organizations that are working to help. But it just seems to fall flat,
my effort feels like a drop in an all-too-dark ocean.

I know I should pray—that it should be my first reaction, but my prayers seem to die out halfway through. They come out of my mouth and then fall short in the air, the pain and the fear swallowing my words whole.

I don't know what to do on days like these. I don't know what to do when we're faced with unimaginable darkness as it seems we are so often.

But the word I keep coming back to is "Celebration."

Isn't that crazy? It seems like the last word that should be on my mind. It seems inconsiderate to celebrate when things like this are happening. We don't know what else to do in the face of death and destruction, but celebration feels irresponsible, joy feels uncaring, sunshine feels insensitive. But still, it's the thing I keep coming back to.

John 10:10 says, "The thief comes only to steal, kill, and destroy; I have come that they may have life, and have it to the full." And I need to hold onto that life part, gripping onto it with both hands. I want to cling to the good things: to the life, to the joy, to the love. I just don't know what else to do!

I'm not saying we should ignore what's happened, or that we shouldn't grieve. I'm not at all advocating for turning our faces away from hurt or pain. We need to grieve, and be quiet, turn off our phones for a little while, and gather together with the people we love. We need to mark what's happened, and process and grieve in whatever way we know how.

But I also want to celebrate because, to me, it seems like the best way to fight back. It seems like the best, most productive thing we can do in times like these, putting a little extra weight on the goodness and love side of the scale.

I want to laugh and kiss and snuggle and tell my friends that I love them. I want to welcome people into my home and be generous with my money and my gifts and my resources. I want to meet people who are different from me, share a meal together, and listen to their stories. I want to find a puppy and smoosh my face into its soft fur. I want to love everyone I can find, and celebrate beauty with everything I have—shouting from the rooftops that the flowers are lovely and that the rain smells like heaven.

There is anger in the world—anger and death and destruction and horrible things beyond comprehension. But there is also beauty in the world—goodness, and love, and new life spilling over. And I choose beauty.

I'm not going to ignore the pain in the world, but I'm going to do everything I can to tip the scale in the other direction.

So today, I pray that we celebrate.

I don't know what's going on in your world as you're reading this today. Maybe today is all sunshine, and best friends, and good news. I hope it is. I hope you don't need these words today. So, if you don't, tuck them away, and go do something lovely. But if you do need them today, I hope they help. Some truly awful things have happened in our world in these last few years, and these words are the only map I've ever been able to put together for how to make my way through. So if the headlines are tragic today, I hope this helps you too.

Telling Our Stories

"I pray that you, being rooted and established in love, may have power, together with all the Lord's holy people, to grasp how wide and long and high and deep is the love of Christ, and to know this love that surpasses knowledge—that you may be filled to the measure of all the fullness of God."

Ephesians 3:17b-19

One of the trickiest moments in my life as a Christian came at the very beginning. My life had just changed, not just a little; it had changed completely. And almost immediately, I was faced with the big question, "How in the world do I tell people about this?"

I was asking the question in a few different ways. One was about my family and friends. How do I share my faith with the people I love so they can know me, and understand what's just happened in my life? In that, I felt a little queasy. What if they weren't supportive? What if I came across people who really don't like Christians, or who disagree with the choices I've made in my life? I instantly felt like I needed to find all the answers, to lawyer-up in defense of God and my dedication to Him.

I also asked the question because my life had changed in such a beautiful way, such a positive way. I knew there were people in my life who were asking the same big questions I had been, who were hurting in the same ways, and I knew that Jesus could help them the way He had for me. It felt like I'd found the cure to such a wide breadth of problems. I wanted to pass it on, but I just wasn't sure how.

Those questions are really tricky. Sharing our faith is really tricky. It's tricky because we're not sure how the person across from us is going to react. We don't want to come across as pushy, or salesy—like we're hocking the latest Tupperware or makeup product in a pyramid scheme.

Truthfully, I think that, no matter how long we've been a Christian, we feel like we don't know enough to share our faith. We know why WE are a Christian, but we feel like we're lacking the theology degree it certainly requires to explain our faith, to defend our faith, or to help someone else grow a faith of their own. But the good news is, we don't need a theology degree to share our faith. What we need more than anything is simply our story.

A few years before I became a Christian, my best friend, Michelle, met Jesus. I was happy for her, but also totally uninterested in doing the same. I had a zillion questions about Christianity and even more doubts about it. When it would come up, I'd pepper her with questions she didn't have answers to, and even when she did, her answers never really helped.

She noticed this after awhile, that her attempts to be God's lawyer, defending and arguing and proving His case, weren't bringing me closer to Him (I've found this strategy never really helps). So eventually she tried a different tactic.

When I'd ask her a big question, or ask her about God, she would answer me with her story. "This is what God has done in my life. This is how He's changed me; this is what He's taught me."

She made it personal; she didn't try to have all the answers. I actually didn't need her to when it came down to it. She wasn't pushy, didn't try to argue with me, didn't try to debate. It didn't feel like she was selling something either, so I didn't feel the need to push back or say no.

She was just putting something on the table in between us, not too far on my side, just showing me, "Hey, this is what God has done in my life." The second part hung in the air, she didn't even have to say it: "and if you want, this is what He could do in your life too." It didn't happen overnight but, after several months of hearing her stories, they started to create a little soft place in my heart, a place of hope, of wonder, of curiosity. I started to be a bit more interested in the things she was saying, wondering if I might want God to do the same things in my life that He'd been doing in hers. Not long after, in the Sistine Chapel with Michelle by my side, I told Jesus I wanted a relationship with Him. I was in. I said yes!

A few years later, God gave me the idea to write a book called *The Lipstick Gospel*. He told me to tell the story of what He's done in my life so that girls just like me can know what He's capable of doing in their lives too. And I think that invitation is for all of us.

Whether we're sharing our faith with our family and friends, talking about God with people who might disagree, or inviting someone to get to know God for themselves, we don't need all the answers. We don't need a theology degree or to know the Greek, the Hebrew, or the Aramaic. We just need to know our story, the story of what God is capable of doing in a human heart, what He's done in ours and what He can do in theirs too.

Those stories change everything. I know they did for me.

You may still have doubts about whether or not your story is worth sharing. What if your story is hard or broken? What if your story isn't some big crazy transformation? What if you've known God your whole life? Or what if you've only known Him for a few months? Do you still have a story worth sharing? Absolutely, yes, 10000x yes, because the details of your story will speak to a group of people who have those details in their story too. There are people in the world who are where you were a few weeks or months or years ago. They're asking the same questions you were—Am I okay? Am I going to get through this? Does God love me? Can He forgive me… even for this? And by telling the story of how God met you there, you get to show them who God is, and how He can transform their lives too.

Confessions & Freedom

"Confess your sins to each other and pray for each
other so that you may be healed. The prayer of a
righteous person is powerful and effective."

James 5:16

A few years ago, I was on a weekend retreat with a group of girl-friends. We all knew each other, certainly, but we weren't best friends, not soul-mate best friends—not yet anyway.

We'd had a long few months of work and needed some time to refuel. So, in the most relaxing, most wonderful weekend, we ate fresh-made pasta, drank exquisite wine, and spent lots of time by the pool and at the beach.

When I left that weekend, my heart felt like it was full to overflowing, but it wasn't because of the wine or because of the pasta, or even because of the beach, if you can believe it. The thing that filled me up so entirely was a conversation we all had while sitting at an outdoor cafe one afternoon.

I can't tell you how we got on the subject, because I truly don't remember. I don't remember who spoke first, or how we got around to confessing the things we did that day. All I know is that I came out of that conversation with the profound knowledge that in one of the deepest, toughest, most rampant areas of fear and insecurity in my life, I am simply not alone.

I think we all have things about ourselves that make us feel inse-cure. I know I do. For some of us, our toughest insecurities are physical, and often those came from being made fun of when we were little. I know that's where mine came from. For others of us, our insecurities have to do with our personalities—parts of ourselves we were taught to hide, downplay, things we've been told are too much or not enough.

But the thing is, we never talk about our insecurities, or at least I hadn't until that afternoon. So I'd carried my insecurity around like an awful secret, and it had never occurred to me until that day that anyone else might be feeling insecure too.

That afternoon we opened up to each other in the most unbelievable way. We went around the circle and admitted to each other what our thing was—the insecurity that bothered us the most. For one girl it was a birthmark, for another it was her nose, and for another, it was the hair on her arms. For another girl, it was her exuberant personality. She'd always believed that she was a lot to handle, more than anyone would really want. She tried to keep herself quiet, and had taught herself to fade into the background when she'd obviously been created to stand out.

We admitted the things that made us feel embarrassed, small, and not good enough—we each had something. But as we talked, we began to notice a pattern. Not one of the things these beautiful women had spent so long worrying about took anything away from the beauty we saw sitting in front of us.

We had never noticed the things the others were insecure about. We had never considered that they were too loud, or too much. We had never seen the birthmark. And, even when they brought their thing to our attention, we almost had to laugh. The thing they were feeling insecure about was like a tiny drop in an ocean of beauty. It couldn't even begin to compare. It was so healing watching this conversation unfold for everyone else this way because it made you think that maybe, just maybe, your insecurity was a tiny drop in the ocean too.

At the end of the conversation, we spent time telling each woman what she actually looked like. With our words, we brought her to a mirror and helped her see the truth about who she really is. We pointed out her gifts, and strengths, and the beauty she had a hard time seeing on her own—and that's what they did for me too.

I walked away from that conversation feeling a thousand pounds lighter because up until that day I'd never told anyone what made me feel insecure. And the thing about keeping things like that a secret is that our secrets grow in the dark. Without any accountability, any light, or any perspective, my insecurities felt enormous, overpowering, like they overshadowed everything good about me completely.

But as I opened up to my friends that day, they were able to flip on a light. They poked a thousand holes in my insecurities that day, showing them for the liars they are, and they helped me see myself in a whole new way. I felt beautiful, and good enough, and for the first time, I felt free.

Are there things you feel insecure about? Have you shared them with anyone? If you haven't, or if you haven't recently, find someone you can open up to. It could be a really good, really safe friend, or a parent, or a counselor, or a mentor. But find someone you trust, and tell them what's going on in your head. Tell them whatever it is that makes you feel unworthy of love because, when you do, it will lose so much of its power over you.

God Can't See Through Roofs

"In him and through faith in him we may approach
God with freedom and confidence."

Ephesians 3:12

The year after I graduated from college, I spent a ton of time with a group of truly wonderful guys. They were hilarious, and adorable, and loved God with their whole hearts. Before I met them, I didn't know guys like that existed, but they do!

They made me laugh, and they made me think, and they picked me up and delivered me right to God's feet, teaching me more about Him than I ever could have learned on my own.

We would joke about a million different things, but one of the things we would always joke about was the idea that God can't see through roofs. We'd be in the midst of concocting some ridiculous plan or scheme, or we'd be joking (just joking!) about doing something we knew we shouldn't. Right about then, someone would jump in and say, "Don't worry about it guys. We'll totally get away with this. After all, God can't see through roofs."

I still say that on occasion—it's one of my go-to terrible jokes. And I love it because it couldn't be less true.

Have you ever been mad at God, frustrated with Him, confused by something He did or didn't do, a way it feels like He totally dropped the ball? My prayers in the aftermath of something like this are always stilted—extra polite, like when you're upset with a friend, but not sure how to bring it up.

Have you ever done something that you think disappointed God?

Your communication with Him turns to radio silence. You just can't bring yourself to face Him, knowing what you've done.

Have you ever felt like you needed to shine yourself up in front of God? Like you need to be on your best behavior when you talk to Him, using big words and referencing the thing you read in your Bible that morning just to earn yourself extra points?

I've done all of those things—feeling like I needed to hide from God, perform for God, keep a stiff upper lip with God—hiding the fact that I'm hurt, or confused, or downright angry with Him. Because He's God, right? He's God. Like, actual God, the God of the whole universe, the one who created the stars and the mountains and the sea.

But the thing I love to remember in moments like these is that I'm not really hiding or concealing very much because God CAN, in fact, see through roofs.

He knows when we're mad, or upset, or confused. He knew what we were expecting, and the ways that fell through. He knows what we did; He was there, He's aware. We aren't keeping a secret by not telling Him. I also don't think He's impressed by our fancy words and good behavior. Because our good behavior next to a holy God still totally doesn't measure up. And our big words aren't fooling Him because He knows how we talk to our best friends and our own dads. He knows how we think, and that movie we quote constantly because it never stops being funny.

There's no pretending with God, or at least there doesn't have to be, and I'm just so grateful for this. It makes me feel so seen, so understood. He knows our thoughts, and our dreams, and our hopes, and our disappointments. He knows all the ways we get it wrong, both in huge ways and in small ones, and the best part is, He loves us through them.

It's fine to be loved for the perfect façade we show the world, but it's a deep, soul-filling, heart-changing thing to be loved for exactly who you are, big mess, ridiculous movie quotes and all. And that's how God loves us because God CAN see through roofs.

He knows us, actually knows us, and He loves us completely. And there's just nothing safer or warmer or better or more transformative than that.

Talk to God today. Have an honest conversation with Him. God knows what you're thinking, but He still wants to talk it through together, to hear your thoughts, and hopes, and dreams, and fears. More than anything else, God wants a relationship with you. So talk to Him today, resting in the deep breath that comes when we realize we don't have to hide or perform for Him anymore. He already knows us and loves us no matter what.

a Season of Newness

"See, I am doing a new thing! Now it springs up;
do you not perceive it? I am making a way in the
wilderness and streams in the wasteland."

Isaiah 43:19

I love winter. I look forward to it for months, dancing giddily in
the first snow of the year. I love winter for its magic. It's a season
full of candles and twinkling lights, sugar cookies and cocoa. It's
a time that invites coziness at every turn—warm chairs and fire-
places calling our names.

I love winter for the tradition—the families that come together,
doing the same things they've done for years. I love the familiarity
of it and also the romance. Everything is enchanting under a light
dusting of snow.

I love winter, absolutely, but by about February, I'm ready to see
it go. There's a heaviness to winter that, on particularly cold days,
seems to chase joy away. Come February, I always find it hard to
get out of bed—my skin not wanting to leave the cozy warmth of
my covers. And after so many months inside, I begin to feel stifled
inside my warm, glowy house. I'm itching for sunlight and fresh air.

And so, with the arrival of spring, I'm always incredibly grateful.

Spring is a time to step out from the heaviness of winter—feeling
the warm sunshine for the first time all over again. It's a season
of newness—fresh life popping up from what was dead for so
many months. Spring is a merciful new beginning that invites us
to become new right along with it.

I think we long for newness in lots of seasons of our lives, and in lots of areas of our lives too. We long for transformation, a new beginning, and whether it's spring right now or not, today is the perfect time to step into something fresh.

But newness doesn't always just happen on its own. Sometimes it requires something from us.

If you've ever had a garden, you know that, before you can plant something new, and in order to give new life room to grow, you have to clear away some old things first.

This is true for us as well.

Every so often, in all of our lives, I think it's good to take an inventory. What is filling your life and your time and your email inbox? What's on your to-do list, in your closets, and taking up space in your heart?

I think every so often we need to re-evaluate—to ask ourselves if this is still good, and right, and helpful, and healthy. We only have so much room in our lives, in our homes, and in our schedules. In order to make space for new things to grow, sometimes there are things we might need to let go of.

So what in your life might need to be cleared away? Are there relationships that you know aren't good for you, or friendships that routinely make you feel small? Do you devote your time to a list of commitments that you secretly dread? Do you have some habits or ways of spending your time that aren't bringing you life? Are you stuck under a pile of clutter, just craving a clean slate?

It can be intimidating to let go of things that are familiar but, once the ground is cleared, we can take hold of something fresh — intentionally planting something good and watching it grow.

Are there any areas of your life where it might be time to take an inventory? Take a few minutes to think through that this morning. What are some new things you'd like to see in your life in this next season? What do you need to clear away in order to give them room to grow?

You Can't Mess Up God's Plan

> "You rule over the surging sea; when its waves
> mount up, you still them."
>
> Psalm 89:9

My life in college was a mess—there is no way around it.

I was drinking too much and making big mistakes. I did too much with this guy; I wasn't enough for this one. I failed this test in school, and I failed even more tests in life.

I was doing my best, or rather, trying to do my best, but it felt like I was running in circles. My story felt like such a random series of events. It felt like I was in the ocean with wave after wave crashing over my head. I was just trying to stay afloat.

When I first heard that God might have a plan for my life, I wasn't relieved, I was sad! Because even if God did have a plan for me, I'd probably screwed it up already. I'd probably doodled hearts, and swirls, and boy's phone numbers all over His perfectly drawn map.

"God wants to use you," people told me. "He has a plan for your life, and He's not going to let you wander out of it, I promise!" But I just had a hard time believing it.

Have you ever watched a sunset from a cliff? Watching the waves from way up high is so different than being down in them.

When you're down in the water, facing the waves straight on, they loom over you menacingly, and they're all you can see. The craziness of life crashes over your head, leaving you exhausted, confused and gasping for air. You can barely see the shore when you're out there. The tide washes you out to sea, and the undertow drags you far away from where you planned to end up.

But, when you back away from the waves a bit, climbing up and getting some perspective, things look so different. When you're sitting up there, high above the ocean, watching the sun go down, a golden path of light stretches out in front of you, leading all the way to the horizon. The waves are still there, absolutely, and life may feel chaotic in the midst of them sometimes. But the waves all exist within that glowing path of light, a path that's wider than anything we can stray from. There's no confusion, only peace, and purpose, and direction.

A few years later, I met a girl I was mentoring at the Starbucks just off campus. I had a hard time saying those words, "The girl I was mentoring," because, even though my life was better than it ever had been, I still didn't feel qualified to be anyone's mentor.

We grabbed our coffees, settled in at a corner table, and she started telling me about a decision she was trying to make.

I nodded, totally understanding where she was coming from. I couldn't believe it, but I had actually been there too. It was a decision I'd wrestled with, something I'd never shared with anyone, but here it was coming up. Something stirred in my heart as I got to use my experience to help her, to show her what was down the path I'd chosen, and to help her pick one for herself.

A week later, I went to coffee with a different girl I was mentoring, and she'd recently made a big mistake. She confessed it to me quietly and instantly began to cry. "I can't believe I did this," she told me, "I'm so stupid! I feel so guilty! Nobody else does things like this! Why can't I get my act together?" I sat there with her for a few minutes, nodding and listening, and then finally I spoke up. "Actually… you're not the only one who's made that mistake… I did the very same thing."

The look on her face went from shock to relief, and then to the best mix of laughing and crying. I've discovered that's often the reaction when we find out we're not alone.

We sat at that Starbucks for hours. We talked through what had happened, how we each got to that place, how I moved forward, and we made a plan for how she could too. My experience was able to help her in hers, and for the first time ever, I saw a sliver of purpose and even goodness in my past.

I thought I was messing up God's plan for my life. I thought I'd made so many mistakes that there'd be nothing left for Him to work with. He couldn't possibly use someone like me to make a difference in the world. He couldn't possibly bring goodness out of the messes I'd made.

But there He was, bringing goodness out of my messes. I'd learned from my messes, I realized over coffee. I'd learned, and I could pass those lessons to the friends a few paces behind me. I could hand them a sweater, a sandwich, and a roadmap. "If you take a left here, it'll be much easier," I could counsel, having taken enough rights to know the difference.

Life may feel chaotic sometimes. We're in the midst of the waves, doing our best, and feeling like we're totally messing things up. But we can't mess things up beyond God's ability to repair. Even our biggest mistakes aren't beyond God's ability to redeem because His plan is bigger than all the waves. It's wider, in fact, it holds them all together. The waves, and even our biggest messes, exist within God's golden stretch of light—He can use them all.

I love the way Lisa Bevere says it. She says, "If you think you've blown God's plan for your life, rest in this. You, my beautiful friend, are not that powerful." Yes and amen to that. Take a few minutes to let that truth sink in this morning.

Climbing Impossible Mountains

"For nothing is impossible with God."

Luke 1:37

A few winters ago, the hardest part of my day happened between exactly 7 and 8 a.m.

The sun was still fast asleep, and my room was impossibly cold. My alarm would go off, and I would hit snooze as many times as it would let me before refusing to be snoozed any longer. I would will my eyes to open, coaxing and prodding them, and that wasn't even the hard part. The hard part was dragging myself out of my warm bed, out to the car (which was usually covered in snow and ice), and praying for it to warm up as I'd drive to our town's Planet Fitness.

It was time to run.

Lest you be impressed with me, I need you know that I'm a positively horrible runner. I tell people that, and they laugh and think I'm exaggerating. But I assure you, I am not.

Running has been my arch-nemesis for years. It was my daily source of torture and shame at the beginning of each dance practice in high school. We'd run the hallways of our school for a warm up, which sounds easy until you realize that our hallways were approximately the size of a concourse at Denver International Airport. It sounds fine until you see that the hallways were lined with football players and all of my classmates—witnesses to my humiliation. It sounds like no big deal until you see that I was always the slowest in the pack, and had (and still have!) some sort of freak reaction to running that turns my face a sickly, splotchy purple.

So let's just say that running and I have never gotten along.

Running has always felt like it had this power over me. It was this mountain that felt impossible to climb, a constant reminder of all of the times I'd tried and failed. It felt like an obstacle I just couldn't overcome. So finally, one day, I decided I needed to learn how to run. I needed to show myself that I could do it—that I could do something hard—that I could overcome a physical challenge and a mental one as well.

And so I took it on. I spent a couple of bucks on a Couch-5K iPhone app and let the automated man's voice (I called him Steve) tell me what to do three times a week for two months.

It wasn't easy.

The biggest battle happened first thing in the morning when I had to choose Steve and my desire for triumph over my desire for an extra thirty minutes of sleep. But, once that was over, I had to take on the road. I had to face my legs that felt like they were filled with lead. I had to face my lack of discipline as I wanted to give up after the first day, and I had to face my fear that I just wasn't going to make it.

The first time Steve told me to run for three minutes, I could have killed him, but I realized that would have cost me my iPhone as well, so I spared his life. And when my first 28-minute run overlapped with a trip to Colorado, I thought the altitude was going to flatten me completely.

But then, on a random Thursday morning, I got up and headed to the gym, and I did it. I ran a 5K all at once—no walking, no stopping, no resting, no cheating. I actually did it!

I learned several things between the hours of 7 and 8 that winter. The first is that there are few better feelings in the world than accomplishing something really difficult. The second is that whatever you're getting up to do will usually make you feel way better than an extra 30 minutes of sleep. But the third thing is this: We're capable of so much more than we sometimes believe.

I'm amazed every day by stories of people doing the impossible. Every single day, people overcome odds and disease and setbacks and circumstances. Every single day, people choose to believe in more than what their surroundings, their bodies, or their situations tell them is true.

Those stories reflect God like crazy because we serve a God who says that anything is possible. We serve a God who brings wholeness from brokenness, beauty from ashes, hope from despair, and life from death. We serve a God who isn't deterred by the word "impossible," so it would be a shame not to follow in his footsteps, don't you think? Even if those footsteps lead you to a treadmill at Planet Fitness.

Are there any mountains in your life right now? Anything that just feels too big to overcome? God's specialty is making a way when there isn't one, doing the impossible, helping ordinary people overcome insurmountable odds. So tell Him about your mountain today, and I dare you to take the first step up it together.

M&M, Thumb Wars, & Church

"Rejoice in the Lord always. I will say it again: Rejoice!"

Philippians 4:4

When I was growing up, and really until I was 21-years-old, Christianity was never a part of my life. I guess it was a part, a very small part though. There were a few short years when my parents made us go to church each Sunday. They did that until one of their children, the more precocious, vocal child of the two (me, of course), complained so much that they finally let us stop.

The church wasn't terrible by any means. It was fine. It's just that the services were boring. (Am I allowed to say that? I hope so.) They really were just boring! It was all hymns and big holy words I didn't understand. I was always itchy and uncomfortable at church—wearing stiff dresses and tights. The worst! So I'd sit there throughout the service, kicking my legs against the pews, waiting and waiting and waiting for it to be over.

My mom was determined when it came to going to church. But my dad was sympathetic. He wasn't letting us off the hook by any means, but he was determined to make it a bit more fun.

One Sunday, right in the middle of the sermon, my dad whispered an almost inaudible, "Hey!" I looked over at him, and he motioned for me to open my hand and close my eyes. I did, and he plopped something small and round into my hand. I opened my eyes to find a peanut M&M. "Where did you get this?" I whispered back, laughing. He reached into the breast pocket of his shirt to grab another one, trying hard not to let the wrapper crinkle.

This began a tradition for me, my sister, and my dad at church.

My dad would keep different things in his pocket each week. Sometimes it was M&Ms, and he'd slip us one when we'd least expect it, just to keep us entertained. Other times it would be Altoids—little minty pops between the hymns and the readings.

On Sundays when he could tell we were really having a hard time, my dad would offer us a hand, low below the pews so no one could see. It looked as if he was going to give us a handshake, but his thumb was stretched high. It was a thumb war challenge, and we were always game. We'd take him on, being careful not to wiggle or squeal or draw attention to ourselves as we battled, and though we'd rarely win, it was just the best.

When I think about my small slivers of faith growing up, this is one of my favorite memories. My dad showed us in a small way that our relationships with God didn't have to be quite so serious, quite so formal. We could laugh, and be lighthearted, and have fun with it. And this is an idea that's colored my faith ever since.

These days, one of my favorite ways to connect with God is to spend some time with Him each morning. Whenever I tell people about my morning time with God, I compare it to any other relationship. If you want to get closer to someone, the formula is pretty simple. You just have to spend time together. The more time you spend together, the closer you'll become. And the same is true with God.

But, as I'm sure you've experienced, if you do the same thing with someone every day, after a while it can grow stale, and this is true with God too. Read your Bible, journal, pray, read your Bible, journal, pray—it can become monotonous sometimes, feeling more like a box to check than a relationship.

Last year, I found myself in a total rut in my time with God. I was doing the check-list thing, absolutely. Read my Bible? Check. Did I remember anything from it? Not really. Did I connect with God through it? Sure didn't. But hey, at least I showed up, right?

And that's when I remembered my dad at church—slipping us an M&M, an Altoid, or challenging us to a thumb war. It reminded me that our relationships with God don't have to look the same every day. They don't have to be so formal or rigid. God is so much more interested in a relationship with us than He is a fully checked off list.

I remembered that it really is a relationship, similar to any other and that when we do new and different things with the people we love, we get to see new sides of them, new dimensions, we get to connect with them in new and different ways. This is true with God too.

When we do new and different things in our time with God, we remind ourselves that He's so nuanced, not one note, not one flavor. God is serious and holy and is there in the rituals, in the incense, and in the silence. He's a big deal, absolutely, and not to be taken lightly. But He also created us with such light hearts, and the world with so many fun secrets and delights and adventures to be had. He created us to laugh, and smile, and play, and love.

And I knew this was my way out of my morning rut.

The next morning, I woke up early, passed right by the coffee pot, left my Bible closed, and my journal too. I headed straight to the garage, where (after some careful maneuvering) I unearthed the black and pink beach cruiser I'd bought on a whim the summer I lived in Southern California. I tossed my leg over one side, and gave a big push, zooming down the driveway, gaining speed as I went.

For an hour at least, I zoomed around my old familiar neighborhood. I zipped through the park, and past the houses I knew so well. I turned corners and turned back again, making loops, not wanting the ride to stop. And as I rode, the wind whipping through my hair, God felt so close, right there with me, laughing, and playing, and enjoying the ride.

Church is no less holy with some laughter and M&Ms, and our quiet times are no less connected when they happen on a bike. If your relationship with God is feeling a bit stale lately, try switching it up—add some whimsy, something sweet, something fun, or something silly. I promise God will still be there, maybe even closer than before.

Grief & Joy

"You will grieve, but your grief will turn to joy."

John 16:20b

I've always hated grief. I don't know if you're allowed to say that, if you're allowed to reject something so timeless and central to the human experience, but I don't care. I just don't like it.

I don't like talking about sad things, or watching sad movies, or feeling sad—let alone the kind of sadness that feels like it could swallow you if you really give into it.

Joy is another story altogether. I love joy. I'm a joy connoisseur—a collector of beautiful things, experiences, and loved ones. I'll take joy with a side of joy with a sprinkle of joy on top, if you don't mind.

But something I've learned is that while joy is more fun, grief can't be ignored.

A few years ago, I heard a man named Ron teach on the subject, and it changed my view of the thing completely. "Grieving your losses is an important spiritual discipline," he began.

He continued on to say that if we don't work through the hard things that have happened to us, we won't be able to help other people. Even worse, we could hurt other people with our hurt.

I'd heard a version of that before, "Hurt people hurt people." Yes. I'd been hurt by people who I knew were hurting. I had also had a pretty clear idea of what this looked like in reverse. Two words: Rebound relationships.

In the wake of my deepest heartbreak, a guy in my French class asked me on a date. I should have said no, but in a grand gesture to prove how fine I was post-breakup, I said yes. He made me dinner, and we drank some wine and ended the evening chatting while lying on our backs on his bearskin rug. (You can't make this stuff up!). After a few general questions about family, travel destinations, and favorite foods, he cut to the chase. "Tell me about your last relationship," he prompted.

Without even the slightest warning from my heart, I burst into tears. Through sniffles and gasps, I tried to explain my last relationship. "I'm totally over it. It's not a big deal," I sobbed. I think I was probably communicating something different.

I left that night thinking maybe I should have given myself a little longer to grieve. That night made me step back and understand there was a mess to clean up—some healing to be had before I invited someone else in.

I was learning I could only run from my grief for so long before it caught up with me in a messy, embarrassing pile of tissues, and I think I'm not the only one.

The truth is, at some point, grief bumps into us all. It's part of our lives in this broken, imperfect, messy world. We don't get to keep the ones we love forever. People aren't always kind, or faithful, or honest, and they don't always take care of us the way they should. We lose a relationship, a job, a friend, or a bit of our identity. Life wounds us all in different ways, leaving bruises, marks, and scars.

But this doesn't have to be the end of the story. If we work through the things that have happened to us, we can actually get past them, walking into our futures with whole, trusting, healed hearts— hearts that can serve others, connect with others, trust others, stand tall as the women we were created to be. Even better, we can help other women through these things once we've worked through them—turning around and offering shortcuts, a sweater for the journey, or just a friend along the way.

But the key here is that we have to work through our hurts. The problems arise when we bury them, when we ignore them altogether, because buried hurts don't stay buried forever—no matter how much we may wish they would.

They stifle our relationships, cause us to be guarded and hard-hearted, they make us afraid, keep us inside, keep us small, and keep us insecure. Sometimes, they make us angry. We get angry, or we just shut down. But anesthesia, as Ron pointed out, numbs everything, not just the bad stuff. We can't numb one emotion without numbing them all.

So here's the kicker for a joy aficionado like me: The more we allow ourselves to feel grief, the more we open ourselves up to feel joy. So what do we do? We grieve.

We face our hurts, ask for help, allow tears to flow so that what's aching inside can finally come out. Once we've faced our hurts, crying them up and out of our souls, cheeks still wet and hearts still tender, Jesus can do his best work—healing, redeeming, and making us new.

What might you need to let yourself grieve? It could be a small thing, or a major thing, or somewhere in between. I hope you begin to face whatever it is today, but know that you don't have to do this alone. If you're going through something hard, please invite someone into it with you: A parent, a friend, or a counselor. I'm a big proponent of counseling. A counselor or a therapist is a great person to help you process what happened, work through the grief, and come out on the other side healed and whole. We don't have to carry our hurts around forever, and we don't have to sort through them alone, so invite someone who knows the way to help you— healing is just around the corner.

It's Okay to Not Be Okay

"Show me your face, let me hear your voice; for
your voice is sweet, and your face is lovely."

Song of Songs 2:14b

We sat on the floor in the dark, facing each other, knees touching.
I was crying—it seemed like that's all I could do anymore. He was
comforting—always comforting. We talked about the deep things
of life, the hard things, and nodded in solemn agreement that joy
isn't always easy to find.

It was a humbling moment—the kind that leaves you feeling
exhausted and wet as mascara stains your cheeks. But it was one
of my favorites because we were closer and more connected than
we'd ever been before.

I'd heard it said, but now I knew it to be true: vulnerability breeds
intimacy, but that doesn't mean it's easy. Getting to know someone
can be a painful, humbling process. To know of someone, or to
see someone is fairly easy. Neither of you is required to risk much.
But to know—to really know—well that's another thing entirely.

The year when my husband Carl and I first started dating, I
watched and squirmed as he really got to know me. I tried to
wiggle away often, preferring to show my shined-up side, the side
who is tall and endlessly confident, always knowing the right thing
to say and wearing my very favorite outfit. I didn't want to be
tearstained and vulnerable, revealing insecurities and fears that
were too ugly for even me to see without cringing.

But, over the course of that year, I watched as he became my best
friend and my greatest love. I watched with amazement as he saw the

mess in my heart, and moved closer instead of away. I would have preferred intimacy without the tears, but no great thing comes easily.

Conveniently, Carl and I weren't the only ones getting to know each other that year. I was getting to know myself all over again, too.

I've always prided myself on being a joyful person. It was the greatest thing about me, the thing that defined me—or so I thought—but that year, it felt like my joy fell apart. I think it had something to do with the fact that I'd just moved across the country and started a new career. I was suddenly living far away from all my loved ones, making all new friends, and beginning a new relationship—the cherry on top of a lot of change and transition.

And, with all of that swirling around me and within me, I wasn't quite so joyful anymore. I was stressed out, worried, sad, and anxious. I cried a lot, hurt a lot, needed a lot of sleep and a lot of time to process. I definitely wasn't brimming over with joy, and truthfully, that scared me.

"I'm not sad, I'm not this girl," I would insist, because if I wasn't joyful anymore, who was I? Joy felt like the thing I brought to the table, the reason someone would like me, even the reason someone would love me. So without joy, I felt like I had nothing to offer. I felt like I was less worthy of love.

So I tried to fake it, fix it, anything to bring me back to who I thought I was supposed to be. But finally, after lots of prayers, and conversations, and even more tears, my soul took a breath. I could finally hear the truth that it's okay to not be okay. That's what Carl whispered to me on the floor that night. "It's ok, and my love for you is not contingent on your joy. Not today, not ever."

Carl has spent years giving me grace and space and permission and love—reminding me over and over that his love for me won't increase once I'm "all figured out." But, at the time, I couldn't say the same for myself. I had a tight definition of who I was and why I thought I was valuable, but that year stretched and strained that narrow, conditional love. It made me ask the questions, "What if I'm not okay sometimes? Is that really okay? What if I am really sad or mad sometimes? What if I have hard days, weeks, or seasons? What if I cry and don't have a good reason? What if I'm afraid?"

God is not scared of my "what ifs," and neither is Carl. And finally, neither am I.

That year was the beginning of accepting myself as I am—full and varied and complex. I started giving myself the grace and the space to experience the fullness of life, not just my own pre-approved emotions. I started getting to know myself without the façade, without the makeup, and without the perfection that I'd been demanding for so long.

It was a painful and beautiful process, and the person I started to find wasn't half bad. She's joyful, certainly, but in a way that's richer and more weathered. Like a relationship that has seen more than a honeymoon season, she's better for the hardship she's endured. She thinks and feels deeply, experiencing all of life with hands wide open. Sometimes she cries, but she always soaks in the fullness of the world like the vibrant green of a rainy day.

That year, I began to learn to love myself for the real stuff. And for the first time in my life, I was willing to sit with myself in the dark and say, "It's ok," and "I love you anyway."

It's scary to let someone really get to know us, but truthfully, getting to know ourselves can be really scary too. It's important, though, because the more we get to know ourselves, the more we have the capacity to love ourselves—and the more we can allow someone else to know and love us too. So take one step forward in that today, and be a little more honest with yourself and the people who love you. Vulnerability leads to intimacy. And while it's not always easy, it's worth it every time.

An Afternoon in Italy

"Every good and perfect gift is from above, coming
down from the Father of the heavenly lights, who
does not change like shifting shadows."

James 1:17

I don't know how long I was sitting there, staring out the window,
watching the rain drizzle down. All I know is that the rain matched
my heart that day—and not in a cozy blanket, hot cocoa kind of way.

Life had been stressful for as long as I could remember: hard, and
heavy, big conversations, more big transitions. It felt like adult life was
bearing down with extra weight in those days. Numbers, metrics,
money, health insurance, to-do lists, and budgets—lots of budgets.

I'm not an escaper, necessarily. I'm not someone who runs from
hard things or hard seasons, or at least I try not to be. But that day,
that's exactly what I wanted to do. I wanted to vacate my life for
a while. And I don't know what you crave when you're dreaming
about running away, but I didn't have to think about it twice. I
wanted to head straight to Europe.

I wanted to wander around Italy, filling my soul with pasta and
cappuccinos and Italian phrases with big hand gestures. I wanted
to read and write and take pictures and breathe. I wanted to
become a professional wanderer, a gelato taster, a photographer
of the faded Italian buildings that set my heart ablaze.

I needed a break, some time to rest, a match to re-light my inspiration, my excitement, and my wonder at the world.

I stared out the window, then back down at my laptop. I poked at the keyboard, wishing the work day was over already. I made my usual rounds between inboxes. I started a blog post then stopped. I felt busy and listless, stressed out and bored. I couldn't make sense of feeling all those things at once, and I couldn't tell you why my soul was craving beauty, rest, and Europe so acutely that day of all days. All I knew is that it was.

Now, if you're anything like me, you don't always give yourself what you're needing or wanting. I'm famous for being tired, but making myself get one more thing done; for knowing I need a night at home to myself, but saying yes to plans anyway. But that day, I decided to give myself a break. I decided to listen to what my heart was craving and actually respond. So I gave up on the work day and headed to a little sanctuary I'd overlooked until that very moment.

You see, for a season, I worked in an office that was right on top of an Italian restaurant—not just a restaurant, but a cute restaurant, one that played croony, Sinatra, wine-drinking music all day and all night. But I'd never ventured into it until that day. I'd always been too busy. (How many lovely things do we overlook because we're too busy? Too many, I'd say!)

And so, fed up and defeated, and unable to muster up inspiration or energy on that gloomy day, I headed downstairs for a stiff drink—a cappuccino, of course.

I found a small table in the corner of the empty restaurant and, as I sat down, I took a deep breath. I allowed the music to warm my gray soul and stared into my cappuccino with nothing more pressing in the world to do than that.

In the hour I sat in that restaurant, I didn't get anything accomplished. Nothing was checked off my list, my life didn't get smoother or less chaotic, and I didn't solve all the world's problems. Nothing happened as I sat there in that restaurant. But also—so much happened as I sat there in that restaurant.

Something about the music and that cappuccino, the moment alone, and the time to care for my insides brought me back to life in a way I sorely needed. Author Anne Lamott says, "Almost everything will work again if you unplug it for a few minutes, including you," and she's so, so right. The color came back to my cheeks and my soul, and my heart began to feel fuller and more delighted by the world than it had in a long while.

The thing is, we may not be able to literally jet off to Italy every time life feels dreary, but in some ways, we can.

We can find bits of Italy in our life and grab onto them with both hands. We can listen to that voice within us that's crying out for fun, or delight, or something delicious, and we can give in. We can take care of ourselves, giving some love and some light and some rest to our tender hearts that are so often overlooked for the sake of efficiency.

So that's what I chose to do that day. There's nothing in the world I wanted more than to escape to Europe, and I got to escape to the Italian restaurant downstairs. It's not exactly the same, but it was certainly close enough.

Take a moment to check in with yourself this morning. You may not be craving the same things I was, but you might be craving something. Do you need rest? Time by yourself? Time with friends? Time with God? Do you need some space to get things done or a break from it all? Are you hungry? Do you need a nap? Listen to what you need today, and then take it one step further and allow yourself to have that thing. And whatever it ends up looking like for you, I hope you get to go to Europe today, wherever you may find it.

When You Relax, You Float

"May the God of hope fill you with all joy and
peace as you trust in him, so that you may overflow
with hope by the power of the Holy Spirit."

Romans 15:13

It was a newspaper ad that started the whole thing. My sweet
mama cut it out and left it on my bed (a successful hint, though
not altogether subtle).

"Snorkel in the Denver Aquarium," the ad read. "Will you go with
me?" she pleaded later, adding a small whimper for dramatic effect.

I wanted to say no. I really don't like snorkeling. I never have.
Peering into a world I don't belong in, brushing up against creatures that are altogether foreign, being so out of control of my
surroundings… "No thank you. I'll wait for y'all on the beach."

But just a few short weeks later I found myself in a black, rubbery
wetsuit, standing gingerly on the edge of the biggest fish tank I've
ever seen. My heart pounded wildly as I caught a glance of the fish
while the guide described the massive turtles and other creatures
that populated the tank.

When it was time, I stepped one flippered foot into the tank and then
the other, sliding my rubbery body into the freezing water. With my
mask on tight, I took a deep breath and then plunged my face into
the tank, ready to face whatever I had just gotten myself into.

My mom paddled around happily, pointing at the colorful fish that
were bigger than my head. I tried to smile at her, I tried to look like

I was having fun, I tried to relax, but every muscle in my body was clenched tight. My legs kept sinking behind me, my upper body wiggling to keep myself above water, and failing entirely. I was ready to get out before I'd even fully gotten in.

The Aquarium Guide swam up beside me and tapped me on the back. I lifted my head to the surface and sputtered, "I think I'm going to get out," sounding like I had a bad cold with my nose plugged up by the mask.

"You can get out if you want to," he told me, "But I think you'll be happy if you stick with this. You've just got to relax! When you relax, your body will float. The more you tense up, the faster you sink."

I thought about it for a second and then decided to give it just one more chance. I put my face back in the water, took a deep breath, and relaxed, consciously and purposefully. As my body relaxed, I floated effortlessly to the surface. And as I did, I realized something—I think this is a lot like following God.

When we follow God with our lives, it's only a matter of time before we find ourselves in a situation that feels foreign, bigger than us, and intimidating, forcing us to face our fears and requiring more of us than we think we have to give.

In situations like these, I think we have two choices: We can go into them tense, trying to keep ourselves afloat on our own, thrashing as we try to maintain control of our surroundings and our lives... or, we can go into these situations having taken a deep breath, relaxing consciously and purposefully, and reminding ourselves that God has this. He is with us; He's in control, and He's taking care of us. When we thrash, we sink; but when we relax, we float.

The thing is that isn't a one-time decision. It wasn't for me in the tank, and it never is in real life. I had to keep relaxing, keep reminding myself that I was okay, keep taking deep breaths. I think trust looks like this in our lives with God too. It looks like reminding ourselves as often as we need to that we trust God, that

He's faithful, and that He has this.

The beauty of this is that when start to relax, start to really trust God, we get to see the amazing things that have been waiting on the other side of our masks the entire time.

The fish were actually kind of pretty when I took the time to admire them. The Aquarium Guide was right. I was happy I'd stuck with this. I would have missed out if I'd given up. After 30 minutes, we got to climb out of the tank. I was shivering and sore, my muscles aching from being tense for so long, but as my dad wrapped a warm towel around my damp shoulders, I felt proud.

I had done something that scared me, something bigger than me, and I had really done it. I had trusted God and allowed him to take me on an adventure, holding me safe and showing me the beauty that I would have missed on my own.

Choosing to trust God sounds simple, but can be a tough thing to do when we're faced with intimidating or uncomfortable invitations. It's something that gets easier the more we do it. The more times we step into the unknown with God, the more times we see Him come through. So let's start practicing this week. Let's start somewhere small. What's one new way you can trust God this week? Maybe it's something tangible, like donating money or food to a place that serves people in need; or maybe it's internal – choosing to believe that God has placed you exactly where you are for a reason, and that you are exactly the right person for the role you are in today.

God Is Better Than A Band-Aid

"For the kingdom of God is not a matter of talk but
of power."

1 Corinthians 4:20

I am, without a doubt, the worst movie date ever. If movies were like food, I'd eat only macaroni and cheese. Part of it is an immature movie palate, I'm sure. But most of it is that I really might be one of the most sensitive people on the planet.

My husband and I have learned one too many times that dark movies, heavy movies, sad movies leave me in a soggy heap. It's all tissues and crying and, "Why is the world such a sad, sad place?" I don't bounce back easily from movies like that. They're total date-night ruiners.

And that's exactly what happened on this night.

We pressed play and, over the next two hours, we watched a story unfold about deep alcohol addiction. We watched this man's drinking steal everything that he loved—ruining his life completely— the movie bringing you right into the action, causing you to feel every emotion right alongside him.

The movie was so hard to watch, mostly because it brushed a little too close to home.

As I watched him drink and drink and drink, I could smell the stench of the stale alcohol, memories of my own days of constant binge drinking flooding to mind. I remembered holding trash cans for friends as they threw up. I remembered sitting by the toilet with people I didn't even know, rubbing their backs as we waited for the ambulance to come. I remember finding that kid barely conscious in the parking lot, having fallen out of his car he was so drunk on a sunny Sunday afternoon.

But it wasn't just other people. It was me, too. In college, binge drinking was what we did. It wasn't a problem, it was a party trick – but one with heavy consequences. I remembered mornings where I was so hungover I couldn't move. I remembered waking up with no memory of the night before and bruises I couldn't identify. I remembered throwing up. I remembered my own night with alcohol poisoning and how my friends saved my life.

As I watched the movie, I got to see darkness deeper and more terrible than I had cared to remember. It felt utterly hopeless. When it was over, I was quiet for several minutes, and then I began to cry. It wasn't a delicate cry, but a deep, gut-wrenching sob. It felt like my blinders had been ripped off and, all of a sudden, I could see things that I'd forgotten about, things that just don't cross my line of sight these days. I'd forgotten how deep the despair in our world can get, and I'd forgotten that I ever spent time sitting in it.

Carl didn't try to keep me from crying, didn't ask any questions. He just pulled me in close and began to pray. As he prayed for me—a soothing, sweet, reminder of a prayer—things started coming back to me.

Jesus, the Cross, hope.

When our lives are good, and clean, and light, and bright, whether they've always been that way, or they've just been that way for a while, I think it's easy to forget just how powerful Jesus is. Sometimes I think we're guilty of talking about Jesus like He's a Band-Aid, or a happy pill, or a nice idea complete with a sing-along album. Those things feel silly and inadequate next to the darkness in our world. But, thank God Jesus is so much more than a quick fix or a bandage. I know from experience that, when we are in a relationship with God, He can actually change and heal the broken pieces inside of us.

I have proof. I am proof.

God changes us. He takes our mess, insecurity, selfishness, and hatefulness. He takes our bad decisions and our past and the things that we can't even forgive ourselves for, and He makes them new. He takes the ashes of our lives and makes something beautiful out of them.

I don't know how He does it exactly, but I know that He does. I know because I've seen it. He has for me, and I know He can for you too.

> Are there any areas of your life or your past that feel broken or unresolved? Are there any areas of your life where you need God's healing, forgiveness, restoration, or redemption? Spend a few minutes telling God about those things this morning, and ask for His help. Once you're done, take a deep breath and know that there's nothing in the world too broken for God to heal.

Showing Up

"Be like-minded, be sympathetic, love one another,
be compassionate and humble."

1 Peter 3:8

I had never seen real poverty before, and the sight of it stopped me in my tracks. It was the first day of my very first mission trip, and we were in a shantytown on the edge of San Jose, Costa Rica. That's where we'd be working that week.

Houses were made of cardboard boxes and scrap bits of lumber. Tin roofs leaked as they attempted to protect their inhabitants from the elements. All the makeshift windows had bars, and kids ran around and through our legs, their faces smudged with dirt and their clothes hanging on by a thread.

As we walked through the town on our first day, our leader stopped at a particularly run-down house and knocked on the door. A beautiful but tired-looking woman opened the door and ushered us in with a warm smile.

We sat down in her living room and, in perfect Spanish, our leader invited her to tell us some of her story.

She has seven kids of her own, and two that she's taken in. Her husband left years ago, leaving her to be the primary breadwinner and to raise their kids alone. Exhaustion was scrawled all over her face. She needed something. Help, hope, something.

We spent the whole week in that town and saw her family as often as we could. We brought her a big bag of food and did construction work to improve the town's infrastructure for when the rainy season came. But I knew we didn't solve all of her problems. We couldn't; I knew we couldn't.

But there's a beautiful bit to this story, and it's the piece I've been holding onto ever since.

If you've ever been in a tough spot—if you've ever had your heart broken, or suffered the loss of a family member, or a job, or something you truly loved—then you know how isolating it can be. You know how easy it is to feel alone.

Part of it is that pain, loss, and fear are naturally isolating emotions. But they're only made worse by the fact that we back away from each other when we don't know how to help.

A friend of mine's dad was diagnosed with cancer a few years ago, and she never knew how to tell people. Even when people did know, they never seemed to know what to say. The thing they said most often was nothing.

We back away when someone's in pain because we don't want to make it worse. We don't know what to say, or how to act, or how to help. So we don't. We back away and hope they know we care.

But we didn't back away from that sweet woman, and through that, I learned something I'll never forget.

We showed up. We sat with her. We asked her questions, asked follow-up questions, and listened to her answers. We sympathized, encouraged, and played with her kiddos to give her a much-needed break.

And even though we weren't able to solve her problems (although I wished with everything in me that we could), I know our showing up was significant. I know because she said so.

When we're going through something terrible, yes we need financial help, or a miracle, or a new job to replace the one we lost. But we also need someone to listen to us, to sit with us, and to not leave even when the stories we tell don't have a happy ending yet. We need to know we're not alone.

When I got my heart broken in college, my best friend Michelle came over immediately. She couldn't fix it, couldn't repair the relationship or bring him back. But she could be there with me, snuggled up close, listening to me tell the same story, again and again, nodding and asking questions. She could show me that I didn't have to go through this alone—which was exactly what I needed.

So today, that's what I hope we do for each other. I hope we show up, bring food, sit with each other, and just listen. I hope we ask follow up questions, pay attention to the answers, and let each other talk for as long as we need to.

We may not be able to solve every problem in the world, in our own backyards, or even in our own homes, but we can show up. We can show up, and in showing up, we can show the people we love that they're not in this alone.

Think of someone in your life who's going through something difficult—maybe their parent is sick, or their child is sick, or they just lost their job or a relationship. Send them a text today and set up a coffee or a lunch date. And, when you see them, tell them that you know you don't have the perfect thing to say, but that you would love to listen. Show them that they're not in this alone.

Grace Clothes

"You did not choose me, but I chose you and
appointed you so that you might go and bear fruit—
fruit that will last."

John 15:16a

There's something truly magical about a great pair of sweatpants.
Your brand of choice might include the elastic at the bottom or
the name of a school down the side. Mine are an old pair of yoga
pants that belonged to my best friend. I borrowed them during
a sleepover and never gave them back—like a sisterhood of the
magical sweatpants.

I'm assuming they used to be black, although now they're a dull
almost gray. They're way too big and have a hole right above the
knee. They've long since passed the point of being wearable in
public, and they're not attractive at all, but they don't need to be.
After all, that's not what sweatpants are there for.

I have always believed that what's happening on our outsides mirrors so clearly what is happening on our insides. You can always
tell the state of my heart by the state of our house. If it's a mess,
unopened mail and shoes strewn everywhere, you can guess my
heart looks just about the same—frazzled, overbooked, chaotic.
The same is true the other way—if fun music is on, wine is poured,
and candles are lit, you know my heart is at rest.

Our outsides so often mirror our insides.

The thing I always remind myself is that the connection between
our outer and inner worlds doesn't have to happen on its own. It's

something we can do intentionally—tweaking our outer worlds to give our inner ones something they desperately need.

My husband, Carl, gets frazzled every so often—when we have a crazy season coming up, or during big weeks at work. You can tell when he's starting to feel this way because he starts to clean. He frantically cleans. He wants surfaces and floors to be clear, wants everything to be put away in its place.

I used to be totally confused by this practice. Who cares what's on the kitchen counter when there are so many important things to be done? But he finally explained it in a way I understood, "When the house is clean, it helps me feel like things aren't quite so out of control." Bringing some order to his outer world helps do the same in his inner world, making it all feel more manageable and less chaotic. I realized that for me, sweatpants do a similar thing.

I don't know about you, but there are some days when I just don't feel good enough. There are days when I feel endlessly critical of myself, holding myself up next to people who seem to have life completely dialed in, feeling like I'm the only one who gets stuck, and feels scared, and has no idea what I'm doing.

I want to be good enough; I want to have a place in the world, I want to matter, I want to make a difference. And in those moments I'm convinced that if I can just be a little more "on," perform a little bit more, change just enough to be more like them in a hundred different ways, then I'll be good enough.

Hustle, hustle, strive, prove.

At the end of the day, I arrive home exhausted, emptied out, discouraged, and frustrated that no matter how much I do, I never quite feel good enough.

But then I wiggle into my trusty pair of sweatpants and remember... there's grace.

Sweatpants are grace clothes—clothes that give you room both to breathe and to be. They don't need you to smile, or to be "on" or to have something funny or witty to say. They're perfectly okay if you need to cry, or feel unsure, or rest, or give up for a minute. They aren't pushing you or pulling you into being someone else; they don't require you to have it all together.

Sweatpants say that you're good enough just as you are, a reminder in our outer world that we need on the inside every single day.

Sweet friend, you are here for a purpose. You bring gifts and talents and words and love and light to the world that only you have, and that we desperately need. Sure, you aren't perfect, and you aren't like her, and you aren't like them. But we never needed you to be. We just need you. We need you to be you, to share your thoughts, and your heart, and your wisdom, and your songs. We need you to share your presence, and your ideas, and your listening ear, and your laugh.

We need more of you in this world. You have things in you that we so desperately need. The world is a more beautiful place because you're in it. We're sure of it.

And all you have to do is be you.

Slip on your favorite sweatpants today, grace-clothes, and allow them to remind you that you're good enough, just as you are.

The Gratitude License Plate Game

"Devote yourselves to prayer, being watchful
and thankful."

Colossians 4:2

The highway was clear and breezy, ruffling my hair, and tickling my face. I hummed along with the radio as I pulled into a gas station for a bottle of sparkling water. I was greeted by an amiable clerk with a sweet southern twang, and he genuinely wished me a happy Friday as I left his small store.

It felt like nice things were strewn across my path that day, just waiting to be discovered. Birds were chirping, and the sweet scent of flowers perfumed the air. I sighed—big and happy.

On another, equally unassuming day, my alarm failed to go off. I woke up with 10 minutes to spare before I'd be late for work—again. With mascara half on and my foot blindly searching for a shoe, I hurried towards the door, only to realize that my keys were nowhere to be found.

The day only got worse from there. Nothing seemed to go right, and everything I did seemed wrong. I was sensitive and insecure, anxious and frantic, sliding quickly towards the end of my rope. Tears threatened to break through the thin veil that was barely holding them at bay.

I stepped outside for a moment to take a breath and look around. I remembered with amazement that just a few days before, the world had been a bright and shining place. What had happened to the smell of those flowers, and where were those darn birds? I couldn't see beauty through my thick, angry fog, and I wondered what had changed between that great day and this awful one. Is it the day of the week, or getting a full eight hours of sleep, or can you really wake up on the wrong side of the bed? What's the tipping point between the best days and the kind where you want to give up and start again?

I thought about it for a long time, and this is what I came up with: I think part of it has to do with our eyes.

When we're a good mood, it's like everything we see plays along. And when we're in a bad mood, frustration seems to abound. Our moods determine what we notice around us, and what we see around us reinforces our mood.

So what if we ask our eyes to go first? What if, even before our moods decide to cooperate, we ask our eyes to look for those beautiful things—not out of a good mood, but in an effort to create one? What if we decide, on purpose, to look for the beautiful things in the world—pulling our stubborn moods along until they're ready to walk on their own?

That's exactly what I tried to do on the Tuesday of the following week. I was running late again, my hair was still wet, and coffee sloshed down my shirt as I walked out the door, forcing me to go back in and change. I sped away from our house, my mood swirling furiously around me, and then I remembered what I'd been learning lately. So I took a deep breath and made a decision: I was going to change my mood.

I knew there were beautiful things in my life and lovely things all around me; I just had to notice. So, like the License Plate Game, I began trying to spot them. There was a beautiful flower on the side of the road, that's #1. "Oh I really like this song!" that song was #2. Someone let me merge in front of them on the highway with a smile and a wave, and I had my #3. I played the game all the way to work, looking for beautiful things everywhere and on purpose.

It took some time, and some intentionality, and at first it felt forced.

But the more I looked for beauty and goodness around me, the more my day transformed.

We don't have to be in a great mood every day, nobody is. But regardless of which side of the bed I wake up on, I want to walk through life present and grateful. I want to see the beauty that is strewn across my path each day—just waiting to be discovered, don't you? Give that a try today. Maybe even play the Gratitude-License Plate Game to get you started.

The Key To Courage

"Be strong and take heart, all you who hope in the Lord."

Psalm 31:24

Just a few months ago, I got an email from a friend who's been thinking about going on a mission trip. At the end of her email, she said, "The idea of this trip scares me so much. Is that normal? I don't know if I'm courageous enough to do something like this. Does the fact that I'm so afraid mean I shouldn't go?" I read her question slowly, remembering all of the times I've asked the very same thing.

I am not a fearless person—let's be clear about this. I am chock-full of fear. I've been scared to death of every decently big thing I've ever done (and every small thing too). I'm a major crier leading up to big changes, and I've never been more afraid than right before I went on an 11-month mission trip around the world.

Ever since I'd read *Eat, Pray, Love* in the midst of my very broken heart, I'd wanted to do something like this. I wanted to travel around the world, get to know God better, and get to know myself better too. This was the perfect opportunity.

I went back and forth a thousand times before I actually signed up. But, after the decision was made, I actually wasn't that scared. I wasn't that scared because I signed up a full year before I had to go anywhere, and I'm convinced that anything sounds easy when it's that far away.

As my departure date loomed closer, however, the fear settled in like a thick black cloud, blocking out the sun and every bit of courage I thought I had. I'd cry myself to sleep at night. My mind was a hurricane of "what if's." I even started thinking totally irrational things like, "Why did my parents let me sign up for something so insane? Don't they love me at all?"

But my fears didn't just stay in my head and my heart – they exploded out into action.

After a particularly long night of crying and worrying, I sent an email that, six months before, I never would have imagined I'd send. "I'm just not so sure this is a good idea," I started. "Is it possible to give up my spot?"I was out; the fear had won—that is, until I found out it was too late to back out. I could get out of going, certainly, but my supporters couldn't get refunds. It was either go or stay home and lose all of their money.

I was stuck.

So I did exactly what John Wayne suggests. Scared to death, I saddled up anyway, and I went. I'm so glad I did.

Venturing out into the world with God changed my life and my faith completely. Getting to see Him out there, interact with Him without distraction, participate in the things He's doing around the world—it's one of the best decisions I've ever made.

My life is forever changed because I saddled up anyway, because I did it scared, and I know I'm not the only one.

The misconception we have about people who do amazing things is that they're fearless. We look at Olympians, people pursuing their dreams, and the founder of the latest, greatest tech startup and imagine that they're somehow different from us. We think they must be missing the fear gene, that they're able to tackle these huge, public things without a quiver or a doubt.

I've had acquaintances look at me as I write a book or travel somewhere new and say, "You're so brave to do these things! I can't believe you aren't scared!"But I am scared! I'm crying myself to sleep each night, a teddy bear tucked under each arm. Everyone is! (Well—maybe not the teddy bear thing, but you never know!)

Everyone who's ever taken a leap of faith, who's attempted something bigger than themselves, has felt scared. Fear is a normal part of doing something big—it's almost a prerequisite. But ultimately, they've decided that, whatever the thing is, is worth the risk. So, with fear and doubt and worry flanking them like an entourage, they've saddled up anyway.

That's how the most wonderful things in the world happen – they happen because someone decided to show up anyway: to hop on that plane, to invent that new technology, to start a family, to write a book, to do it even though they were scared.

If there's something in your life right now that you're considering doing, but something that scares you more than you can even explain, don't wait for bravery or courage to show up in the form of not being scared anymore—because I'm convinced that's just not the way it works.

Gather your people around you, bring your teddy bear, and take the leap even though you're afraid. Be courageous sweet friend, because we need you to be. We need you to do the thing, to serve the people in that country, to sing the song that God has placed inside of you. And yes, you will be afraid, but yes, God will be with you every single step of the way.

Don't Talk About My Friend That Way

> "We demolish arguments and every pretension that sets
> itself up against the knowledge of God, and we take
> captive every thought to make it obedient to Christ."
>
> 2 Corinthians 10:5

There are seasons in life when I just cannot give myself a break. Do you ever have times like that? Every moment, every glance in the mirror, every action is a reminder of all the ways I fall short—of all the things I could be, could do, and ways I could look but don't.

I think things like, "You really should go to the gym more. You are really looking gross these days. Of course you failed, you always do. Could you possibly be more annoying?"

I make a simple mistake like forgetting to bring my lunch, and my thoughts are entirely unforgiving. "You always do stuff like this! You are so forgetful and irresponsible! You can just be hungry until we get home. That'll teach you to remember things next time!"

I crack down on myself hard. I think that if I am just a little bit meaner, just a little bit harsher, if I just raise the bar a little bit, I'll be motivated enough to leap over it. I'll meet the sky-high expectations I have for myself and stop being such a disappointment.

For years, more years than I can count, this is how I've talked to myself. I've been my own worst critic. I've criticized my body, and my mind, and my actions, and my skills. I've held myself up to my friends, and coworkers, and women I've never even met. "Why can't you be more like her?" I'd ask myself. "You have got to get it together!"

As I say these words out loud to you, I feel like I'm peeking out from a dark corner. Anyone else? Does anyone else do this? Is it just me?

It feels totally vulnerable to admit to these thoughts. Mostly because I feel like I'm way too nice of a person to say things like this, and that's true! I would never talk to someone else like this! I have all the grace in the world for other people—they're human, they're in process, they're doing the best they can.

But I am the exception, the lucky winner that gets to be the object and source of all of my disdain, and it wasn't until a girlfriend of mine uttered one simple sentence that I realized how ludicrous this whole thing really is.

We were getting ready to go to dinner, when I peered into the mirror and let one of my thoughts accidentally slip out. "I can't believe I let myself gain so much weight. Seriously, I'm so big, I look terrible, and the worst part is that it's my fault! If I was just more disciplined and not so lazy, I wouldn't be in this mess to begin with."

Mean, right? I still can't believe I said it out loud, but I'm so glad I did, because my friend didn't skip a beat. She didn't ask for clarification or sweep it cleanly under the rug. She turned to me with glowering eyes and snapped, "Don't talk about my friend that way."

I was instantly both so embarrassed I could disappear and so grateful I could cry. I felt caught red-handed, and heroically defended all at once. I was the attacker and the victim. She was coming to my defense, ready to fight the one who was hurting my feelings, knowing full well that the assailant was me.

As we drove to dinner, we talked about the way we all talk to ourselves sometimes. "We think we get a free pass to be cruel because we're being cruel to ourselves. But we don't get a free pass to treat anyone that way, and we shouldn't have to put up with treatment like that from anyone, especially not ourselves."

She was right. Of course she was right. And her words have stuck with me ever since.

There are enough naysayers in the world, and the more I've thought about this, I've realized that I don't want to be another one.

At least we can get away from the naysayers, but we're stuck with ourselves. If we're our own worst critic, we're stuck with our own worst critic right there in our ear. Every time we brush our teeth, every time we take a chance at work, every time we fall asleep, she's there, telling us we're not good enough, that we should be different or that we're a disappointment.

And I've just decided I don't want to play that game anymore.

Life is far too hard, and far too short to be our own worst critics, and it never seems to help us get better anyway. Good things don't come out of shame; good things come out of kindness, support, and encouragement.

So these days, I try to talk to myself the way I would a friend:

"Good job, sweet girl."

"You tried, and that's really saying something."

"You are beautiful."

"I'm so proud of you."

Maybe you are never your own worst critic, and if that's true, I want to give you a hug and a high five and ask you to teach us all of your ways. But if you are, if the thoughts in your head speak to you this way sometimes, let me grab them by their collar, look them straight in the eye, and say, "Don't talk about my friend that way!" You don't deserve to be treated that way, not even by yourself.

Take some time this week to start paying a bit more attention to your thoughts. What kinds of things are you saying to yourself throughout the day? Are you your own worst critic, or do you talk to yourself like a friend? Let's start paying a bit more attention, and start making intentional choices with our thoughts. Let's start talking to ourselves the way we would a friend.

The Story Your Bible Tells

"The only thing that counts is faith expressing itself
through love."

Galatians 5:6b

When we were leaving for vacation not long ago, my husband, Carl, picked up my suitcase and groaned as he felt the weight of it.

"What the heck do you have in here? It feels like your suitcase got heavier overnight!"

"It did," I told him. "I put my Bible in the front pocket."

"Your giant one?" he asked, referencing my NIV Study Bible that's roughly the size (and weight) of two bricks laid side-by-side.

"Yes," I replied without budging. "That's my Bible, and I don't like reading any other."

I was given my Bible just a few months into my life as a Christian by my college pastor, Bill. After hearing what God was starting to do in my life, he guided me to a closet just outside the sanctuary of our church. He pulled out a thick, sturdy Bible, one of the ones they sold after church on Tuesday nights. I fumbled for my wallet, but he shook his head. "Take it; it's yours. Use it well, okay?"

I felt so honored when he handed it to me, like something important was being passed on and entrusted to me. It's one of the best gifts I've ever been given, and I've used the same Bible ever since.

After several years of hard use, the binding started to break, and the cover began to rip, but I wasn't ready to let it go. So I took it to a sweet little lady in Denver to have it re-covered. Part of having it recovered was getting to pick the phrase to be stamped on the front. I thought about it for a long time, wanting to pick just the right thing, and I finally settled on the second half of Galatians 5:6.

Her English wasn't great, and my handwriting is downright atrocious, but I was pretty sure we were on the same page as to what I wanted it to say. In the neatest handwriting I could manage I wrote, "The only thing that counts is faith expressing itself through love."

When I picked up my newly bound Bible, it was perfect—sturdy and strong with a new leather cover—and, stamped on the front in gold leaf were the words, "The only tning that counts is faith expressing itself through love."

"Wait a minute… the only tning? The only tning?!"

It seems we'd had some sort of miscommunication.

I would later, carefully, dab a bit of gold paint just above the "n", optimistically trying to give it just the right amount of height. It still most certainly says, "The only tning" but it looks like maybe it once said "thing" and the h has just started to rub off. It's imperfect, and it's mine, and I love it. My gosh, I couldn't love it more.

My Bible has been my constant companion, my lifeline, my anchor, and I never leave home for more than a day without it. Together, we've been to Ghana, and Jamaica, and Mexico, and Romania, and Nepal, and Rwanda, and more. It's made its home with me in Boulder, Colorado, and Gainesville, Georgia, and Nashville, Tennessee, comforting me and guiding me on the journey in between.

I've dripped tears all over it in the wake of breakups, and it was there on a gorgeous July evening when Carl and I got married. It's helped me figure out what to do when I was deciding between this job and that, and it comforted me as I proceeded to lose both this job and that.

We've seen so much change together, so much life, and through it all, it's taught me about God—about who He is, what He's about, what's important to Him, and how much He loves me.

My favorite thing about my Bible—next to the Story it tells of course—is the story my Bible tells.

It's a time capsule of my life with God, a travel journal of the road we've walked together. It's full of notes next to things that changed my life five years ago, and another note next to the same thing as it changed my life just last week.

It's full of reactions, circles around things I think are funny, hearts next to things that really hit home. There are notes pressed in there, encouragements and prayers from friends throughout the years. There are the occasional dollars from countries around the world and, if you open to the right page at just the right time, you'll find pink pressed Bougainvillea flowers that a precious little girl gave me in Cambodia.

The famous English Preacher, Charles Spurgeon, once said, "A Bible that's falling apart usually belongs to someone who isn't." I love the idea that our lives could be so reflected in the pages of our Bible, and I so hope that's the case for me.

There's nothing more I'd want my life to be full of than God's word, notes from lessons learned along the way, prayers from best friends and loved ones, and pressed Bougainvillea flowers— all there to remind me that the only "tning" that counts is faith expressing itself through love.

Do you have a Bible that's special to you this way? If not, why not make today the day you get one? You can find them at your local bookstore, or online. There are tons of versions, types, and helpful tools inside of them. Reach out to someone you look up to, someone you trust, and ask what kind of Bible they prefer, and if they have any advice. Also, find some time where you can thumb through a few, see how they read and how they feel in your hands. Your Bible is the perfect place to write notes, to reflect, to keep special things hidden and tucked away, the perfect companion for the journey of your life. So, if you don't have a Bible that's really your Bible, I think today is the perfect day for that to change!

Permission to be Terrible

"I will sing to the Lord all my life; I will sing praise
to my God as long as I live. May my meditation be
pleasing to Him, as I rejoice in the Lord."

Psalm 104:33-34

Kindergarteners are my favorite kind of people. They're funny
and quirky and always seem to be sticky. They're also my favorite
because they're fearless.

Have you ever spent time with kindergarteners? If you get a
chance, go up to a group of them and ask them this: "Who of you
are artists or singers or dancers?"

I guarantee that before you can finish your sentence, you'll have
half the class up front pulling out all of the stops—whipping out
their best tree or twirl or rendition of "The Sun Will Come Out
Tomorrow." Now try that same thing with a group of college students—or even better, a group of professionals.

My dad tells the story of when he was at a conference with 400
law enforcement professionals — experts in their field, people with
PhDs and fully loaded guns.

The speaker asked the same question, "Who of you are artists or
singers or dancers?" There were a couple of nervous coughs as
everybody averted their eyes, not wanting to make the rookie mistake of making eye contact with the guy up front.

Not one person raised their hand.

You'd assume that, as we get older, we'd become more confident. You'd assume kindergarteners have way more to lose. After all, they have no filter, and their peers are way more vocal about their disapproval. They also don't have full control of their bladder function yet—which has to bring you right back down to size, right? But, time and time again, I can promise that you'd find more reckless confidence in a group of 5-year-olds than in a group of 400 professional adults.

Doesn't that just make you wonder?

I think there's a point, probably somewhere around middle school, when we pick a lane and decide to stick to it. We discover (or maybe just assume) that we can eliminate a lot of humiliation if we avoid things that we might not be good at right away. And, although in some cases there may be some truth to this, it's not a truth that lends itself to any kind of freedom, or any kind of fun.

When I was little, I loved to sing. But as I got older, while I still loved to sing, I stopped being able to sing in public. I had to basically be sedated anytime I tried, and my voice squeaked out as a shadow of what I (and the walls of my shower) knew it was capable of.

I was talking to a friend about this several years ago. "I love to sing, but I just can't do it," I told him. "I'm terrified of what it'll sound like, of what people will think."

He nodded thoughtfully and waited a moment before he spoke. You could see that he had an idea, but wasn't sure how I'd react.

"Steph, what if you gave yourself permission to be terrible? What if you didn't expect yourself to be good; what if that wasn't the point? I mean, what's the worst-case scenario—that people will think you're a bad singer? Most people are terrible singers! What if you just gave yourself permission to sing and took all the pressure off of the outcome? I bet you'd be able to sing much better and, more than that, I bet you'd enjoy it."

He was right. What was the worst-case-scenario? Was it really that bad if people thought I stunk? For the first time, in that moment, my desire to sing and to do something I enjoyed outweighed my fear of what other people would think—so I started to sing.

I started taking guitar lessons and, for awhile, I even led worship. I was singing in front of large groups of people—actually surprisingly confidently. I wasn't half bad and, more importantly, I really, really enjoyed it.

And it made me wonder…

What would happen if we, as confident, degree holding, weapon wielding (or not…) adults, decided to paint? What would happen if we decided to sing or learn to play the guitar or take a dance class?

What kind of freedom are we missing out on by limiting ourselves to the things we know that we're good at? And what would our voices, paintings, and dancing be like if we weren't choked by fear? Who knows? We might even be amazing! Or, we might not be, and I think that might be even better because then we could just do it for fun.

So let's go for it. I dare you, and really, I dare me too. Let's sing loudly, and super off-key; let's paint terrible trees that look more like green clouds on sticks; let's take a tap class and stink it up right there in the front. Let's do the things we love just because we love them!

How much fun could we be having if we did things we might not be good at? Kindergarteners are finding out, shouldn't we?

Is there something you used to love doing but haven't done in forever—or is there something you've always wanted to try, but you've always been too scared to? I think today is the day: check into those guitar lessons, look up dance classes in your area. Whatever the thing is, I say we go for it!

Worry & Wagons in Africa

"Can any one of you by worrying add a single hour
to your life?"

Matthew 6:27

The summer after I graduated from college, I went on a 10-week mission trip to Ghana, West Africa. I fell in love with the country and the people immediately. We worked with wise, wonderful pastors and their families—warm, Godly people who taught us to think, pray, love, and to see God more deeply than we ever had before.

One afternoon about halfway through our summer, one of the pastors told us we were going to visit a village that had been having a hard time lately. "It's a bit of a journey," he told us, "But we should be back by dark." So we all piled into our bus and drove three hours outside of the small town where we lived, but our journey, we found out, was only just beginning.

When we arrived (in the middle of nowhere, it seemed), the pastor led us to a tractor with a wooden wagon attached to its rear. "Hop in!" he instructed, explaining that the village we were to visit couldn't be accessed by even the rough dirt roads. We still had a two-hour tractor ride to go. We grabbed a seat on the makeshift benches, and we were off—bumping down what was certainly not a path, deep into the African bush.

The ride to the village was actually fun. We held on tight and laughed and warned each other of oncoming tree branches, feeling our benches rocking back and forth and slipping precariously towards the open end of the wagon.

But on the way back, I started to worry. It was getting later in the day, and dark clouds were approaching, slowly but surely. If it rains, I realized, we're hours from the closest shelter. The ground will get muddy; we'll break the axle or a wheel; we could easily get stuck. And if we got stuck, it was going to be dark before long, and the weight of spending the night, soaking wet in the African bush started to weigh down heavily like the clouds. "Who even knows what animals live out here," I thought, my eyes growing wide.

Life felt wild, and I felt exposed and unprotected within it. The "What ifs" slammed into me with every jolt of the wagon, my bruises multiplying quickly. I looked down at my hands holding onto the sides of the wagon. My knuckles were white. I wasn't having fun anymore. I was worried. No, let's be honest, I was terrified.

As we made our way forward, the tractor slowed at one point, and we picked up a woman carrying a sack of rice in one arm and her baby in the other, hitching a ride for the long trip into town. And as I held on and gritted my teeth, worrying about every bad thing that could (and I thought certainly would) happen to us, I looked over at the mother and her baby. The baby was sprawled across its mother's lap, cooing happily, staring up at the sky and watching the trees pass by.

How can the baby just relax like that? I wondered, a hint of accusation in my thoughts. Doesn't he know that we might be in danger? Doesn't he sense there are things that could go terribly, terribly wrong? Then I realized that babies, of course, don't work that way; they don't worry about things in the future or get tricked into the idea that worrying about them in advance might soften the blow if the worry ends up coming true. But that's something I've believed more times than I can count.

When my boyfriend Kyle and I were dating, I constantly worried that he'd break up with me. A small, fearful voice inside my heart said that if he did break up with me, at least I'd have seen it coming. That would help a little bit, wouldn't it? It was better than being blindsided.

It's the same voice that tells me it makes sense to worry about my mom and dad's health every day. They're totally fine, perfectly healthy, "But one day they won't be," the worried voice whispers, convincing me that worry is like bringing an umbrella. If you bring an umbrella, it's sure not to rain.

But worry, I'm learning, just doesn't work that way. Worrying about our relationship ending didn't protect me from pain when it did eventually end; it just robbed me of the joy I could have been experiencing along the way.

Worrying about something happening to my parents doesn't keep them safer, and it doesn't protect me from the grief I'll feel when something eventually does. Instead, it has me grieving both then and now. It's multiplying the grief instead of softening it.

My worrying about what could happen to us there in the middle of the bush didn't make the situation better. It didn't keep us safe or save us from anything bad happening. I was as helpful to the situation as that sweet, giggling baby. In fact, I was probably less helpful because I bet you could feel my anxiety a million miles away.

What did happen was that I missed out on the adventure. I missed out on the fun of the ride. I stopped paying attention and noticing that I was riding in a wagon pulled by a tractor in the bush of Africa. That's an experience to really pay attention to—it's not one we have every day.

That's what worry does. It doesn't prepare us, doesn't help us, and doesn't lessen the blow. It empties today of its strength and its joy. Because usually, the things we worry about don't happen or don't happen the way we think we will. Even if they do, God is there in the midst of it taking care of us, providing for us, helping us, and we're usually surrounded by people who love us who are there to help us too—we don't have to go through it alone.

So, these days, I'm really trying to take a lesson from that baby. I'm trying to take in the scenery of life, trying to relax and enjoy the journey a bit more. I'm trying to loosen my grip—remembering that my white knuckles don't help anyone. They just make me miss the beauty of the ride.

What is one thing you know to be true about God, one thing that brings you comfort about Him? Is it that He's good? Sovereign? In control? Is it that He sees you and hears you? That He's with you? That He loves you? All of those things are true, and we can reach for those truths anytime we need them.

The tricky thing is that trying not to worry is ultimately like walking in circles around our worry, never taking our eyes off it. Trying not to worry doesn't help. Our focus and our energy are still on the thing we're worrying about. So try this instead: Replace the worry with the thing you know to be true and solid. Let that one thing you know about God be your stability—the thing you hold onto that keeps you safe.

You Don't Have to be Perfect to be Loved

"For you created my inmost being; you knit me
together in my mother's womb. I praise you because
I am fearfully and wonderfully made; your works
are wonderful, I know that full well."

Psalm 139:13-14

For as long as I can remember, I believed a gigantic lie. I believed
that, in order to be loved, I had to be perfect.

My quest for perfection was endless. Everything from my eyebrows
to my personality was under scrutiny. I wanted to be the smartest, the
most organized, the most well-liked, the funniest, the one with the best
hair, and the best clothes, and the best butt. Grace was nowhere to
be found; no part of me was safe from my scrupulous dissatisfaction.

I thought if I could just get it all right, all at the same time, that I'd
be worthy of love. (Saying that out loud is hard, isn't it? Have you
ever had that thought?)

For years I tried and tried, and performed and performed, always
coming up short, and always believing that, if I could just work
harder, download one more productivity app, and hit the gym one
more time that I'd get there. I'd be the plate-spinning, world-changing, delightful, beautiful version of myself that I've always wanted
to be—perfect, and therefore loved.

It was an exhausting way to live, so exhausting that one day, I
just fell apart. It was too much to carry. I couldn't do it anymore!
My perfect façade cracked and then shattered, and I came face to
face with my imperfection in front of the person I was most afraid

would leave when he saw it—my boyfriend (who's now my husband). Not only did I fall apart, but I fell apart BIG, in the middle of a crowded restaurant, with sobs that couldn't be contained with a quick dab of my napkin. As I sat there, an embarrassing, snotty puddle of tears, Carl did something that changed everything.

He said, "Steph, I know you're not perfect. Do you know that I know that? Did you think you had me fooled?" He was joking, but also deeply serious.

He continued, "I love you. Stephanie, I love you and your bad days and your messy hair. I love you when you're crabby; I love you when you don't make sense. I love you when you're sad or mad or frustrated. I love you when it doesn't seem like there's any sparkle in the world—or like you forgot to be sparkly in it. I love you when you're lost and confused and can't figure it out. I love everything about you—everything."

He looked at me, his eyes full of resolute love, showing me something I never imagined I'd see. He knew I wasn't perfect, and he loved me anyway. And that kind of love changes you.

It changes you because it's a human, flesh-and-blood representation of something God's been saying all along: "Perfection isn't the point, kiddo. You're perfect because I'm perfect because I gave you my perfection and took every bit of your mess. Oh, one more thing: you're loved more than you could ever imagine—exactly as you are."

That was the first day I began to understand that perfection isn't a requirement for love. It isn't from God, and it isn't from other people either. We don't want perfection from each other, and we certainly don't need it! Perfection is creepy, Stepford, inauthentic.

We keep up the façade because we're afraid that when people see the real us, they'll back up, move away, or think poorly of us. But, what really happens (with people we can trust, of course!) is that those people come closer. They fall more in love with us because they've seen the best parts of us—the quirky, off-kilter, slightly nerdy things—the parts that are so special, and so entirely lovable. When we open up to them about our real selves and our struggles, they know us even better; they feel trusted, honored, and safe. They might even open up too because now they know that's allowed. They know that perfection isn't a requirement in this relationship, so they can put their guard down too.

Perfection has never been a part of the equation, has never been a prerequisite for love. So, let's stand tall and bravely step out in a new truth today: We are not perfect, and we are so, so loved.

Let's put that truth into action today. Let's give it a shot, step out on top of that idea and see if it holds. Let's try taking down our façade a little bit, allowing someone into part of our world. Let's tell our story in a way we haven't before or, to be honest about a struggle when we would have normally said, "Oh, I'm fine!" When we do that, we invite the other person to do the same and prove to ourselves and to them that we don't need to be perfect in order to be loved.

A Full Life

"He brought me out into a spacious place; He
rescued me because He delighted in me."

Psalm 18:19

Did you ever read a book in high school that had absolutely no
margins? You know those books, the ones that seem to weigh a
thousand pounds and take you a year to get through despite your
two-week deadline? I always dreaded those books, wondering why
the author couldn't have included a picture or two, or at least some
space between her thoughts.

Doesn't life feel this way sometimes?

We have 24 hours in a day, and we cram those 24 hours full until
they're like an over-packed suitcase, oddly shaped and threatening
to burst. *If I could do just one more load of laundry, or a few more errands,
or take one more class, or get one more email written…* We do this, jam-
ming our lives full to the brim, like one of those books, leaving no
margin at all.

That's how my life felt in a particular season a few years back
(and many times since!). Carl and I went to Washington, D.C.
for my grandmother's birthday, but we still had a ton of work to
do, so we fit phone calls and emails between family events, sneak-
ing away every so often. We arrived back home on a Tuesday to
a messy house and a pile of the to-dos we'd neglected over the
weekend. Then, somehow, in the midst of coming home from the
trip, cleaning, having several rounds of friends stay with us, Carl's
birthday, work trips for both of us, and normal things like, you
know, showering and sleeping, I had to finish the final edits on a
book I'd been working on.

All of life's craziness seemed to converge in that one week.

Worst of all, I kept saying yes: yes we can stay in Washington another day, yes we have time to go to dinner, yes we'd love to have you, yes I can talk on the phone, yes I can get my book done by then, yes, yes, yes. And, even though those yeses were all good, important things, they were packed so tightly together that I was left with no margin at all.

The thing about this kind of living is that it's okay, for a while.

It's okay to run at full speed; it's okay to have seasons when all else falls by the wayside for the sake of this one important thing. It's okay to fill in the margins sometimes, to pack a page as full as it can get. Without packed margins, I wouldn't have finished my book. There are times when life has to be lived this way. But we can't live this way forever. We have to stop, we have to slow down, we have to leave some room in the margins again—and that can be hard!

Once you've been living a packed-to-the-brim life, it's hard to live differently. It's hard to let moments breathe, to allow items to stay on your list for a day or so, to leave them unchecked. It's hard to shut your computer, to let your mind relax, to say "enough is enough." It's hard to slow down because it feels like you're wasting time—there's always more to do.

But it's important because the kind of life we want to live doesn't happen all smashed together like that. More is not always more, and when we pack our margins full, we don't leave room for full, beautiful life to unfold.

Full life happens in the margins.

Full life happens over lingering dinners, instead of rushing off as soon as you get the check. It happens on long walks, or when you drive around just to enjoy the scenery. Full life happens on

Saturday mornings when you stay in bed an extra hour to cuddle, and when you sit down to enjoy your coffee instead of inhaling it on the drive from one place to the next. That's the kind of fullness I want, not the kind I had in that season.

So this is the work I've been doing in my life ever since. My schedule is still crazy sometimes; there's still a lot going on, but, more than ever, I'm trying to leave some room in the margins for life to happen.

I'm trying to leave some space to watch the leaves turn, to write because I feel like it, and to watch a movie with Carl. I'm trying to put down my phone, and let the laundry stay undone for just one more day.

Mostly, I'm learning that a full life isn't always a full life and that full life happens best when we leave some room in the margins.

Is your life full of life these days or just plain full? What are a few small changes you could make this week to give your life some room to breathe? Author Bob Goff is famous for quitting something every Thursday. Today may or may not be Thursday, but maybe there's something you could quit or say no to today. It's hard to say no; it's one of my least favorite things. But saying no is one of the best ways to leave some room in the margins.

A Little Take, a Little Give, & a Big Side of Grace

"Rejoice with those who rejoice; mourn with those
who mourn."

Romans 12:15

My girlfriends are one of the best parts of my life—hands down.

I have a heart-full of them, best ones, new ones, forever ones. There's something so indescribably wonderful about female friendships, this side-by-side, shoulder-to-shoulder kind of living we can do when we choose to live life together. There's nothing in the world like it, nothing at all.

The thing I find myself forgetting about friendships, though, is how difficult they can be. They aren't always difficult, certainly. Much of the time they really are midnight phone-calls, and sleepovers, and weekends away. They make your heart 10x bigger as you realize that you truly aren't alone in the world, not even for a second. But I forget, every so often, what it takes to get you to this connected, we're-in-this-together kind of place.

A few years ago, I had to have a hard conversation with one of my closest friends. We had had a miscommunication when we were texting earlier in the week that left both of us frustrated and the conversation unresolved. This doesn't happen all the time, but it did that day—a conversation where both of us were a bit bruised by the other.

The heart of the issue was that we both needed things from each other and, that day, our needs clashed in midair. I needed a favor, and she needed not to be needed for a while, both at the very same moment.

This is the tough thing about friendship. Sometimes we find ourselves in different places, needing each other for completely different reasons, and sometimes, this makes friendship really hard. A family member dies the same week that a friend gets married. A promotion is given on the same day a job is lost. We can be single and married, both at the same time, pregnant and wrestling through infertility in the very same year.

There's a piece of scripture that points to this perfectly, "Rejoice with those who rejoice, and mourn with those who mourn." But if you've ever been in two totally different places with your friends, you know this isn't easy. It's not easy to be in your best friend's wedding just a week after a big breakup. It's not easy to mourn with a friend after you just got engaged. It's not easy to think of what your best friend needs when your eyes are focused on what's going on in your life.

What my friend needed from me that day was my love, and my understanding, and my friendship, and my grace. And unfortunately, I didn't do that well at first, focusing on what I needed from her instead. But this is what friendship requires of us. It requires us to get out of ourselves for a moment, to consider what our friend needs instead of what's at the top of our needs list. It requires us to mourn with those who mourn, even when we're celebrating, and to rejoice with those who rejoice, even when our heart is breaking.

We never do this perfectly. We give it a shot, and sometimes we mess it up. We bruise each other every once in a while and have to have the hard conversations that move us from broken to better. We give a little, we take a little, we rejoice, and we mourn. And with a helping of honesty, and a heaping side of grace, we get to go through it all together.

Friendship is difficult. It's not all sleepovers and trips to the beach. But it is also those things, and those things are so much sweeter when we've listened, and loved, and been there for each other along the way. So think about your friends for a moment. What's going on in their lives? What might they need from you? It may be a hard thing to give with where you are in life right now but do your best. And if you've been hurt by a friend recently, or if you have a feeling you've hurt a friend recently, make the phone call, have the conversation. Your friendship will be so much better for it.

The "All Is Lost" Moment

"Weeping may stay for the night, but rejoicing
comes in the morning."

Psalm 30:5b

You're not supposed to be home at 2 PM on a Thursday.

That's what I kept thinking to myself the day we lost our jobs. There wasn't money to pay us—me, my fiancé, and dozens of my friends—we could take our things and go home, effective immediately.

We did what any sane humans would do following such a shocking announcement. We headed to the Mexican restaurant down the street for margaritas. It wasn't yet noon, but days like that change the rules entirely—11 AM margaritas weren't just appropriate, they were absolute necessities.

We told the story over and over again over lunch, as we would for the next several weeks, "What did they say to you?" "Can you believe this?" "Why?" "How?"

We were confused and hurting, but from our places around the table that day, things somehow still seemed sort of okay. It seemed like it could all turn out okay when we were in the same boat together, laughing and crying into our rapidly emptying margaritas.

By 2 PM I was back home—home when I should have been at work, alone when I should have been surrounded by my friends. *You're not supposed to be home at 2 PM on a Thursday,* I thought to myself. And with that thought, the weight of what had changed, of what I'd lost, the fact that I was suddenly drifting out to sea without a paycheck or a plan, settled onto my chest. It would be months before it would lift back off again.

Those next few months were a swirl of job applications, resume tweaking, hoping, and praying and waiting. I watched as my severance ran out, and my savings account started shrinking like it had sprung a small leak.

I was scared, and I was sad, and I was mad, but mostly I was scared. But there was one small thought that kept me going, like a flicker of a tea light in the dead of night: God does His best work in moments like these.

There's a moment in every story called the "All is lost moment." It's the moment when the protagonist has given up, when the relationship looks too broken to fix, when the problem seems unsolvable, when the audience is forced to wonder if things really will be okay. We love this moment in stories. It keeps us on our toes, keeps us engaged, and everything working out in the end is so much sweeter when we thought it really might not happen. In life, however, we don't love this moment. At least I don't.

We want a backup plan for our backup plan. We want our severance check to overlap with a signing bonus, with a relocation stipend to boot. We want one step to glide seamlessly into the next without a moment of doubt or fear or wonder if it's going to work out in the end. But the thing I reminded myself with as much gusto as I could muster was this: God does His best work in the "All is lost moment."

The Bible is a story swirling with God meeting people in these places. They've hit a dead end. It seems like there's no way this could possibly work out well for anyone. But that's when God gets to show off the most. That's when He awakens an army from a valley of dry bones, an angel shows up, or an old woman conceives. That's when a baby is born to a virgin, is killed, and then comes back to life, saving the world and everyone in it.

That must have been the biggest "All is lost moment"—the Saturday before Easter, as Jesus' disciples wondered, "What just happened? What do we do now?" But God never leaves the story there. He never leaves His people high and dry; He always provides, and His provision is always better and more abundant than the very thing His people were begging and pleading for to begin with.

And that's what God did for me then, too.

The finances came in at just the right moment; opportunities opened up just seconds before we'd given up. He opened doors we never would have dreamed to pray for, and He was with us every step of the way.

God has never hung me out to dry. He has never abandoned me. He has always come through. And you know what? He'll do the very same thing for you too.

If you're in the middle of an "All is lost moment," I'm praying that this truth sinks deep into your heart, providing even a tea light of hope on the darkest of days. God never leaves the story there; He never abandons His kids; He never leaves us high and dry. He will do something wonderful in this and through this, He WILL take care of you! Just keep sticking close to Him. You can trust Him.

Let's Show Up For Each Other

"Greater love has no one than this: to lay down
one's life for one's friends."

John 15:13

Something I've been thinking about a lot lately is friendship. Let's be honest—something I think about all the time is friendship.

In my life, in my faith, in my relationships, in what God is calling me to do in the world I've never found a resource (other than God Himself) more powerful or more transformative than having a great group of girlfriends by my side. I'm just convinced that life is better (and certainly more fun!) when we do it together.

I've always loved friendship and having great girlfriends, but I gained a new appreciation for them a few years ago when Carl and I moved to Nashville. I was in a new city where I didn't know anyone, and I suddenly found myself without girlfriends. It was one of the loneliest seasons of my entire life.

The toughest part about it is there's no blueprint for how to make friends as an adult. It seems like this weird, hard thing that so many of us need to do, but nobody knows how. So I started trying to figure it out. I've learned a lot about friendship since then. Recently, I stumbled upon a simple trick to having better friendships—a trick I discovered because I almost got it wrong.

So what's the trick? We have to show up for each other.

The week before Christmas was my friend Kaitlin's birthday. She invited me and a bunch of girls to go to dinner at a great new restaurant here in Nashville and, when she invited me, I said an enthusiastic, "YES! Of course, I'll come!"

But then the day of the dinner arrived, and I have to be honest, I didn't want to go. Yes, I wanted to celebrate Kaitlin—of course, I did! But I was getting sick, and feeling pretty terrible. The only thing in the world I wanted to do was to stake my claim on the couch and stay there for a week.

I thought about the dinner, and I thought about Kaitlin, and then I had a thought that I think so many of us have—a thought that robs our friendships of so much. I thought: *I can skip it. Right? She probably won't even notice if I'm not there.* I figured, there would be a lot of girls there celebrating her. She wouldn't even notice my absence. *It really doesn't matter if I don't go, does it?*

Then I remembered the birthday party I threw for Carl a few months before.

It was his 30th birthday, and I wanted it to be perfect, so I invited his closest friends in Nashville to a party at our house. I worked on the party for months, making sure every detail was just right. When the night of the party came, our friends arrived right on time. Well, most of them, but not all of them. A few of them weren't able to make it at the last minute for totally legitimate reasons. I knew it wasn't personal, and it wasn't even my birthday, but it still hurt my feelings.

When we invite people to show up for us, regardless of the occasion, it's a vulnerable thing. We're putting our hearts on the line, and until that night, I had never thought about it that way.

So as I was getting ready for Kaitlin's birthday dinner, and thinking that she probably wouldn't notice if I wasn't there, Carl's birthday flashed through my mind. I absolutely remember who didn't come. Their presence was missed, and even though their reasons for missing it were totally legitimate, their absence made me sad! But, even more, I remember who did come. And I know Carl does too. Our house was packed that night—filled with the scent of barbecue and the roars of laughter from some of his favorite people. It was such a special night, and it's because so many people showed up for him.

So I knew that I had to show up for Kaitlin. Yes—she would have understood if I had to back out. I was legitimately sick, after all. But I also know how much it's meant to me over the years when people have shown up for me, and I knew I wanted to show up for her.

That night was a blast. I'm so glad I didn't miss it! Not only was it so much fun celebrating Kaitlin (I got to sit right next to her at dinner!), but I also met great new friends! I laughed so much that night, and I came home with such a happy and full heart.

It could not be more tempting to back out of things. It doesn't matter what I'm committed to—a few hours before I'm supposed to leave, I never feel like going. And it's so easy to think that people won't notice—that our presence really won't change things. There will be so many people there; it really won't matter. But that's simply not the truth. People notice when we don't show up. They really do, just like we notice when people don't show up for us. But even more—people notice when we DO show up.

Showing up is the best way to show someone we care about them, and amazing things can happen when we do. You never know who else is going to be at dinner, or at the party, or at the small group. Friends of friends are the best way to make even more friends, and those friendships begin in moments like these. So let's show up for each other, shall we?

Next time you're invited somewhere, say yes. And if you say you'll go, go. You're showing your friend that you care, that you're trustworthy, and that you love them. You're going deeper in your friendship by spending that time together, and you never know what other friends you'll make along the way.

May God Bless You with a Chocolate Croissant

"Taste and see that the Lord is good; blessed is the
one who takes refuge in Him."

Psalm 34:8

Sometimes there's nothing you need in the world more than a chocolate croissant—or at least that's how I felt this morning.

There's just something about it, the flaky outside, and the dense chocolate inside, about the way that those two elements melt into a cappuccino that propelled me to hop in the car, still in my PJs, and drive to the nearest coffee shop to find one.

Truth be told, I don't even think it was the croissant that I was craving, but rather the experience that one would offer because you don't just eat a chocolate croissant. You don't grab one to go and eat it in the car with one hand while you're steering with the other. No, a chocolate croissant doesn't do on-the-go very well.

What it does do just perfectly, is linger.

The flakiness of the pastry demands a plate, and I just learned the hard way that if it comes with a chocolate drizzle (as all the best ones do), it needs more than a few napkins. It's big, and a bit floppy and usually saves a bit of chocolate in the corners of your mouth for later. It's not to be taken lightly or eaten quickly. It demands more of your time and attention. A chocolate croissant invites you to slow down a little, and as soon as you do, you're able to listen.

And that is what I was actually craving this morning, time to listen.

Life moves so fast, doesn't it? I know mine does, and I love the hustle and bustle of a busy life. However, the thing I've noticed over the last several years is that when I'm moving at the speed of life, I have a really hard time hearing from God, and I bet I'm not the only one.

God is there, make no mistake. He's there speaking, and guiding, and teaching, and loving, But when my life is moving so fast, I don't always make time to stop and chat.

It's like when you have friends over for dinner, and you want everything to be just perfect. You're chopping, and plating, and setting the table, and wiping up something sticky on the counter. You're so busy making everything perfect for your loved ones that you barely notice when they walk through the door.

I've missed whole dinners, whole parties, whole weekends with the people I love because I was so busy trying to make everything perfect for them. I forgot to stop and be with them and actually notice that they're there.

This is how I often am with God. I'm moving so fast that I realize I can't hear Him anymore, that we haven't connected in as long as I can remember. And it's not because He's not speaking. It's because I haven't taken the time to listen.

And I think that's what I really needed this morning as I craved my chocolate croissant. I needed some time to be quiet, to be still, to just be with God, some time to listen to Him.

So this morning that's exactly where I've been: listening, connecting, and getting chocolate drizzle everywhere.

My heart is so full.

And if you need a little extra help slowing down and listening, well then may God bless you with a chocolate croissant today too.

Today, I invite you to join me, or rather, to join Him. Slow down, take a second, take a moment, don't start your day quite yet. Steal some silence, put away your phone, take a deep breath, take your coffee out onto the porch. Take some time to just be with Him, to invite Him into your life, and into your day all over again. You don't even have to say a word. Just spend a few minutes together in comfortable silence. Let Him remind you that He's there and that He loves you.

Beyond Your Comfort Zone

"For since the creation of the world God's invisible
qualities—his eternal power and divine nature—
have been clearly seen, being understood from what
has been made, so that people are without excuse."

Romans 1:20

Being from Colorado, I've spent my life surrounded by nature
enthusiasts. Sadly, I have never been one of those people. I'm what
some would call "indoorsy"—preferring a hot tub to the slopes, a
hotel to a tent, and a great new restaurant to anything cooked over
a camping stove. I don't hate the outdoors—not by any stretch.
I've just never understood people's passion for it. At least, I hadn't
until a few years ago.

It was my best friend Kelsey's bachelorette party, and my favorite
kind of weekend. It was full of good food, great wine, and my best
friends. Yes and amen! But there was one particularly irksome
activity penciled into the otherwise perfect itinerary. We were
going tubing down a creek in the Colorado mountains.

For most people, this would sound like no big deal. Most of the
girls even seemed excited, but not me. It wasn't in my normal rep-
ertoire of activities, which made me think that: 1. I was going to
embarrass or hurt myself, or 2. I was going to really hate it. Either
way, I would have rather stayed home.

Unfortunately, the weekend wasn't about me. So I took a deep
breath, slipped on my suit, and grinned the whole stinkin' way
down to the creek. Standing at the water's edge, I gingerly dipped
in a toe, trying to gauge what I was getting myself into, and just

as quickly yanked it back out. The water was freezing! I couldn't believe we were actually going to put our bodies in it. I couldn't believe people thought this was fun. But, ever the team player, I saddled up a double tube with my best friend, Michelle, and off we went, the current carrying us through a slightly dialed up version of a water park's Lazy River ride.

I was doing fine until I saw the first rock. My hands gripped the handles tighter; my stomach was in knots. We were heading straight towards it, and there didn't seem to be a way around. The water level was too low, and the creek was a minefield of them. Sometimes we managed to avoid the rocks, sometimes our tailbones gave them a solid high five, and sometimes our tubes got lodged up on top of them, forcing us to wiggle and scoot until we could finally break free.

When we first got in the water, and when we first noticed the rocks, I was absolutely scared. I was counting the minutes until I could get out, until this whole thing was over. But, after awhile, it started to feel like an adventure. "Butts up!" we'd yell to the tubers behind us, all of us reaching our hips towards the sky to avoid smacking the rocks. Other times, the current would take us straight into a fallen tree branch, hanging over the water off the shore. We'd have to make ourselves as flat as possible, shielding our faces and closing our eyes, trying to limbo our way underneath it.

Tubing was everything I was afraid it was going to be, but, despite myself, I was having a blast. I liked being on this adventure. It required something of me—quick reflexes, balance, and some amateur navigation skills. It was so different from my everyday life which was, to my amazement, a good thing!

Between the rocky patches were long stretches of deep water. We got to float, the current slowly turning us around, giving us a 360-degree view of the mountains that nestled us close. I had forgotten how beautiful Colorado is, or maybe I had never noticed in the first place.

While we floated on these long stretches, Michelle and I got to catch up. Surrounded by nature, with our cell phones safely in the car, we got to have conversations that unwound slowly in a way that phone calls and text messages never seem to permit. In a quiet moment in the conversation, I surveyed my friends, in various positions on their tubes, talking, laughing, trying to wiggle themselves off of a rock, and genuinely having a fantastic time. My heart was warm, and my cheeks couldn't stop smiling.

I took in the sights and the smells in a way I hadn't in so long. Breathing deeply, I allowed the warmth of our friendship, the peacefulness of the water, and the zing of adventure to re-light a place in my heart I had completely forgotten about. I felt alive and whole and happy beyond words. Best of all, out there in nature, God felt so close. *Maybe this is why people like the outdoors,* I considered with sudden clarity.

Those few hours we spent on the creek will go down in the history of our friendships as one of the most fun things we've ever done together. It was unexpected and out of my comfort zone completely, but I think that's why I loved it so much.

It turns out that there are beautiful things waiting just beyond our comfort zone. When we're brought to the end of ourselves, we see things differently. We can see God even more clearly when normal life isn't fogging up our view. We notice things we haven't seen before, both around us and within us.

Today I dare you to try something outside of your comfort zone. Maybe it's a dance class or even just a new coffee shop. Maybe it's signing up for a mission trip, or going on a hike, or going to that new small group. When we're outside of our comfort zone, we learn so much about ourselves, we see life in a new way, and we see God in a whole new way as well. What might be hiding just beyond your comfort zone? I can't wait for you to find out!

Comparison Food Poisoning

"For we are God's handiwork, created in Christ
Jesus to do good works, which God prepared in
advance for us to do."

Ephesians 2:10

Have you ever been hit square in the face with comparison?

You're walking along through life, feeling pretty confident in your own skin. You feel good enough, tall enough, strong enough, successful enough, small enough, like you're in just the right place and stage of life, and then it happens... WHAM! Comparison.

It feels like you're being smacked with a 2×4: You see someone who has something you want but don't have, or something you didn't even realize you wanted that bad, or someone who is all the things you feel like you can never be. Ouch.

Sometimes it happens with us physically. You are feeling fine in your skin, beautiful even, and then you see someone who seems to knock your own beauty right out of the park, leaving you feeling small, hideous, and stupid for ever thinking you were good enough.

Or maybe it happens with relationships. You're single, and feeling good about it, and then your phone buzzes with a photo from your last single friend. It's a photo of her and her boyfriend, snuggled together, tears in their eyes as she holds up her hand that's sporting a sparkling diamond. You were doing fine, but now it feels like you've come down with the comparison equivalent of food poisoning—sudden, strong, and totally debilitating. *Why her? Why not me? What's wrong with me? Why can't doesn't my life look like hers?*

I came down with comparison food poisoning earlier this year. I was speaking at a sorority event in Georgia and, before it began, I had some time to chat with my wonderful hosts. As we were talking, one of them asked me, "I want to share my story, but it feels like the world doesn't need it. It's already being done by somebody else and being done better. How do you get over this?" I'm well acquainted with this question, so I had an answer all ready to go.

I said, "Listen, other people may be sharing similar stories, or teaching similar things, but they don't have your story, or your way of sharing it. The story you have, and the exact way you will share it will resonate with a group of girls that might not resonate with her. And, even if they resonate with both of you, there's still not too much goodness or encouragement in the world. I think we can officially call the market saturated when every single person in the world knows Jesus, and knows themselves, and loves themselves, and knows how much they're worth. But until that happens, the world needs your voice. So you have to keep sharing it!"

It's my favorite answer to give, and one I believe in wholeheartedly. It's something I think about all the time in moments when it feels like my voice may not matter, like my message is already being heard.

But then... completely out of the blue... comparison struck. One of the girls at the event mentioned another writer, and how much her blog has impacted her life, and that was it. It was sudden and violent, like food-poisoning always is. I was totally overcome with comparison.

Now listen, I totally know the truth here. I had just shared the truth. Right? I love this other writer! And on most days, I am the biggest fan of other women doing anything—even if what we're doing is similar. But for some reason, in that moment, on that day, none of that mattered. The truth I knew, the truth I usually know, couldn't stop comparison from coming in and almost knocking me out. My face grew hot; my hands were clammy, my insides were immediately in a knot.

All of a sudden, I couldn't think about anything except for how I'm not good enough. I couldn't think of anything but how far behind I suddenly felt. I couldn't think of anything except for the fact that the place I thought I occupied in the world was totally occupied by somebody else, and that somebody else was doing it better.

Here's why I wanted to tell you this today, because I have a feeling I'm not the only one who feels this way sometimes. If you struggle with comparison sometimes, you're not alone. I do too. Sometimes I have a handle on it, and sometimes I totally, completely don't.

But here's what I know: Comparison is the thief of joy. It really, truly is. We get nowhere when we compare ourselves to each other. We just lose the ability to proudly and confidently be ourselves—contributing to the world in a way that is totally our own, in a way nobody can steal or diminish.

So we can't succumb to comparison. It happens, absolutely, but we have to fight it.

We have to fight it by admitting it to the people we love, opening up the windows to the broken parts of our heart, letting people in to help us figure it out. We have to fight it by repeating the truth to ourselves—that God loves us, that He created us with a purpose, that the way God created us is absolutely good enough, and that God's economy works differently than ours—there's more than enough to go around.

God has a place in the world for you and for me. He has a story, and a plan for each of us, and nobody can take those things away.

So, sweet friend, here's to fighting comparison with everything we have, and to singing our song anyway as we practice believing that how God created us is good enough and that there's more than enough goodness to go around.

Have you ever been hit in the face with comparison? Maybe you have comparison food poisoning right now. Or maybe you're in a good place when it comes to comparison. But no matter where you are, I don't think we can ever hear this reminder enough. Find a piece of paper and write yourself a note to keep where you can see it. Write, "Comparison is the thief of joy. I don't need to compare myself to anyone. I am good enough. There is a place for me. There is more than enough to go around."

Markers of Where God Showed Up

"You know with all your heart and soul that not one of all
the good promises the Lord your God gave you has failed.
Every promise has been fulfilled; not one has failed."

Joshua 23:14b

I don't know if you're allowed to say you don't like a section of the
Bible, but I'm going to go ahead and say it. I don't love reading
the book of Exodus: the story of the Israelites wandering around
the desert. If you haven't read the story or haven't read the story
recently, Moses leads the Israelites out of Egyptian slavery, through
the desert, and to the promised land—the land God has prepared
just for them. It's such a frustrating story, though, because the
Israelites just cannot seem to get it together!

The story begins with God literally parting the sea, saving them
from their enemies, allowing them to walk through the sea on dry
ground. Amazing, right? But the moment they reach the other
side, they start complaining, saying, "We're tired; we're hungry;
we're sick of the food you magically made fall from the sky." And
it only gets worse from there.

God does amazing thing after amazing thing, and, about four
seconds after every miraculous instance of provision, they forget.
They begin to doubt God again, to complain, to worry, and they
turn to other things besides God to take care of them.

I think I dislike this story so much because as I read how many
times God has come through for them and how many times they
forget all about it, I cringe because I know that the story isn't just
about them. The story is very much about me.

God has done amazing things in my life, and I know He has for you too. He's provided jobs and money when I had none. He's given me a whole new shot at life after I've messed up my old one (more than once). He's pulled me out of bad situations and comforted me in seasons I wouldn't have gotten through otherwise. The list of ways God has shown up and done just absolutely miraculous things in my life is LONG.

But here's the thing: I forget constantly. I am so grateful, so over-the-moon at His goodness and presence and provision. Sixty seconds later, I'm on to the next thing. Before long, another problem arises, and I'm sweating and cry-ning (a Wilson-family word for a combination of crying and whining) and mad at God for letting me get into this situation in the first place when, of course, it's usually my own doing. I'm pretty sure He's going to fail me this time, and I start to look a heck of a lot like those Israelites. So often, I just can't get this trusting God thing right.

But there's something they do to help with their forgetfulness—those Israelites—that I really love. God has just parted the water for them again (yes, a second time!), and, as they cross, God has Joshua (their leader at this point) instruct 12 men to each pick up a stone. When they get to the other side of this river, dry and safe, Joshua stacks them up one on top of the other. When they ask him what this sculpture is for, this is what he says:

"So that all the peoples of the earth might know that the hand of the Lord is powerful and so that you might always fear the Lord your God." (Josh. 4:24)

Joshua tells them to use these stones to help them remember what God has done for them, who God is. And when people ask about the stones, he says to use them to tell the story of what God did so that others can know Him too.

I don't know about you, but I need these stones in my life. I need things to remind me of who God is and what He's done, because, quite frankly, otherwise, I start to forget. And forgetting is such a hard thing, because when I come to the edge of the next river, the next tricky situation, the next painful problem, and I need God all over again, I want to remember that He was there for me last time. If I can remember that, it helps me trust Him this time too.

So, over the years I've been collecting stones: memories or markers to remind me of days and places and times when God came through. If you walk through my house or even just flip through my Bible, you'll see so many of them.

There's a tile cross from Sevilla, the city where our relationship began; a bookmark from Ghana that reminds me of the passion for missions God gave me while I was there; the pub crawl t-shirt I was wearing in Rome the day I met Jesus. My favorite stones are my journals, stacked neatly side by side on a shelf in my office. I love them because they chronicle my life. They're the stories of the rivers I've walked through and how God carried me through every single one. They're first-hand accounts, evidence of His goodness and provision and presence in my life, written in my own handwriting.

God is so faithful, and we're so infuriatingly forgetful. But when we stack up these stones—reminders of times when God came through—it reminds us that we could trust Him then, and we can trust Him now too.

What are those markers for you? Do you have any? As you walk through life, and into life with God, keep your eye out for moments and mementos that you can bring home with you. Gather a few shells from a beach where God taught you something new. Bring home a paper napkin, or a book of matches from the restaurant where you saw God's redemption at work. Start keeping a journal so you can remember the rivers in your life and how God always carried you across. But, whatever your markers are, keep them where you can see them— reminders of the last time God came through, and that He will this time too.

Celebrating the Ones We Have

"All beautiful you are, my darling; there is no flaw in you."

Song of Songs 4:7

Before you get married, you picture every detail of it perfectly. The wedding, certainly, but also every event, step, and festivity along the way.

In watching so many of my friends get engaged, I had flipped through countless engagement photos. They were lovely, such wonderful keepsakes. The photographers captured their personalities and their love so beautifully. I couldn't wait for when it was our turn.

But when our turn did finally come, I was a wreck. The day before pictures I stood in my closet, trying on everything I could find, and nothing fit the bill. I grabbed my keys and zipped out to the closest little shop, hoping they'd have just the thing to make our photos perfect. It was in one of those dressing rooms that I had a particularly horrible moment.

Can I just say that dressing rooms are one of life's cruelest forms of torture? Why in the world would stores that are trying to sell you on the fact that you look good in their clothes create such tiny spaces with such horrible mirrors, and even worse lighting that brings out every single flaw until you're crawling out of there, hands empty and insecurity dragging behind you like toilet paper stuck to your shoe?

That's what happened in that dressing room. I put on the dress I'd chosen and looked in the mirror, and was horrified at what was there looking back at me. I'd been working out and eating healthy to get ready for our wedding, but it seemed like the body staring back at me hadn't gotten the memo. It was all dimples, and wrinkles, and pudge, and flab. *It's the lighting and the mirrors and the angle,* I tried to tell myself soothingly. But still, the body that stared back at me felt so discouragingly flawed.

But as I walked out of the store, swimming in self-pity and frustration, I had one fleeting, possibly life-changing thought.

What if I never have a perfect body?

It wasn't a discouraging thought, but a daring one—something I'd never allowed myself to think before.

I've always been the person who is striving to improve. I can always be a bit smaller, a bit more toned, a bit stronger, and look a little bit better in those jeans. For as long as I can remember, I've been working for that day when I finally look good enough—perfect in every outfit, every mirror, from every angle.

And in that tiny, fleeting moment, I wondered what would happen if I just gave up.

I'm not talking about health. I know the benefits of water, broccoli, and exercise. What I'm talking about is the incessant pressure we put on ourselves to be smaller, better, and prettier. Really, what would happen if we just gave up?

What if perfection wasn't the target anymore? What if health was? What if we accepted the things about our bodies that are totally normal, and totally imperfect? What if we got over the fact that we're short, or tall, or heavier in the middle, or skinny up top? What if a lack of cellulite wasn't the requirement for beauty and love and really cute underwear? What if we just decided that good enough is good enough and that we're going to celebrate our bodies instead of refusing to love them until they reach a certain size? What if we never have perfect bodies, but learn to love the ones that we do have?

Bodies do miraculous things. My best friends are starting to have babies, and their bodies are creating tiny humans, the cutest little darlings I've ever seen. This is seriously a miracle! My body is able to love Carl; it's able to wrap its arms around his neck, able to have dance parties in our bathroom, and able to kiss his perfectly soft cheeks. My body is able to run a 5K (well—it used to be able to, at least) and do Pilates and take long walks. My body is able to sleep, and eat, and heal itself when I'm sick, and rock a great pair of jeans.

We are all different. We, as women, are all shaped differently, all molded uniquely, and I just wonder what would happen if we gave ourselves a pass, a get-out-of-jail-free card, and allowed ourselves to just enjoy how we are?

Our bodies aren't made to be statues of perfection. They're meant to make babies and make love. They're meant to dance, to sleep, and to snuggle. They're made to eat cookies, and eat icing with a spoon, and run, and be strong.

Our bodies are amazing, and I just wonder what would happen if we started treating them that way.

> Do something to celebrate your body today. Eat icing with a spoon, or go for a run, or cannonball into a lake, or romp in the snow. Our bodies are capable of such amazing things, so let's celebrate them today.

Turning Around

"Don't urge me to leave you or to turn back from
you. Where you go I will go, and where you stay I
will stay. Your people will be my people and your
God my God."

Ruth 1:16

I know this is disappointing, but I really don't like to hike. It's disappointing because I'm a Coloradan, born and raised. But even the beautiful Rocky Mountains could never inspire me to spend a Saturday sweating my way up a trail.

Despite my distaste for the activity, not long ago I went on a hike with my aunt, jumping at the chance for some quality time with her.

At first, the hike was exactly as we expected. It wasn't easy, but it wasn't impossible either. *Maybe this hiking thing isn't as bad as I thought,* I considered with surprising optimism. We talked as we hiked, catching up, telling stories, and getting lost in conversation. But that became exactly the problem: we'd lost ourselves in the conversation. All of a sudden we looked around and noticed the trail markers were nowhere to be found.

We decided to keep going. We figured we'd come across the trail once we made it to the top. So we began to blaze a trail of our own, not knowing what obstacles lay ahead. Our makeshift trail was much harder than anything we'd encountered so far. It was steep, a series of slippery rock faces and small cliffs.

I led the way, climbing up the first of the small cliffs that were almost as tall as I was. I found a sturdy branch to hold onto and then brought my foot up as high as I could to wedge it into the lowest crevice. With a place to push off of, and the branch as my anchor, I hoisted myself up. One step closer to the top.

But my aunt was still behind me. So, holding onto the branch to keep from slipping, I turned back around. "Put your foot there," I instructed her, showing her what had worked for me. "Hold on here, and when you get close enough, I'll grab your other hand to pull you up." Slowly but surely, we made our way to the top. I'd go first and then turn around and help her up too.

We made it to the summit safe and sound (a total accomplishment for this non-hiker), and I proudly told the story (adding as much drama to the situation as I could get away with) to anyone who would listen.

When we're navigating the terrain of our lives, we have two choices. We can either overcome an obstacle and continue on ahead, or we can stop, turn around, and help the person behind us.

When we stop, when we turn around and share the tricks of the trade or an encouraging word or offer each other a hand, I truly believe that's one of the kindest things we can do for one another. It's a perfect demonstration of the truth that we don't have to navigate this life on our own.

A few years ago, I had the incredible opportunity of visiting a small rural town in Cambodia. The town had overcome a lot in the last ten years or so, and I got to visit an after-school program that the organization I traveled with had helped begin.

When we arrived, we were greeted by a group of the giggliest, wiggliest, most adorable kiddos you've ever seen. We ran and played, and I picked them up and spun them around until I thought my arms would fall off. Then I got to meet their 24-year-old leader, a guy named Kollel.

"Why do you do this?" I asked him. "Why do you spend your time here with these kids?"

"It's because I looked up to my kid's club leader when I was their age. He inspired me, and taught me, and made me better, and I want to do the same and be a role model for these children."

I had goosebumps everywhere, which is really saying something in the oppressive Cambodian heat.

Our lives are a journey, and after we make it past a particularly rough stretch, we have two choices. We can either continue on, or we can turn around and help those a few paces behind. My life is so much better because of the people who have turned around and helped me, and I bet you can say the same.

So as we navigate terrain in our lives, that's what I hope we do too. I hope we turn back around, show the person behind us which crevice works best, and offer them our hand as they climb up too.

Take some time today to reflect on obstacles you've overcome in your life so far. Maybe you've made it through a bad breakup, the loss of someone important to you, a big transition, a steep climb in your career. Then think about some people who may be a step or two behind you. Maybe it's someone you work with or the kids in the youth group at church. Maybe it's your best friend's little sister, or a friend walking through something hard. Once you have that person, or those people, in mind, invite them to coffee. You don't need to have all the answers or a quick fix to the problems they're facing, but you do have so much to share with them—all the things you learned when you walked that path before. They'll be so glad to have a friend to walk with them along the way.

God Uses Imperfect People

"But he said to me, "My grace is sufficient for
you, for my power is made perfect in weakness."
Therefore I will boast all the more gladly about my
weaknesses, so that Christ's power may rest on me."

2 Corinthians 12:9

I don't know about you, but I love having guests in from out of town. I love having our house filled with people, love making sure the guest bathroom is in order, love putting freshly washed sheets on a bed I know someone I love is going to sleep in soon. So I was over the moon when I heard that my little sister was coming to stay with us for the weekend.

And I don't know how your mind works, but as soon as I heard she was coming, I began to make plans. But not just plans like, "Let's take her to Pancake Pantry," deciding to brave the lines that always wrap around the block.

Instead, I made bigger plans, like how we'd all be closer by the time she left, how she'd get to know her new brother-in-law better than ever before, and I pictured us setting a good example for her in relationships by showing her what our marriage looks like, up close and in action. I pictured us being at our very best—light, and free, full of joy, and fully in love. And I pictured her going home to my parents with a glowing report and an encouraged heart, having seen how great marriage can be.

But, as you can imagine, that's not exactly how things went down. It wasn't anyone's fault—not hers, not ours—but she just caught us on a bad weekend. We'd both been out of town until the night before she arrived. It was a busy time at work for both of us, and it seemed like every crazy logistical-adult-y thing that could happen that week did. So, while we were thrilled to have her here, we were also totally preoccupied, worried about life and work. We were bickery, short-tempered, and totally on edge—a combination that made me feel like we were setting a poor example instead of a good one.

On Saturday night, as Carl was out running some late night errands, just trying to get things checked off of his ever-growing list, my sister and I sat snuggled up on the couch as I started to cry. "I wanted to show you how great marriage is," I told her through sniffles. "I wanted to show you how amazing our life is. I wanted to set a good example for you!"

As I cried, my sister leaned over and put her hand on my knee, reminding me yet again that she's always been the smarter of the two of us—always comforting and counseling her older sister.

With grace in her eyes, she told me exactly what I didn't know I needed to hear: She told me that it was okay, that she was happy she got to see another side of us and our lives this weekend. She was happy about it because it's real, because it's raw, because it's normal. She said what I totally didn't expect her to say, that we were actually setting an awesome example for her—showing her how to do life with someone when it isn't perfect, and when it's actually pretty hard.

And then she said something that just unwound my tangled, disappointed insides in a way I could never have imagined. She said, "Steph, you guys are enough. Just as you are, right now, in good moments and in bad ones too, you guys are enough. You are good enough. You don't need to try to be anything else."

Deep breath, sob, sigh.

I've always had this idea that I need to be pulled together, and shiny, at my best and perfectly "on" in order to make a difference in the world. But since that weekend, God's been teaching me something altogether new. He's been teaching me that we, as we are today, are enough to make a positive difference in the world. It's not because we have our words perfectly chosen, or our outfit carefully selected. It's not because we're at our best, or because we and our husbands are at our most synchronized and charming. It's because we're us, because I'm me, and you're you, and God is in us, and when we let people see us as we really are, God's able to show them what He's capable of in a heart and a life that's surrendered to Him.

So that's where I've been ever since—totally imperfect, just trying to figure it out. And apparently, according to my sweet little sister, and according to God, that's enough. I just thought you might need to hear that today too.

That's what I want to invite you into today, sweet friend. Take a deep breath and know that you are enough. You don't need to perfect, or perform, or be "on" in order to make a positive impact in the world. You just need to be you. God is in you and with you and, because of that, you as you are right now today, are enough. So take a deep breath and remind yourself of that today as many times as you need to.

There's Still Beauty, There's Still Joy

"In this world you will have trouble. But take heart!
I have overcome the world."

John 16:33b

On a random Thursday, that still feels like yesterday, I got a phone call.

My heart dropped, I instantly felt sick, and I began to cry—not light tears, but the kind of visceral sobs that wait deep in your soul for a day when you really need them. Carl rushed over immediately, sitting on the couch next to me, squeezing my hand hard. Somehow he knew that I didn't need tender love in that moment, I needed gripping, fierce love that could guard me, even just the littlest bit, from the blow I was in the process of receiving.

My cousin died. He was young, perfectly fine, and then he wasn't—heatstroke killing him almost instantly on a hike with our family.

He was always bigger than me—tossing my cousins and me into the lake when we were younger, gently but with a terrifying yell. We'd climb back onto the raft, slippery in our one-pieces, trying to evade him, while secretly hoping that he'd send us flying just one more time.

It didn't feel real. How could someone who had always been there all of a sudden be gone? The sadness of it left me feeling hollow—as if something core and central to me was carved out and left cold. The suddenness of it terrified me, leaving me with white knuckles as I grasped for anything that felt solid and sure.

I cried off and on all day, feeling like the slightest wind would knock me over. By the end of the day, my head was aching, my heart was searing, and my soul was exhausted, but Carl still insisted that we go on a date. He knew that out of all the things I needed that day, what I didn't need was to be alone.

We pulled into a restaurant we'd never seen before in a tiny town in North Georgia. It was a treasure—a perfectly timed gift.

We pored over the menu like kids in a candy shop, pointing at items and oohing with delight. We started with fried green tomatoes with pimento and goat cheese. Then we shared the honey-sriracha fried chicken, with a summer salad and their homemade grits on the side— topping it all off with peach and rhubarb cobbler.

We ate and laughed a little and talked about nothing important. The restaurant around us glowed with twinkle lights and candles, and the food was delicious. It was the best meal, we agreed, that we'd had in a long, long time. It was exactly what I needed.

After dinner, we wandered down a hill following what sounded like a movie and found the community sitting in a large park, pic-nic-style, watching Madagascar 2 on a big screen. We stayed for a while, breathing in the smell from the popcorn stand and listening to families laugh. Then we walked back to our car, hand-in-hand, watching the sun go down.

My eyes filled with tears as we walked, realizing that, over the course of the meal and the movie and the walk, I'd actually felt a tiny sliver of joy.

That was a terrible day, a devastating loss. It's taken a long time to heal, and we will never, ever forget. The world is a dimmer place for having lost my cousin's warm heart and twinkling eyes, and our family will never be the same. But even on the darkest of days, in the saddest of seasons, there's still beauty, there's still joy.

And that's what I got to see that night, right when I needed it the most. Tucked right there in the midst of my grief—miracles twin-kled up at me, like lightning bugs on a warm, Georgia evening.

There were big miracles like love, and family, and people who carry you through the hardest days of your life. And there were little miracles like fried green tomatoes—the best I'd ever had.

And with each one, little by little, my heart started to fill back up with hope—flickers of light reminding me that darkness can't overcome us after all.

Have you ever been through a dark season? Maybe you've been through one before, or maybe you're in the midst of one right now. When we're going through something hard, or grieving a big loss, nothing makes it feel better immediately. It didn't for me. But the thing that does help me is knowing that God is with me in the midst of it, and that, no matter how dark the night gets, God's light is always stronger. So in whatever you're going through today, whether it's big, or small, or totally earth-quaking, hold this truth close to your heart, "In this world you will have trouble. But take heart! I have overcome the world." - John 16:33

Let's Pay Attention

> "Carry each other's burdens, and in this way you
> will fulfill the law of Christ."
>
> Galatians 6:2

Something you may or may not know about me is that I'm super sensitive and, until a few years ago, I hated that about myself. For years, I equated sensitivity with being high maintenance. I always believed my feelings made me a lot to handle, so I always wished I could get rid of them. I wished I could be tougher, feel less, hurt less easily. I wished I had thicker skin.

For years, I tried to make that happen. I covered up my tender heart with alcohol, with boys, and with being extra busy—anything to keep me from feeling all the things one feels as they wander through this messy, hard, wonderful world.

Life just feels heavy sometimes, doesn't it? I know that's not just me.

I had coffee with a new friend last week, and she said something I can't get out of my mind. She said, "Empathy is really, really hard." and she's so right! It hurts to hurt when the world hurts. It's gut-wrenching to mourn when the world mourns because it seems like there's just so much to mourn. It feels 10000x easier to turn off our feelings, to numb ourselves to the world, to care less, to just be less sensitive to it all. But even if that is the easier route, it's certainly not the best route. We know it's not.

In the years I spent numbing my heart and dulling my sensitivity, I lost so much, because you can't numb yourself to the bad without numbing yourself to the good. I saw a snippet from a conversation with author Glennon Melton recently that said:

"Q: Glennon, why do you cry so often?
A: For the same reason I laugh so often. Because I'm paying attention."

That's really how feelings work, isn't it? Joy and grief are two sides
of the same coin. We have to feel one in order to feel the other. It's
similar to how our greatest liabilities, the things about us that feel
the hardest, are actually so often another side of our greatest gifts
and strengths.

My sensitivity may make me crumble when I watch the news, but
it's also my sensitivity that allows me to feel giddy over just how
much I love my people. It's my sensitivity that allows me to savor
the gifts and delights of this world fully. One time, I teared up
while eating a really great grilled cheese sandwich. I'm telling you,
it really was that good.

It's my sensitivity that helps me experience the world and then
write about it. In the same way, it's your feelings that make you a
fantastic sister, friend, mom, or wife. It's your feelings that prompt
you to care enough to help, to make a difference, to fight for people
who can't fight for themselves, to advocate for a cause.

Empathy may be hard, as my new friend said, but she also pointed
out that it's the very thing that connects us, that motivates us to
help—it's the very thing that makes us human.

So here's my challenge for all of us even when life feels heavy: let's
keep feeling.

Don't numb your heart to the bad, because we need you to feel the
bad. We need you to listen, to care, to act, to join in and to give
whatever you can to the people who need it most. Keep your heart
tender and open so you can make the bad better, and so you can
experience the heights of the good. Because even when our world
feels like it's falling apart at the seams, there are still beautiful,
wonderful, hopeful, glittery bits of life to behold and be held—it
would be such a shame to miss them.

So here's to feeling our way through this world—to doing the hard, human work of empathy, and to doing the deep loving that makes it all so worth it.

Facing and feeling our emotions can be scary, especially if we haven't done it in awhile. But it doesn't have to be scary or happen all at once. Take just one step in that direction today. Pray and ask God to open your eyes just a little bit more than they were yesterday. Ask Him to help you see what people around you are needing, what they're going through, and how you can help. Ask Him to open your eyes a little bit more to the beauty swirling around you. And finally, ask Him for the courage to face and really let yourself experience the things going on within you. Don't forget—your emotions are not weakness. Your emotions carry so much strength.

Bad Attitudes & Gratitude

"I trust in your unfailing love; my heart rejoices in
your salvation. I will sing the Lord's praise, for he
has been good to me."

Psalm 13:5-6

When Carl and I first moved to Nashville, we had a really hard
time going to church. I don't know if you should admit that out
loud, but I just did. So if you're there too, know you're not alone.

We'd been showing up because we knew we should—because we
knew it was a better option than lazing around in our pajamas
all day, but it was a struggle. Our lives were busy, we were in the
midst of a gigantic transition, and church just felt hard—like an
obligation we wished we could get out of.

But it wasn't just church that felt like an obligation—it was spending time with God in general. I was still spending time with Him,
but it lacked the enjoyment, the intimacy, and the connection I
usually feel when I do. Again, I don't know if you're supposed to
admit that, but that's how I was feeling.

One Sunday in the fall was particularly tough. Carl and I were
cuddled up on the couch, wanting to do nothing more than to
watch football until bedtime. Without much enthusiasm, and
much later than we should have, we finally talked ourselves off the
couch and dragged ourselves to church.

We arrived just after the service began, and found seats in a sea of
enthusiastic worshipers. Everyone around us looked happy, deep
in their bones happy, like worship was seeping out of their pores.

They were experiencing something with God in that moment, something special and intimate—something I hadn't felt in a while.

Toward the end of the worship set, the pastor prompted the congregation to praise God for all He's done and, I have to admit, I did not want to. I didn't feel grateful, or worshipful, or any of the other things I wanted to feel in that moment. I felt cynical, vaguely cranky, and was still longing for my soft spot on the couch. But in that moment, I realized I had two options: I could either make the best of it or maybe I should just leave. But I didn't want to walk out of church—that felt extreme. So I took the pastor's suggestion, and I decided to give praise and thanksgiving a try.

I started small, and randomly.

"God, thank you for the coffee I drank this morning. Thank you for the lunch we're going to eat after church." It was hard at first, awkward and stilted, but as I added to the list, I started to pick up steam.

My list grew longer and more profound, and I began thanking Him for the deeper things He's done throughout my life that I forget about sometimes—the things we lose track of if we don't stop, pause, and look back. I went through my storehouse of favorite memories with God, like old buddies getting together and telling the same stories they've told for years.

But then I started remembering more recent events. I thought about what God had done in the last six months—how close He was to us when we lost our jobs, how I felt like He was physically there, holding me up when my knees had given out with sadness.

I thought about our wedding, about Carl, and about how I would never have met him if it weren't for God. I thought about the move to Nashville, and how perfectly He'd lined up everything for us, from our jobs, to our apartment, to our budding community. And, as I flipped through those memories, I felt something stirring in my chest, something I hadn't felt in awhile: worship.

The more I remembered, the more thankful I became, and the more thankful I became, the more I could relate to what the people around me were feeling. I felt like worshiping, not just on the surface, but deep down in my bones, just like I used to. And, before I knew it, my bad mood had casually slipped out the back door.

I may be wrong, but I think gratitude might be the key to connecting with and worshipping God.

I'm usually zipping through life so fast that I barely find time to toss a "Thank you!" out the window like gum onto the highway before I'm onto the next thing. But, when I slow down enough to notice, when I have my eyes peeled for God's goodness, and when I remember all the times He's shown up before, worship flows a lot more easily.

Our relationship with God is just that: a relationship. And, just like in any other relationship, there are seasons when we feel so in love we could just sing about it, and seasons when we feel like we'd rather just sit on the couch and watch football.

Thankfully, our mood and how close we feel to God doesn't actually impact how close He is to us. God promises us He'll never leave us, so no matter how cranky we are at church, He's not going anywhere.

But our gratitude does change things—not God's relationship to us, but our experience of God, because when we take the time to notice and remember how good He is, it's impossible not to praise Him.

> What are three things you're grateful for today? God is so good and takes such good care of us. Take some time to notice and to thank Him this morning.

Cleaning Out Our Junk Drawers

"Arise, come, my darling; my beautiful one, come
with me."

Song of Songs 2:13b

Carl and I are moving in a few weeks, and I'm discovering there's nothing more revealing than packing up everything you own. It's so revealing because it uncovers all you've stored up over the last year, or ten. It forces you to finally face up to your junk drawers and find the notes, the gum wrappers, and the spare change that have been cluttering those spaces for longer than you can remember.

When it comes to packing, I'm more of a "shove everything into boxes and then figure it out when we get there" kind of packer, but Carl insists it makes no sense to move things you don't want to keep. So I've been working hard to take inventory and throw out the junk. It's a long, exhausting process, but it's a liberating one.

A few years ago, I started thinking about the same process but with our minds and our hearts instead of our homes.

It began at a dinner with some of my girlfriends. My friend, Krista, had been learning a lot about how we see ourselves as women, and she wanted to tell us what she'd been discovering.

"We pick up labels in our lives," she began "They're the things people say about us over the years, the way we're identified, the categories people put us in."

I thought I understood what she was saying, but I asked for some examples, just in case.

"Maybe you were dubbed the smart kid in school or the dumb kid," she began, "or maybe you were the jock or the popular girl— or maybe you were the bigger kid in your family or the trouble-maker of all your cousins. Do you know what I mean?"

I knew exactly what she meant. In fact, we all did.

"I took some time to think through my labels last night," she told us, pulling a piece of paper out of her bag.

"I want to do it," my friend, Sarah, chimed in, "Do you have more paper?" We agreed; Krista had us all curious! How had people labeled us throughout the years? We all wanted to know! So Krista passed a sheet to each of us, and we sat there quietly, thinking, writing, and eating our last bites of dessert.

"Well?" one of my friends finally broke the silence. "What did you guys find out?"

We went around, and each shared the labels we felt had stuck the most. Our dinner had taken a somber turn, but we could all tell we were in the midst of something important.

For me, my stickiest label was that I was high-maintenance. Two dif-ferent boyfriends spat those words at me in the midst of our break-ups. They'd each retracted the words later, apologizing for being so mean, but it was far too late for that. I'd been both believing and fighting against that label for years. And as I sat there at the table, I was noticing for the first time just how much it had affected me.

My friends were carrying around rough labels as well, and they covered the spectrum: The nerd, the underachiever, the fat girl, the mean one, and more and more and more.

When we'd made it around the circle, we looked at each other in disbelief. We hadn't realized that those labels were weighing quite so heavily, but they were! They were coloring the way we saw the world and ourselves inside of it. And that's what these labels do.

They change the way we interact with the world, and we can see that playing out all around us.

Do you have a friend who believes she's not desirable? That impacts the way she carries herself. She doesn't come across as confident or inviting, and the result just proves her point.

Do you have a friend who doubts she can accomplish big things? Chances are she won't even try them or, when she does, she won't try them wholeheartedly. It makes her fear come true when, if she just believed differently, it wouldn't!

The things we believe to be true about ourselves have ripple effects in our lives. That's why it's so important to take an inventory every once in awhile.

Our lists surprised us—we didn't realize the depth of those insecurities, or quite how much those labels had gotten stuck. But with those words staring up at us, we knew what we had to do.

It was time to clean out our junk drawers.

We moved from the table into my living room, curling up and getting straight to work.

First, we called the lies out for what they were. I scrounged around my house for as many Bibles as I could find, and we went on a hunt for the verses where God tells us who we are. We went through line by line, comparing those labels to God's word. It turns out that God rarely agrees with the mean kid in middle school, or our ex-boyfriends, or our friend's mom and all of her opinions. Who knew?

And then, armed with truth and in an act of defiance and bravery, we took the papers with our labels outside, and we burned them. They lit slowly, and then we watched as the paper was engulfed in flames, shriveling into a crisp and then disappearing into a pile of ash. It was a perfect physical demonstration of what we wanted to happen to those labels that had crippled us for so long.

Our insecurities didn't disappear that night, but in a big way, they started to. Because from then on, when the labels would try to creep in and define us again, we could remember back to that night. With that pile of ash in our minds, those labels didn't have quite as much power over us as they used to.

The labels we've been wearing around for so long can be sticky – they are tough to get rid of, like a stain, or gum on the bottom of our shoe, but calling them out is the first step. And that's the step we took that night. We cleaned out the junk drawers inside of ourselves, finding the names, the hurtful words, and the labels hidden within—and together, we took a step toward God's truth.

Song of Songs 4:7 says, "All beautiful you are, my darling, there is no flaw in you." Can you imagine what life would be like if we believed God's labels instead?

What labels have people put on you throughout the years? I bet a few came to mind as you heard about ours, but once you have them in mind, it's tempting to feel discouraged. What do you do about them? How do you take them off?

The thing that helped me more than anything was to talk about them with a counselor. That's what a lot of us did after that night. It felt so good to shed light on those labels and to come clean about how we'd been feeling. Our insecurities diminished so much because of what we did together that night. But several of us wanted to take it one step further. We wanted to take them off for good. Counseling has been incredibly helpful to me in several seasons of my life, and this was one of them. So, if you're noticing some labels you've been wearing, and if you are ready to take them off for good, talk to a counselor about them. I can't recommend it enough.

Stop Being Brilliant. Start Being You.

> "In all these things we are more than conquerors
> through him who loved us."
>
> Romans 8:37

A few years ago, I had the privilege of speaking to a group of students at Belmont University. I love speaking; I love college students—everything about it should have been perfect. The problem was, even by "Belmont talk: Version 6" I still had no idea what I wanted to say.

There's this thing I sometimes do when I'm writing—most of my brain is trying to string thoughts together, but there's this chorus in the back of my mind that says, "Be brilliant, be brilliant, be brilliant," like a train chugging down the tracks.

Now, I'm sure you can imagine, but writing when those words are leaning over your shoulder is almost impossible.

Lost in my screen, my brow furrowed, I wrote in fits and spurts. My talk was in less than 24 hours, and I was stuck. I tried one tactic, then decided I hated it, deleting furiously and starting again. Nothing I wrote was good enough; nothing I wrote was brilliant.

Finally, after hours of wrestling with my laptop, I abandoned it for the moment, wrapped a blanket around my shoulders, and wandered into the living room pathetically. Ignoring the couch completely, I plopped onto the floor feeling very sorry for myself, and very scared that the morning would come and I'd still have nothing to say.

I lay on the floor for a long time, staring up at the ceiling. *What can I say that's brilliant? How can I organize my thoughts in a way that's life-changing? How in the world am I going to make this perfect?*

But after a good long time, I finally had a thought. It struck me with an abrupt pop, as the best thoughts always do: *What if I stopped trying to be perfect, and just tried to be me?*

The thought stopped me in my tracks because it's not a thought I'd had much recently. It's a thought I think very few of us have on a regular basis.

Whether you're a writer, or a businesswoman, or a student or a mom, whether you're a wife, or a paralegal, or a teacher, or nanny, I bet you have a similar refrain going through your head. "Be great, do this perfectly, don't make mistakes, don't screw up."

I think we all do that. We all want that, we all want to be great. We want to be the best moms, the best wives, the best employees, the best students, so we put that kind of pressure on ourselves—the pressure to be really great, to be brilliant, even —the pressure to be perfect.

But the thing I realized as I was lying there, pathetic and stuck in my quest for perfection, is this: The pressure for perfection is paralyzing!

I knew what I wanted to say to the students at Belmont, but that pressure formed a barricade, blocking my thoughts and ideas from coming out like I needed them to. So, from my position, teary and overwhelmed on my back on the carpet, I repeated that new thought in my mind a few times. *What if I stopped trying to be perfect, and just tried to be me? What if we all did that? What if we all stopped trying to be perfect, and just tried to be ourselves?*

Instead of trying to write the world's most perfect talk, what if I just showed up and shared the things I know? What if, instead of trying to be the perfect mom, you just showed up and were you? What if we did that for our husbands, and our employers, and the students we're teaching?

What if, instead of trying to be perfect, we just showed up and were ourselves?

My friend Ally does lots of speaking, and she gave me a piece of advice she learned along the way. She learned that when she's trying to be perfect—trying to write the perfect talk, deliver it exactly like she practiced, never straying from the notes—she delivers her very worst talks.

On the other hand, when she shows up and is open-hearted, having a conversation with the audience and just being herself, that's when she does her best.

So what if we showed up open-hearted instead of perfect?

What if we all took off the pressure to be brilliant and decided to just be ourselves? What if we truly believed that the things inside of us, without the pressure, or the striving, or the working for perfection, were actually enough? I can't imagine how life-changing that would be.

> Who you are is good enough. What you have to offer is good
> enough. What's inside you is good enough. It really is true! So
> today, instead of trying to be perfect, show up and just be you.
> Offer your heart to your students, your kids, your employees,
> your clients. Share your heart, your stories, the things you know,
> and the things that are inside of you, and do it bravely. Show up
> and be you today, and I promise, that's enough.

Let's Be the Kind of People Who Go

"For God did not give us a spirit of timidity, but a
spirit of power, of love and of self-discipline."

2 Timothy 1:7

If you haven't met Michelle, let me introduce you to her now. She's
my best friend, my soulmate, the yin to my yang. We met when we
were eight years old and have been best friends ever since. We've
been through everything together for almost all of our lives. We've
weathered straight across bangs, countless breakups (not with each
other), and more than one set of braces. She knows me deeply.
She's my person, feeling more like my sister than a friend.

I look up to Michelle for a million different reasons, but one, in
particular, has kept coming up recently. Michelle is the kind of
person who goes.

Michelle puts her airline miles where her mouth is—traveling
to all corners of the country just to visit. She's been to Austin,
and Atlanta, and Portland more times than I can count, throwing
inconvenience to the wind to be near her best friends.

I've always wanted to be that kind of person—the person who
buys the plane ticket. I want to travel, to make the trek, to visit
my people because I know it's worth it. That face-to-face time, the
being there, it makes life richer, better, and more complete.

But being the kind of person who goes just isn't easy. Our lives
are so busy; it usually feels impossible to leave. When you even
consider it, you're met with the sudden sense that you might just
be the glue that holds your world together. (Is that just me?)

My cousin passed away suddenly a few summers ago, and my dad and I sat on the phone for a long time, debating what to do about the funeral (which was a long and expensive plane ride away). We both had meetings and deadlines and were facing the busiest weeks we'd had all year. Our schedules were already bursting at the seams with things we weren't going to have time for, and then we got the phone call.

The tragedy brought our worlds to a halt, and we had a choice to make: were we going to stay or were we going to go? In moments like these it can sometimes feel like the stronger thing to do is to stay at work. Like if we never miss a day, no matter what we're going through, it means we're more resilient, tougher, or more dedicated somehow.

But as we paced on either end of the phone, weighing the options, we realized all at once what the right answer actually was: we had to go, because those are the kinds of people we want to be. And so we did. It was expensive and inconvenient—costing us money and time and progress, but it was worth it. It was so worth it.

We arrived just as the wake was beginning and, as we gave a round of hugs, we both started to cry. We knew we had made the right decision.

We spent that weekend in my grandmother's living room, eating crispy bacon and blueberries by the handful. We gathered around a long table dotted with heaping plates of pasta and carafes of Italian wine. We talked about my cousin, about life, and about nothing at all. It was so needed. We needed to be there, holding each other's hands and crying together. We needed to show our support, to receive the support of others, and to have the time to reflect on such a beautiful life.

But stretching far beyond that weekend, the decision we made was a fundamental one.

I think we all want to be the kind of people who put relationships first, but so often our schedules tell a drastically different story. We stay late at the office and answer emails during dinner. We spend money on the junk near the register at Target, instead of putting it towards a plane ticket to see our friends. We want to go, we tell them, but work is just so busy this time of year. But it's always that way, isn't it?

So that decision to go was a dagger to the heart of all of those excuses. In the purchasing of the tickets and postponing of our plans, we declared that family is actually more important than work. We put our airline miles where our priorities really are — with the people we love.

That's something I want to continue doing. I want to do the uncomfortable thing—spending the money and the time and the trek to the airport. I want to leave my weekend routine and the laundry that needs to be done, declaring that people are my priority and proving it.

I want the face-to-face, the in-person. I want to make new memories instead of dragging out the old ones when I need to feel connected. I want the dinners and the sleepovers and the time lounging on the couch. I want to see and experience this crazy world with the people I love and, sometimes, that means hopping on a plane. But it's always worth it.

I want to be the kind of person that goes—just like Michelle.

> Be honest with yourself for a minute today. Do your relationships come first in your life? Do they really? Maybe they do, or maybe you know you could do better. Either way, let's put our money, our time, and our energy where our hearts are even more this week. Let's be the kind of people who go.

Syrup Fasts & Shame

"I have swept away your offenses like a cloud, your sins like the morning mist. Return to me, for I have redeemed you."

Isaiah 44:22

I sincerely doubt I did something terrible. I was a pretty good kid overall, but I had done something to disappoint my family, and that day, their disappointment was more than my little 10-year-old heart could bear. I had disappointed them, I'd let them down, and I deserved to be punished. But as I waited for the hammer of punishment to crash down in the form of no ice cream, no TV, and definitely no weekend time with friends, nothing happened!

I knew they were disappointed because they had told me they were, but they knew I was sorry. They weren't going to punish me. "We forgive you," they told me. You've got to be kidding me!

We all know, we've all been there. Having someone be disappointed in you, and worse, not punish you at all, is enough to make the guilt explode right out of you. If they're angry or punish you, at least you feel like you're even. But we weren't even that day. I'd messed up, and I certainly didn't deserve the love, kindness, and grace they were giving me. So, I reasoned that if they weren't going to punish me, well then I was going to have to do it myself. I couldn't think of another way to set this right.

So, with all of the drama in my 10-year-old heart, I picked up their love and their grace and I handed them right back, declaring with a flourish that I just did not deserve them.

I began by yanking my blankets off my bed—declaring loudly, and very seriously that I didn't deserve a bed. I refused to go back into my room—not wanting to sleep in a bed I hadn't earned, a bed meant for girls better than me. Instead, I tied large sheets over the banister in our upstairs hallway, creating a makeshift tent, fully intending to live there for the rest of my days (not realizing that I was further inconveniencing my parents by blocking the path to their bedroom door).

I sat at the breakfast table the next morning, my shame hovering around me like a cloud. As my mom passed me the syrup. I waved it away sadly. "I don't deserve syrup," I said and proceeded to eat my pancakes dry.

Although I've become slightly less dramatic with age, I still find myself living this way. I am guilty of acting this way with Carl. I inevitably do something wrong (just one of those things that happens in marriage), and then I over-do it trying to earn back his favor instead of accepting the love and forgiveness he freely offers me. I do this with my girlfriends sometimes too—convinced that if I'm the perfect friend, if I do everything perfectly for long enough, it'll outweigh whichever way I dropped the ball this time.

I do it the very most when it comes to my relationship with God. I feel like God's watching me, just waiting for the moment I mess up. When I do mess up, when I do fall short, when I'm sure I've disappointed Him, I get to work trying to earn back His love, favor, and closeness.

It looks a little something like this: Spent most of my quiet time this morning thinking about those four pounds I want to lose? Shame! Read two whole chapters of the Bible to make up for it. Haven't gone to church in a month? Heathen! Sinner! God couldn't possibly want to be close to you now! Give away a whole ton of money to the church to the point where Carl asks, "Did you not get paid this month? Where did all of our money go?"

But the thing is, my parents didn't work like this, Carl doesn't work like this, my girlfriends don't work like this, and God most certainly doesn't work like this. God isn't sitting there with a clipboard, keeping track of our rights and wrongs, and when we do get things wrong (um… every day, pretty much), He doesn't push us away, shun us, shame us, or give up on us.

That's the beauty of the Gospel, the beauty of what Jesus did for us that day on the cross. He took on every single disappointing thing we've ever done, and every single disappointing thing we will ever do, and He was punished for it so we wouldn't have to be. It's that simple, that beautiful, and that hard to receive. (Is that just me?)

So, because of Jesus, when we do get things wrong, as I did that day, and do pretty much all the other days too, we don't have to hide from God, or try to earn back His love, or punish ourselves. We get to come back to Him and say, "I messed up. I'm so sorry. Will you help me do it differently next time?" And He brings us back into His arms (because He never wanted us to leave them in the first place), gives us a seat at the table right next to Him, and passes the syrup our way.

Are you feeling guilty about anything these days? When we do something we think might be wrong, we're so tempted to hide from God, but hiding never actually helps. Instead, when we can be up-front with God about what happened, confessing it to Him, and asking for His help, it helps us get through whatever the thing is, it helps us live a better way, and it also brings us closer to Him. Shame is never from God, and having an honest conversation with Him is the perfect way to get rid of it. So do that today! Talk to God about anything that's making you feel guilty—be honest about it, confess it, and invite Him into it. Ask Him to forgive you, and to help you live a better way. He'll do it. I know He will.

Stop & Wait for Your Soul

"Come to me, all you who are weary and burdened,
and I will give you rest."

Matthew 11:28

I once read a story about an American woman who was traveling
with an African tribe. They were heading to a destination that was
four days away by foot. Well, on the first day, they covered twice the
distance they were supposed to have covered. And so on the second
day, the American woman woke up ready to hit the road again,
excited about the prospect of reaching their destination early.

But when she went to gather the troops, instead of finding them
chipper and ready to go, she found them resting and relaxing with
no intentions of continuing on that day. When she urged them
to get ready and stressed the point about the early arrival, they
stopped her saying, "We need to allow our souls time to catch up
with our bodies."

I can't shake this story from my mind. It resonates so much with
me because so often I am that American woman. I fill my days to
the max, and if I find myself ahead of schedule (which let's be
honest, rarely happens), I add even more to the day.

And I think this is something we all do. Our lives are so full—there's
no space for rest, for prayer, or for reflection on who we are and
who we're becoming and where we're going. We are efficient and
accomplished. We achieve our goals and reach our destinations.
But, by the time we get there, we're so brittle and exhausted, so disconnected from ourselves and our souls, that the destination never
feels as fulfilling or as full as we hoped it would. We are racing ahead
of our souls and not giving them even the hope of catching up.

That is where I found myself after a particularly crazy season. I'd been sprinting for months—years—my whole life, really. And it was finally taking a toll on me. I was sick and exhausted. I felt disconnected from my heart, disconnected from God, disconnected from the part of me that usually felt so vibrant, and creative and full of life. And so finally—I decided to do something about it.

I had a break from work and a few months over the summer that I hadn't quite packed full yet. So when my best friend mentioned the spare bedroom in her apartment in Southern California, I knew that that was the perfect place to stop and wait for my soul.

And that's just what I did!

There's this Italian phrase that I love to pieces but had never put into practice. It says, "Il dolce far niente" which means, "The sweetness of doing nothing." And that's exactly what I did that summer. I put my toes in the sand, took a long road trip up the coast, and bought a pink and black beach cruiser to ride around town. I spent many afternoons painting with my best friend in a sunny spot on the floor of her apartment while drinking chilled white wine and eating hummus and pita chips for lunch.

I gave my soul time to catch up with my body, and when it was time for the next leg of my journey, it had made all the difference.

My life doesn't look exactly like that anymore. My days are mostly busy now, and I don't spend as much time painting and drinking white wine as maybe I should. But I have learned to stop every once in awhile—to give myself time to pray, and reflect, and think, and dream. I've learned that every part of my life is better and richer and that I travel through life so much more lovingly and gracefully when I've given my soul time to catch up with my body.

So that's what I'm doing at this very moment. I'm sitting in a wrought iron chair in a cafe, nibbling on a shortbread cookie and sipping an iced latte with just a hint of lavender. I'm praying, and reflecting, and dreaming, practicing "Il Dolce Far Niente" and soon, I'll be ready for the next leg of the journey.

Luckily, we don't have to move to Southern California to rest and reflect and pray. We can do it in our favorite chair in our living room, or at a nearby cafe, or on a walk around our favorite park. Find just a few minutes today to practice "Il Dolce Far Niente," to give your soul time to catch up with your body.

It's Okay. You're Okay. God is Here.

"No one has ever seen God; but if we love one
another, God lives in us and His love is made
complete in us."

1 John 4:12

Have you ever gone through a hard season and needed God but
felt like He was nowhere to be found?

In the few weeks after I got back from a long mission trip to Ghana,
I was totally overwhelmed. I had experienced so much, grown so
much, laughed so much, cried so much, and seen God do so much
that I felt like I arrived home and collapsed into one big heap.

I had so many thoughts, and feelings, and so much to think about
and sort through, and I had no idea how to go about any of it.
I was a mess. I didn't know who to talk to; I wasn't sure they'd
understand. I kept reaching out to God, but I felt like I kept getting
His voicemail and that His mailbox was full.

God felt far away, and I couldn't figure out why.

A week after I got home, I was praying a frustratingly disconnected
prayer to God when my phone rang. It was my sweet friend Lacey.
She was near my house and wanted to take me to lunch.

I hugged Lacey when I arrived, and we settled into a table and
ordered. Then she turned to me, her face a reflection of kindness
and concern, and she asked, "Steph, how are you doing?"

I didn't plan to tell her everything. I had funny anecdotes from the trip all cued up and ready to go. But instead, the truth slipped out.

"I'm a mess! I have so much on my mind; I'm processing through so much, and I have no one to talk to about it. And, in the midst of this, God feels a million miles away, and I have no idea why."

Lacey nodded seriously and then started asking me questions. She asked about my trip: the funny stories, the hard stories, what God had been teaching me, and how I felt like I'd grown. But she didn't just ask those questions; she asked follow-up questions, inviting me to talk more when she could tell I needed to. It was as if my mind was an over-packed suitcase. She gently took it from me, laid it down on the floor between us, and slowly started pulling things out of it one by one.

And at the end of the lunch, after she'd heard everything I had to say, she said the one thing I needed to hear more than anything: "It's okay, you are okay, exactly where you are today is okay. You're not supposed to be anywhere else; you're not supposed to have this all figured out yet. You, right where you are right now today, are okay."

And with her words, my soul took a breath.

When I walked out of lunch that day, I felt lighter. I felt lighter, and understood, and almost put back together. As I got into my car to head back home, it hit me: God was right there! He hadn't left me, not at all. He'd just shown up in a different way for me that day—in a way I really needed, but couldn't have thought to ask for.

Author Glennon Doyle Melton says, "God approaches us in the disguise of other people." And that's exactly what He did for me that day.

He showed up in the form of Lacey, in the form of a dear friend who took the time to ask and took the time to listen. He showed up through a friend who could say the words I needed to hear. "It's okay. You're okay."

So today—whatever you're going through, whatever feels weird and complicated and confusing—I want to tell you the same thing she told me: It's okay. You're okay.

It's okay to be where you are; it's okay to allow other people into that—asking them to pray with you and talk you through it. It's okay not to have it all together—nobody expects that of you. And even when it feels like it, God hasn't left you.

God promises us that He'll never leave us or forsake us, not today, not ever. He just shows up for us in different ways sometimes, and it's always in the way we need the most.

God IS showing up for you today. It might not be the way He has before, but I promise He's there. So take a moment and reflect. How is God showing up in your life today?

Everything Will Be Okay in The End

"And we know that in all things God works for the good of those who love Him, who have been called according to His purpose."

Romans 8:28

The season when I lost my job was one of the darkest, and most painful of my life. It wasn't the job itself necessarily, although one day I was doing something I loved, and then the next I wasn't invited to do that anymore. But the losses that came with that season were bigger than that.

The community I'd joined there in Georgia felt steady, solid, like it would never let me down. It felt like a family. I had buddies there beside me. I had warm, kind, and wise mentors leading the way, teaching me how to love God and other people in whole new ways.

It was the same for my husband Carl (who at the time, was my fiancé), and for the huge group of our friends and co-workers who were let go too. Our lives were planted there, we were planted there, and we'd been growing there for years, thinking we had years more to go before it'd be time to move on.

But then we were asked to leave. It happened suddenly, and it happened coldly. It's like they forgot they knew us, they forgot they'd been mentoring us for years, they forgot they'd called us family. We weren't thanked for our hard work; we weren't recognized for what we'd contributed; we weren't supported as we stepped into the next season. We were just shown the door and it felt like a betrayal. The family support system we thought we had there turned out to be a cardboard cut-out of the real thing. That's the part that hurt the most.

The part that made it so scary and confusing was that when we were shown the door, we tripped out into the sunshine with no idea what to do next.

The only thing we had on the horizon, now that we didn't have jobs or a discernible future, was a dinner party my roommate, Lacee, and I had planned for the very next night. But, at this point, a dinner party seemed like a bad idea. To have a party at a time like this felt insensitive—like a bright light when all you want to do is pull the covers over your face. Thinking we were doing everyone a favor, we offered to cancel, but our wise friends refused. "You must have this party. We need a reason to come together. We need a reason to celebrate." And so we did.

Lacee and I zipped to the store and returned arms laden with the ingredients for the richest lasagna we knew how to make. If this wasn't a time for comfort food, we didn't know what was. We mixed and shredded, layered and baked, and as we lit the final candles, we heard the first knock.

One by one, our friends trooped through our door, looking heavy but relieved not to be alone. Almost ceremoniously, they set their offerings on our table: a loaf of bread, a bowl of salad, a bottle of wine, until our table was overflowing with food that would last us for weeks.

We scrunched in closer than necessary around the table—relieved to have some company to help us carry our heavy hearts. Our faces glowing in the candlelight. We talked and laughed and refilled our plates. We told happy stories and sad stories, the wisdom and love at that table bringing us to tears.

We had many nights like that in the weeks and months that followed. We had slumber parties, dinner parties, and cookouts by the lake. We grew closer during that terrible time in our lives, learning each other's stories, and dreaming about the future in closer, more tangible community than any of us had seen in awhile.

None of us wanted to lose our jobs. None of us wanted our time working there to end, especially so suddenly. But even that first day, God's presence and provision were palpable.

There's a quote I had taped up in my locker in middle school that I'd forgotten about until that season. It says, "Everything will be okay in the end. If it's not okay, it's not the end." Nobody seems to be sure who said it. John Lennon, maybe? But when we've invited God to be a part of our lives, I absolutely believe that quote to be true.

We all have hard seasons. There are seasons in our lives where positively nothing feels okay, but God's not done with the story yet. God is not in the business of leaving things broken and messy. He's not a God who sees a hard situation and shrugs, "I guess I'm not really sure what to do with this one!" He's a God that brings life from death, beauty from ashes, hope from despair, light from darkness, and healing from the most broken, mixed up, and messy situations. That's who He is, and we can stand on those promises. We can lean our lives against them; we can trust Him to do that.

Losing our jobs in that season is one of the hardest things I've ever been through, and for weeks and months after, most of the time I felt like I was lost in the darkness. But sprinkled throughout that darkness were moments like this one—tucked around the table with best friends, our faces glowing in the candlelight. There were little reminders that God was hard at work in the midst of the things that still weren't okay, assuring us that by the time He was finished, they would be.

Are there any parts of your life that feel broken or unresolved, any parts that still don't feel okay? Write a journal entry about those things this morning. Talk to God about them, invite Him into them, and then ask Him to bring healing, goodness, restoration, and redemption into each and every part of them. Make sure to leave some room on the page and revisit it from time to time. That way you can write down how God shows up because you can be sure that He will.

A Glorious Before & After

"For all have sinned and fall short of the glory
of God, and all are justified freely by His grace
through the redemption that came by Christ Jesus."

Romans 3:23-24

Several years ago, I started dating a new guy and, a month or so
into our relationship, he asked to hear my testimony. I love sharing
the story of what God has done in my life, and so I rolled up my
sleeves, and told him what happened.

At the end of my story though, I looked over at him, and he had
tears in his eyes. Not the good kind of tears, the bad kind. He
hated my story, every bit of it. He wished I hadn't told him. The
stories I had told him didn't reinforce what he knew to be true
about me; they made him question it.

His disappointment felt like a sandbag weighing on my heart. I
was embarrassed, I was ashamed, I was sorry, but mostly I felt
stupid. How could I have thought I was redeemed? How could I
have been so blind to think my actions would never have reper-
cussions? The disappointment on his face was burned into my
memory, a delayed punishment for all I'd done.

For the first time in my Christian life, I began to wonder if
redemption was possible, or if forgiveness was like a pity invite
into heaven, but not a clean slate like I'd always imagined. I began
to wonder if I'd always live with this shadow over my life—if love,
relationships, marriage, and sex would always be tainted by my
past, by the mistakes I'd made before.

A few years later, I was on one of my very first dates with a new boyfriend when he asked me the question I'd come to dread.

He wanted to hear my story.

My heart froze. I didn't want to tell him. I didn't want to watch his face change, couldn't handle his disappointment. So I gave him the clean version, relying on clichés and platitudes, and glossing over the messy parts.

Before he could press me for any more details, I vacated the hot seat and ushered him into it. "Your turn!"

Before I knew it, I was swept up in the story of his life. He didn't hurry, didn't blush, didn't apologize. His story wasn't clean, and he didn't gloss over the messy bits. He told me the hard parts and the great parts, the disappointing parts, and the painful parts. I was nodding emphatically as he spoke, amazed at how many moments, revelations, and experiences we had in common.

When he was finished with his story, I was in tears. The good kind, for sure.

I was looking at a man who was nuanced and well-worn in the best way. I was looking at a man who really knew God, not because it was the right thing to do, or because he was a perfect Christian. He knew God personally because he'd needed Him, just like me. I didn't know it at the time, but that man would soon be my husband.

When he was finished, we sat quietly for a long time. Then I finally broke the silence and said, "Can I try my story again? I think I left out some important parts."

That day, Carl reminded me of something I've known all along but forgot for a while: our stories are not something to be ashamed of; they're something we can proudly stand next to, a glorious before and after.

We have a past, every single one of us. Some of us wear ours more publicly—divorce papers, bankruptcy, an affair; while others of us can carry our mess more privately—pride, greed, selfishness. Every single one of us has things to be ashamed of if we really want to play that game.

But shame isn't a game I'm willing to play anymore. I don't think any of us should.

Allowing ourselves to sit under a mountain of shame after what Jesus did on the cross is a tragedy. Jesus paid for our sins and gave us grace, and freedom, and redemption, He gave us a clean slate, a fresh start, and a new life. Shame doesn't have anything on us anymore.

And in response to that freedom, we need to tell our stories.

We need to be honest about what we've been through and how God saved the day because we need to remind each other what He's capable of: "If He can do this for me, He can do this for you too!" We need to remind each other that God is bigger than even the biggest messes, that there's no limit to His ability to save, redeem, and restore.

Share your story with someone this week. It doesn't have to be the whole story or all of it all at once. And there's always the small chance that the person across from you won't react the way you're hoping they will. But remember that someone's inability to fully grasp the depths of grace and the heights of redemption doesn't mean it isn't true or real. It doesn't take away from the truth of how God has transformed your life. And that's really what He's done. So share that transformation with someone this week. Show someone else what God is capable of doing in their life through what He's done in yours.

The One Who Invented the Light

"Not only so, but we also rejoice in our sufferings,
because we know that suffering produces perseverance;
perseverance, character; and character, hope."

Romans 5:3-4

You didn't mean to get into this tunnel, but either you took a wrong direction, or a wrong direction took you. Or you just were walking straight ahead, minding your own business, when you found this tunnel blocking your path. There was no way around; you couldn't turn back and go the way you came. You had to go straight through, and the path was far from easy.

Tunnels come in a million different forms, and in each of our lives, we'll walk through more than we can count.

In my life, I've walked through tunnels of devastating breakups. I've grieved the loss of family and friends, I've wrestled deep, crippling insecurity. I've lost myself in drinking and partying, I've ached my way through being perpetually single, and I've been let go from my job on more than one occasion.

Our tunnels are our testimony—the desert, the valley, the spot between a rock and a hard place where we just didn't see a way out.

I hate tunnels, if I'm being honest. I would much rather be in perpetually happy, peaceful, sparkling seasons of life. (Wouldn't we all?) But the woman God has made me into is a direct result of the learning that came in those dark places. It's in those places where we see God do His very best work, and I wouldn't trade that for the world.

Are you in a tunnel right now? You might be. This might be a particularly hard semester at school; you might have just gotten your heart broken, you might have just lost someone you love, you might be sick. You might be in that crazy season of having a newborn baby; you might be starting life over in a new city, you might be starting a new business or a new job.

There are seasons of our lives that are just plain hard, and you might be in one of those today. But if you are, I hope you keep going. I hope you keep putting one foot in front of the other, doing the hard work, showing up day after day, being brave in whatever way you know how. Keep going through the tunnel because there will be a day when you burst into the light, a bit dusty, and certainly tired, but stronger, better, and closer to God than you ever dreamed.

Tunnels do that to us if we let them. We learn fortitude in the tunnel; we learn to be a little bit scrappy. We earn some scars and calouses from doing the hard work the hard way. It's in the tunnels that we learn what we're made of, shocking ourselves when we're capable of far more than we ever dreamed. Tunnels teach us the meaning of perseverance and faith as we trust that there's a light far before we can actually see one. It's in the tunnel that we learn what hope and joy and love really are and how they're worth fighting for every single time.

When we can't see anything but the darkness that engulfs us, what we really find is God. We find that there's a steady hand guiding us through the tunnel, and it's in the moments when we can't see our own hand in front of our face that we learn to trust the one who invented the light.

> You may be in a tunnel right now—I think so many of us are. And if you are, I promise that you won't be in there forever. It feels like you will be. I know it does. But you'll make it to the other side— stronger, tougher, wiser, and closer to God than ever before. Keep going, sweet friend. You can do this!

Honest & Messy

"For it is by grace you have been saved, through
faith—and this is not from yourselves, it is the gift of
God— not by works, so that no one can boast."

'Ephesians 2:8-9

I met Jesus for the first time in the Sistine Chapel on a spring break
trip to Italy. It was a moment that changed my life completely—a
change emphasized by the fact that when I met Him, I was hungover
and un-showered. To make matters worse, I was wearing the free
pub crawl t-shirt we'd been given during our escapades the night
before. That's how I showed up at the Pope's house. Needless to say,
I wasn't a prime candidate for anything that day.

I always had this idea that if I was ever going to become a Christian,
I was going to have to clean up my life first. I thought there was
no way God would want to know me if I didn't, but that day, Jesus
showed me that wasn't true. It was never about being the perfect
candidate or cleaning up our lives. It was about a relationship with
God—something that, because of Jesus, we can't disqualify ourselves from, no matter how stinky, hungover, or inappropriately
dressed we may be.

That truth transformed my life completely.

After a while, though, as God changed my life in small ways and
huge ways, my understanding of the whole thing started to shift.
I wasn't a mess anymore, not in the same ways, at least. My life
was so much cleaner than it had ever been, and my behavior was
so much better too. And so, somewhere along the way, I started to
forget how much God had done in my life, how it was God that

had transformed me. I began to think that it was my good behavior that had done the heavy lifting. My behavior also earned me a place in what felt like the "Good Christian Club." That's what people thought of me. They thought I was a good Christian, and, to be honest, I liked it that way.

But the problems began when I started believing that I had to keep my life perfectly cleaned up in order to keep up that image and, even worse, in order to stay close to God. I had a checklist of things I needed to do to be the perfect Christian, and I clung to it with white knuckles.

I was so afraid of getting it wrong; I wasn't in a relationship with God anymore. I saw God as a taskmaster, and I felt as though we were both always disappointed in me.

The harder I tried, the more distant I felt and the more frustrated I became. Why wasn't this working? I was doing all the right things. If there was a Christian honor roll, my name would have been on it. So why did God feel so far away?

Finally, on a Friday morning, everything broke. I was on the brink of some major life decisions. I had no idea which way to turn and, that morning, the pressure of it all felt like it was crushing me.

I collapsed in a heap on my bed, and I began to sob—the kind of sobs that can only come from a girl who had spent as long as she could remember performing for a distant God. "Are you really there?" I choked out, tears streaming down my face. "If you are, I need you to show up right now! I can't do this! I can't do this without you. It's too big, too scary. I need you... please be here!"

In that moment, I didn't need a checklist. I didn't need to be a good Christian or receive a plaque for being on the honor roll. Those things weren't strong enough to hold me. The only thing that was strong enough in that moment was Jesus himself. Lying there on my bed, for the first time in a long time, I felt like a messy person, and to my surprise, it was such a relief.

Jesus told the Pharisees that He came not for the healthy but for the sick. He hung out with people on the fringe, people who were stinky, and hungover, and even inappropriately dressed. He loved them just as they were, and made a way for them to be close to God. And as they were loved by God, they were transformed by God. Being good enough was never part of the equation.

That's where Jesus and I had begun, and it felt like heaven to sit there, honest and messy, with Him all over again. He sat down in the thick of the mess with me that morning and took my hand. He didn't try to clean me up or make me presentable. He didn't even try to fix me. He just sat there with me, and it was that moment on my bed when something cracked.

It was like my "Good Christian" ceiling was smashed open. Light poured in along with peace, and joy, and love. I wasn't in this alone, I realized for the first time in a long time. I didn't have to perform, or fix myself, or earn my way into God's grace. He'd been offering it to me all along.

On that day, I gave up my spot on the honor roll. I'm not interested in proving myself, and I don't care whether or not I look the part. I'm not shined up, not all the time, and when I am, I had absolutely nothing to do with it.

I'm sitting beside Jesus now—not performing for Him. I'm messy, and honest, and tucked up close to the giver of grace. And truly, there's nowhere in the world I'd rather be.

There is nothing in the world you could do to make God love you more. And there's nothing in the world you could do to make God love you less. God loves you—not because of anything you could ever do, but because of Jesus. Because of what Jesus did for you, you're in good standing with God. He loves you, and He wants a relationship with you! Spend just a few minutes reflecting on that this morning.

God's Grace In This Season

"There is a time for everything, and a season for
every activity under the heavens."

Ecclesiastes 3:1

If I had to describe my life to you right now, I'd use just one
word: small.

Life feels incredibly small to me these days, tucked in, routine, and
unglamorous. I have to tell you, I couldn't be more grateful.

My life tends to swing like the pendulum of a grandfather clock,
heavily to one side, and then heavily to the other. There are big,
busy seasons, packed full with travel, and there are quiet, tucked
away seasons where I just get to be home.

Summer is always a big travel season for me and Carl. In a few
weeks, we'll be leaving for almost a month. We're going to a friend's
wedding in Mexico, then straight to a middle school camp in
Wisconsin where we volunteer, and then to my yearly family vacation in at a lake in New Hampshire. Adventure upon adventure.

But in the meantime, we're hanging out here at home, and the rest
and familiarity of it just feels like heaven.

We slide into a routine when we're home for a long stretch. I
wake up each morning an hour before Carl does, and I tuck into
my favorite little chair in the corner for some much-needed time
with God. When I hear him stirring upstairs, I'll bring Carl some
coffee, and then we both get ready for work. Carl puts on real
people clothes and goes to his office. My work attire consists of an

array of sweatpants, and makeup is nowhere to be found. When I'm traveling and out in the world a lot, I miss these sweatpants days, so I'm savoring them while I can.

Carl comes home from work at the end of the day, pretty much as soon as he gets hungry. Then, we pretend we're on an episode of Chopped as we gather whatever's in the pantry to make a creative concoction for dinner. Sometimes, when I'm in charge of dinner, we just eat Kraft Mac and Cheese, and not one bit of me is ashamed.

Date nights are small too. I love exploring the restaurants here in Nashville, but we'll be doing so much exploring in the next busy season, that I'd rather just be home right now. So we opt out of big date nights in favor of frozen pizzas and a Netflix marathon. I light my favorite candles, and we curl up in our signature spots on the couch, and I usually fall asleep before the movie even gets started. Bliss!

My life may not sound glamorous or exciting these days, and you'd be right, it's not. But the peace of it, the familiarity of it, the routine of it, the rest in it, is totally evidence of God's grace and love for me in this season of my life. I need these things. I need this time. I need life to be exactly as it is right now, especially because I know it won't be this way for long.

We'll be on the road and on new adventures before I can even believe it. Life will feel big again soon, which makes it all the more important that we soak in every last one of these small days in between.

Whether your life is big and busy right now, or small and tucked in, there's a chance it doesn't feel glamorous or particularly photo-worthy either. But from my cozy spot on the couch, I want to remind you (and me) that it won't always be this way, and there's so much beauty and purpose and grace right where you are today.

Wherever you are right now—in a job that's not your favorite, waiting for a relationship, taking care of sweet babies, plugging away at your homework, or curled up on the couch in gray sweat-pants that match mine—there's beauty and purpose and grace there. We just have to take the time to look for it.

So that's my challenge to you today.

There are quirks and special details about this season that are unique from any other, and you won't want to look back later and realize you've missed it. So wherever you are—whatever the season may look like—I challenge you to curl up and enjoy it.

That's what I'm up to these days. I'm living up every last one of my cozy, indoor days before I venture back out in the world. And because I soaked in all the goodness of my days in this season, I know I'll be able to do the same in the next.

> What does your season of life look like right now, and what would it look like for you to fully embrace it?

You are Making Progress

"Consider it pure joy, my brothers and sisters, whenever
you face trials of many kinds, because you know that
the testing of your faith produces perseverance. Let
perseverance finish its work so that you may be mature
and complete, not lacking anything."

James 1:2-4

They say that patience is a virtue, but I have to say, sometimes I'm
just the worst at it.

The same thing happens every time I try something new: writing a
new book, working on a project, getting back in shape, or learning
a new skill. I'm dedicated, I'm focused, and I'm ready to take it
on. And about a week in, I look around and think, "Am I making
ANY progress?"

I feel so ready to see transformation, action, or a finished product,
but each day I wake up to the frustrating knowledge that change
doesn't happen overnight, no matter how much I want it to.

Have you ever felt this way? Have you ever looked at your life
and thought, "I'm working my tail off, why aren't we there yet?"
Maybe you were in that place recently, or maybe you're in that
place right now. Well, friend, I've noticed something these last few
weeks that's given me hope for all areas of my life, and I can't wait
to share it with you.

These last few weeks, I've noticed that I know how to cook.

Now, you may be wondering why my culinary skills should provide you hope as you're studying for the GRE or trying to get out of debt, but hear me out.

Just 12 months ago, I was a disaster in the kitchen. The thought of having to make anything other than sandwiches for dinner made me freeze and usually made me cry. If we ate well, it's because we went out, or because Carl cooked. (He is a fantastic cook, which didn't help my self-esteem any).

I would help him in the kitchen sometimes, usually washing dishes, but every once in awhile he'd give me a bigger task like chopping a pepper—it usually didn't end well. I'd take the foreign pepper in my hands, examining it for clues. Then, I'd set it down on a cutting board, because I knew that much at least. I'd gingerly pick up one of our all-too-sharp wedding knives, (Must they be that sharp? Isn't that a safety hazard?) and then the chopping would begin.

By chopping, I mean I'd awkwardly try to maneuver the knife through the pepper, dividing it into smaller, yet hopelessly uneven pieces, while trying not to cut off a finger. Carl would catch a glimpse of my plight out of the corner of his eye, and he'd laugh kindly, come over, and reposition the knife in my hand. He was loving as he did it, but it still felt like a knife to my heart. "You're not a good wife," his correction seemed to say; "you're a failure as an adult."

He wasn't thinking that at all, but still, I wanted to quit, and I did, probably once a week. I'd stomp out of the kitchen listing loudly and with big gestures all of the things I am, in fact, good at, but I'd always come back. Because the truth is, I really like food, and I really wanted to learn how to cook. I'd slink back into the kitchen and watch Carl work. And slowly but surely, I started picking up a thing or two. Slowly but surely, I got better!

Last week, we invited some friends over for dinner, but Carl had to work late, so, when it came to making dinner, I was on my own. I love Italian food, and it's become my favorite thing to cook, so I made a plan and got to work.

Our main course was baked ziti, cheesy and delicious. I'd made it a few times, although the first time I made it, sauce exploded all over the stove, the kitchen counter, and even onto the floor. But that didn't happen this time. I'm telling you, I'm becoming a pro! On the side, we were doing a Caprese salad with the plumpest, most beautiful tomatoes I've seen, and fresh mozzarella, which I'm convinced is just the greatest thing on earth. And, to top if all off, I made these incredible peach dumplings with bourbon sauce.

The dinner was amazing, the conversation even better, and all of it happened without a single tear, without help, and without burning the house down. I can't believe I'm going to say it, folks, but I can actually cook.

So here's why I'm telling you this, and why my accomplishments in the kitchen should give you hope. It's because I literally could not cook a darn thing one year ago—not a thing. It was a source of shame, of great frustration, and honestly, it felt like an entirely impossible mountain to climb—but it happened. I took it one day at a time, I kept going, and over the course of a year, it became a total victory in my life! That's what happens when we keep putting one foot in front of the other. Things change, we grow. (I have to remind myself of this all the time.)

So if you're feeling frustrated today, or if you're feeling like nothing's changing, happening, growing, progressing, I implore us (you and me) to keep going. Things are changing; we're just too close to see it. We have to take a deep breath, and step forward in faith, believing that if we keep moving, we'll make progress. And this time next year (and even next month!), we can turn around and be amazed at how far we've come.

What's one way you've grown over the last year? What's something you can do now that you couldn't a year ago, something you've learned or accomplished? Take a minute to reflect on that today. That's amazing! That's a big deal! What's something you want to have accomplished a year from now? Take some time to think about that too, then write down one small step you can take today that will get you on your way. As a little extra inspiration, here's one of my favorite quotes these days:

"A year from now you will wish you had started today."
Karen Lamb

Still Dancing

"Gray hair is a crown of splendor; it is attained by a righteous life."

Proverbs 16:31

Spring is here, and my birthday is coming up. This has always been my favorite time of year. I've always loved birthdays, although I have to admit that my enthusiasm for them has begun to trickle off lately. It's not that I don't like birthdays; I am never one to turn down an excuse to celebrate, but it's hard to be excited about something that the women around me are starting to dread.

It's a conversation that's beginning to rumble amongst women my age. A few gray hairs have started to arrive, wrinkles on our foreheads—just a few, but still. We're getting to the point of having mortgages, and people are having kids, and even my girlfriends and I catch ourselves saying things like, "When we were younger," as if our best stories are behind us.

A friend of mine asked me, "How are you doing?" as my birthday approached—as if something sad, and hard was about to take place.

Now here's the thing… this makes me mad.

It makes me mad in the same way that it used to when college graduates would warn me of the perils of the "real world" after graduation. "Stay in college forever!" they'd tell me. Okay, what did they want me to do, never graduate? It makes me mad because, in telling me that, they were telling me to run away from the inevitable, (You can't stay in college forever!) which is, of course, a lose-lose proposition.

Dreading aging is like fighting gravity – it's just not a battle we're going to win. And that leaves us with a few choices.

The first is to be afraid of growing older. We can complain about it, pretend we're not aging, dread each birthday as if that's going to stave off the passing of the time. We can refuse to celebrate, hoping that if we don't acknowledge our day, it will be like it never happened.

But, the thing is, if we start that today, it only gets worse from here. If we're dreading turning 22, how will we feel when we're 32? If we're dreading turning 32, how will we feel about 62? I just can't stomach an option that only gets progressively worse. There has to be a better way to think about the passing of time, doesn't there?

I think there is!

The second option, as I see it, is to be grateful for every single year and the blessings that it contained—to pop open the champagne and kiss our loved ones and dance until the sun comes up, and to do that for the rest of our lives. (My sweet Gramie was doing this well into her 90s!) With this option, we celebrate with full gratitude the fact that we got to live on this beautiful earth for one more year – something that is never a guarantee.

Proverbs 16:31 says, "Grey hair is a crown of splendor. It is attained by a life of righteousness." I love that.

Getting older is a privilege denied to many. Reaching the point of having gray hair and wrinkles is a gift – it means we had a full life, years upon years to do marvelous things with extraordinary people, both family and friends.

So instead of dreading the passing of time, or sweeping it under the rug, I want to focus on spending it well. I've lived many amazing years so far, and I want to keep going – whether I get two, twenty, or two hundred. I want to earn my gray hair and wrinkles—living life to the full and wringing out all of the beauty and the laughter it has to offer.

I'm refusing, right now, today, to allow age to be my enemy. Instead, I'm deciding that it's a gift. I am choosing to believe that every year gets better – that each stage of life is better than the last and that it's only getting better from here.

95... I'm coming for you and, if I'm lucky, I'm going to be wrinkly and still dancing when I arrive.

Whether you have a birthday coming up or not, I think this is something that's tricky for all of us. There's just no manual to teach us how to handle getting older. But no matter how old we are, instead of trying to hold onto the past, or trying to stave off the future, what if we decided to live fully in the present? What if we decided to embrace today to the best of our ability — to fill it with people we love, and to use every gift and talent we have to make the world a better place, and to stuff each day positively full of gratitude? I think if we did that today, and tomorrow, and the next day too, we would stop dreading the passing of time, and instead find ourselves living a truly full life.

The Desires of Our Heart

"Take delight in the Lord, and he will give you the
desires of your heart."

Psalm 37:4

From the day I stepped foot on the beautiful campus at the
University of Colorado in Boulder, I knew one thing: I wanted to
be a journalist. I was sure of it. It was the perfect fit, the perfect
plan, and I had mapped out every step along the way for how I
was going to get there. But of course, as so many of our plans do,
this one changed.

It began when I became a Christian while studying abroad in
Spain, but the plan changed completely on my first ever mission
trip in Costa Rica. God swooped into my life over the course of that
short trip. I'd met Him, certainly, but it was like I'd been watching
a movie by reading the script. When I showed up in Costa Rica,
God became larger than life like the 3D IMAX version. God and
Christianity and the plan God had for my life exploded into light,
and action, and color.

So, on our last morning there in Costa Rica, I took a deep breath
and handed my life plan over to God. "Here, take this, I'd love to see
what you can do with it." I didn't expect for Him to take away my
desire to be a journalist, but that's exactly what He did. I couldn't
believe it, but it was true. I didn't want to be a journalist anymore.
But good gracious, I had no idea what I would do instead.

A month or so later, I found myself in the mountains of Colorado
at a spiritual retreat with my best friend, Kelsey. The heart of the
retreat was to give us the space and quiet to experience God in a
whole new way. Yes, please!

One evening, they told us we were doing something a bit unusual. They had us line up and hold the shoulders of the person in front of us; then they led us outside. As we passed through the doorway, a woman with the most comforting face would smile at us, say, "Are you ready?" and tie a blindfold over our eyes.

For the next 20 minutes, we wound through the snow in the Colorado Rockies, led by the person in front of us. They wanted to give us the feeling of being led in the dark so we could see that, even when life feels dark and confusing, God still has a plan. He's still leading the way.

At first, I was nervous, and I couldn't stop giggling, but with the reassurance of the shoulders in front of me, the crunch of the snow under my feet, and the total silence of the snowy mountains, my soul took a breath.

"God, where do you want me to go?" I asked, knowing that my life was going to be different from the one I'd been planning for so long. He didn't say anything for a long while. I crunched in silence, taking deep breaths and waiting. And then, out of nowhere, a thought popped into my mind. It didn't feel like an answer from God, directly. It felt like my answer. It felt like the core of who I am in the deepest, tenderest parts, got the courage to speak up in the cutest little mousy voice, with one hand boldly raised:

"I want to work in college ministry," it said, my life finally quiet enough to hear the little voice.

That answer was so surprising, so out of left field for me. It was absolutely nothing I'd ever considered or planned before. As soon as the thought popped into my mind, I felt the rest of my rational self reel around in surprise to look at my brave little mouse self with wide eyes. "You DO?"

The little voice was right. That's what I wanted, that's what God's plan was for me, and the answer came out of my own little heart.

There's this verse in the Bible that I love, but I feel like sometimes we interpret it differently. It's Psalm 37:4, and it says, "Take delight in the Lord, and he will give you the desires of your heart." This sounds like a genie situation, doesn't it? Take delight in the Lord, and rub the lamp, and He'll give you three wishes, but only three, so you better make them good.

But this isn't how I see it.

God answers our prayers, absolutely, but thank God (literally), He doesn't just give us whatever we ask for. (If He did I'd have been married four times already, to all of the wrong people). Instead, I think of this verse like a heart transplant, or a desires-of-our-heart transplant.

When we're writing the story of our lives on our own, we want what we want for a zillion different reasons. Sometimes those things aren't good, and a lot of times they are. But good desires and God desires aren't always the same thing, and I have always found that God's are so much bigger and so much better.

That day in Costa Rica, when I invited God to take over my plan, what I was really praying for was Psalm 37:4. I didn't want my desires anymore. I wanted God to give me His desires for my life. I wanted His desires to become my desires, and that's exactly what happened. I found myself desiring new things, things I never would have dreamed of before, but things that fit me and my heart and my life like a glove.

"And He will give you the desires of your heart."

If you're anything like me, you have plans for your life—good plans, fun plans, exciting plans, plans you've spent many a night thinking through.

But what if God had better plans, bigger plans, more beautiful plans? They may be different from what you've planned all along, or they may be a different form of the very same thing. They may surprise you completely like mine did.

"You DO? That's what you want? I never saw that coming!"

But those plans are the very best kinds.

What if you invited God into your plans today? What if you prayed the same prayer I did and told God you want more than just a good plan for your life, you want His plan for your life? Talk to Him about it today!

The Magic Cure to Everything

"Now the Lord is the Spirit, and where the Spirit
of the Lord is, there is freedom. And we all, who
with unveiled faces contemplate the Lord's glory,
are being transformed into his image with ever-
increasing glory, which comes from the Lord, who is
the Spirit."

2 Corinthians 3:17-18

I remember exactly where I was when it happened and exactly
how it felt to hear the Gospel for the very first time. It felt like
magic! I was in Palma De Mallorca, Spain, sitting across a check-
ered table cloth from my best friends, Kelsey and Michelle, as they
laid it all out for me. When they were done, I remember saying,
"Why doesn't everyone KNOW this? This is like... the magic cure
to everything!" And that's exactly how it felt.

But I think after we've been a Christian for a while, after we've had
the mountaintop experiences twice over already, after we've been
on the mission trip, heard the worship songs, and after it feels like
we've heard all the sermons before, the Gospel starts to feel just a
little less magical, doesn't it?

It's not that it's not good news because it absolutely is! We know
that. But the way we react to it is sort of how we react when we
hear the most steady, solid person in our lives say, "I love you." We
hear it, we appreciate it, and we say it back, but it doesn't feel quite
as miraculous as it once did. We know it's there, so we don't really
think about it too much anymore.

A few weeks ago, I was getting ready for bed, slipping into my favorite plaid pajama bottoms when, in a sudden download of memory, I remembered just how magical the Gospel really is.

I don't know how, and I don't know why but, for some reason in that moment, I could remember with crystal clarity just how much power God has to change everything, and how He's changed absolutely everything in my life.

I was a messy, heartbroken, insecure, (often intoxicated) sorority girl from the University of Colorado with absolutely no interest in becoming a Christian at all. I thought I had life dialed in. I thought I knew what I was doing and that if I could just achieve this one thing, join that one sorority, get that one grade, and of course—lose the Freshman 15 I'd gained—I'd be the woman I'd always wanted to be, and I'd finally be happy.

But the truth was, I was miserable. My life was a mess; my heart was so broken, I could feel it in my fingertips. The pain of the loss I was going through was radiating all the way through me and into the rest of my life as well. I was drinking ALL THE TIME, doing things with boys I shouldn't have because I thought it'd help me move on, hanging out with people who I'm pretty sure didn't even like me and, in all of it, I hated the fact that I had to be me.

I remember thinking one day that I felt like I was the last choice in gym class, and I was furious that I ended up with myself on my team.

But then I met Jesus, and He changed everything.

In a lot of ways, it felt like the lights were turned on in my life when I became a Christian. It's like something sparked in my heart, bringing me back to life when I didn't even realize I'd been dead. Color flooded my cheeks, this indescribable joy filled my heart, and I could laugh again—easily and often—and, as author Anne Lamott says, "Laughter is carbonated holiness."

That is what I have to remind myself of on days when I feel like the Gospel isn't really that big. That happens sometimes—we forget. We forget what God did for us last week, let alone what He did in our lives years ago. I forget just how much becoming a Christian changed me. I forget what really happened along the way and start to think I've always been this way. But I haven't. I'm telling you, I most certainly, most definitely haven't!

The power of the Gospel is real; God is real! God can change us, heal us, redeem even the hardest things in our lives, and put broken things back together. So let's remind ourselves of that today.

Take some time today to remember what God has done in your life. When we remember what He's done in our lives, we remember how big, and how good He is, and we remember that we can trust Him with the things we're going through today. If your relationship with God is new, or if you don't feel like you've gotten to see Him do a whole lot quite yet, remind yourself of what you've seen Him do in other people's lives. At the very beginning when I first met Him, the best evidence of God that I had was what He'd done in my best friend Michelle's life. That works too. Because the things you've seen Him do in someone else's life, He can (and will!) do in yours too!

Lipstick On The Mirror

"We are therefore Christ's ambassadors, as though
God were making his appeal through us."

2 Corinthians 5:20a

It's really hard to be a Christian when the people around you aren't. It's hard because you feel a bit like a fish swimming upstream, like you're walking down on an escalator going up, like you accidentally turned the wrong way down a one-way road. (Have you ever done that? No, no, of course, you haven't. I haven't either.)

It's tricky because you're trying to live your life the best way you know how, and you want to share this amazing thing you've just learned about God and about life, but you don't want to come across as pushy or preachy. Just like it's been since our playground days, being different from the people around you can just plain be hard.

I wrestled with this a lot when I came back from my mission trip to Costa Rica. I felt new and different and excited about God and the path we were heading down together. The only problem was that the people around me weren't walking down that path.

I was at coffee with my friend Sam—wise and hilarious and strong in his faith—when I told him about my dilemma. "I don't know how to be around my roommates now. I don't want to come across as preachy or pushy. I want them to know that they can still talk to me. I still want to be their friend. But I also want to be true to myself—true to what God is doing in my life, because I'm excited about it. Also, God is doing such amazing things in my life, and I want to share it with other people—which brings me back full circle. I don't want to be preachy or pushy. I have no idea what I'm doing."

Sam considered for a moment before he said words I have never forgotten. He said, "Steph, you may be the only Christian your roommates ever really know."

Wait. What?

"Are you saying that I'm supposed to represent Christianity to them in its entirety, that I'm responsible for what they think about Jesus? That's supposed to make me feel better?!"

He held up his hand and laughed. "Hang on a second. I wasn't done. You aren't responsible for what they think about Jesus, or Christianity as a whole. That's not what I'm saying. You don't need to preach, or perform, or be perfect. But you can show them something they may not get to see anywhere else. You can show them who God is, and what He's all about if you just let them see your relationship with Him. So that's all you have to do. Just live your life with God. Learn the lessons He's teaching you, go on the adventures He's taking you on, live your life with God honestly, and just let them see it."

He was right. I couldn't believe I had forgotten just how impactful that could be.

A few years before, I was in the mess of one of the darkest times of my whole life. I was reeling from a recent breakup, depressed, painfully lonely, and achingly insecure. I was getting ready to go out with my girlfriends one night—convinced that if I just looked good enough, and drank enough, and if some cute guy gave me some attention, I'd feel better. That's how it works right?

So before we went out, I headed to the president of our sorority's bedroom—she was the master at doing hair, and I knew I needed all the help I could get. I sat in a chair pulled up to her desk, a big mirror leaning back against the wall as a makeshift vanity.

As Carolyn teased, and sprayed, and shaped my hair, my eyes wandered down her huge mirror, taking in the photos and clippings and ticket stubs taped along the side. Just as I was about to look away, my eyes landed on a quote. It was in the top, right corner of the mirror, and I couldn't believe I'd missed it before. It was written in pink lipstick in round, perfect letters.

"Look at the nations and watch—and be utterly amazed. For I am going to do something in your days that you would not believe, even if you were told."

In that instant, the world screeched to a halt. My eyes zoomed in on the words, and everything else faded away, quiet and fuzzy in the background. My insides had gone cold, and somehow warm all at the same time. That was it. That was the quote I wanted to define my life. I squeezed my eyes shut tight, trying to picture a life that was so good I wouldn't believe it even if I'd been told. I couldn't picture it, but I wanted to keep trying.

That was the first time I'd ever seen scripture—the first time my life had ever intersected with the Word of God, and it happened because of Carolyn.

Carolyn probably didn't know it at the time, but she really was the only Christian in my life. She was the only example I had of anyone who knew Jesus, of what Jesus was like, of what life as a Christian could look like. She's the only example I had.

But Carolyn didn't push or preach or judge. She didn't isolate herself from us or try to be perfect. She was just herself—she just loved God in her way, honestly, and let us see it in little ways. She didn't write that verse on the mirror for me or thinking I might see it. She wrote it for herself—a reminder she needed in her life. But she did it in a place where it could be shared, where I could bump into it as well.

Sam was right. We can't control what other people think about Jesus or Christianity. We don't need to preach, or perform or be perfect. We just need to be ourselves—following God, learning the lessons He's teaching us, going on the adventures He's taking us on, living our lives with God honestly—and just letting other people see that.

And I'm proof—it really can change someone's life.

How can you do this in your own life today? Maybe it's as simple as having a quiet time (or reading this devotional) at a coffee shop where people can see you. Maybe it's writing a verse on your mirror in lipstick. Or maybe it's sharing a little bit more about what God's doing in your life with a friend. We don't have to perform, or perfect, or push, or preach. We just have to live our lives with God honestly and let other people see it.

Comfort Isn't There, but God Is

"However, as it is written: 'No eye has seen, no ear
has heard, no mind has conceived what God has
prepared for those who love him."

1 Corinthians 2:9

"Do you have peace about it?"

Has anyone ever asked you that as you're getting ready to make a
big decision? They definitely have for me, and I love the question.
I'll take peace with a side of peace every day of the week!

The problem is, as I've been making the decisions that have brought
me closest to God, that have been the most meaningful, the most
transformative, the most beautiful, and the most rewarding—if
you were to have asked me in the midst of those decisions, "Do
you have peace about this?" I would have decisively said, "No!"

When I think of peace, I think of a hot shower on a cold morning,
a fluffy bed at the end of a long day, or a hug from my dad. And
none of those decisions have felt like that.

As I left home to study abroad, when I walked away from my
major just a few months before college graduation, when I went on
my first mission trip to Costa Rica, I felt a lot of things, but none
of them was anything close to a fluffy bed at the end of a long day.

Instead, they felt like knots in my stomach, and tears rolling down
my cheeks. They felt far too big for me, like certain failure. They
felt overwhelming and, on a great many days, I wanted to give up.
I bet I'm not the only one.

If you read through the Bible, most of the people in it had terrifying assignments: go someplace you've never been, build a big boat in the middle of the desert, walk through the ocean, fight a giant, give birth to God's child.

Now, I wasn't there, but I'll bet those things didn't feel like a hot shower on a cold morning either. So lately I'm wondering if peace, the way we usually think about it, is actually more the definition of "comfort," and I'm not so sure that comfort is the path to the plans God has for our lives—not the best ones anyway.

As God and I walk along the journey of my life together, we always pass comfort along the way. We pass comfort, and he's at a warm house, with a cup of coffee and a rocking chair waiting there just for me. Every time we get close to comfort, I slow my pace and start untying my shoes. I'm ready to kick them off and relax for a little while. But every time, God walks right past comfort, turning around to look at me—my shoes half off—and asks, "Are you coming?" So I lace my shoes back up and continue on, and eventually, we come to the edge of a cliff.

He reaches out to hold my hand and asks me if I'm ready. "We're going to jump," He tells me, "But it's going to be so worth it, and I promise, I'm here to catch you."

God and I have stood at the edge of more than a few cliffs together: traveling around the world for a year, writing books, starting a company, leaving my home to move across the country, getting ready to get married—just to name a few. And, in those moments, at the edge of those cliffs, comfort is nowhere to be found. He's back at the cabin in his rocking chair with his coffee—lucky guy! I'm not comfortable; this doesn't feel easy; I don't think I can do it; I'm absolutely not sure about this, and I'm always, always crying.

But you want to know who is there? God. God is there, and that tips the scale just enough to outweigh my fear. So together we jump.

On the other side of those fear-filled decisions have come the sweetest parts of my life. I am who I am, I know God the way I do, and I'm living a life more beautiful than I ever could have planned on my own because I trusted God and took those big, scary leaps. God is right there with us, taking us to places that are more beautiful than we ever could believe, even if we were told.

So as we're making big decisions in our lives, what if we stopped asking, "Do you have peace about this?" Thinking that if this the right thing to do, we should be comfortable, and sure, and know for a fact that this is going to work out. We should be sleeping like a baby, happy, calm, and confident about this whole thing.

Instead, what if we said things like, "God, I'll go," or "I trust you," or "Send me!" or "Whatever you have for me, I'm in."

God tells us not to be afraid. He tells us to be strong and courageous, to trust him, to have faith and not to doubt. I think it's because sometimes, following God takes us beyond our comfort zones to a place where we really need that advice. It's scary sometimes, but it is always, always good. Every single time, it's better than we ever could have asked for or imagined. Life with God always is.

Are you trying to make a big decision these days? Are you struggling to figure out what to do with your life— a particular part of it or the whole dang thing? If you are, know that you are not alone. Most of us are in that place right now; you're in good company. But as you're deciding, weighing the pros and cons, and praying about it, know that the right thing may not feel like the comfortable thing. You may feel afraid, you may feel anxious, you may cry a little or even a whole lot, like me. But remember that feeling this way doesn't mean you took a wrong turn. The biggest, best things in life feel a little scary around the edges. They require a lot from us. They require us to trust God. But remember: God is with you, so keep going. Be strong and courageous. You can do this, it will be so worth it, and He'll never make you do it alone.

Like Sunlight On the Water

"Whatever is true, whatever is noble, whatever
is right, whatever is pure, whatever is lovely,
whatever is admirable—if anything is excellent or
praiseworthy—think about such things."

Philippians 4:8

Elizabeth Gilbert writes, "I want God to play in my bloodstream the way sunlight amuses itself on the water."

Isn't this such a beautiful thought? Every time I read those words, I have to sit back and close my eyes. I can see the sun dancing on water, and I get goosebumps as I think about what it would be like for God to be in my life, around my life, and dancing through my life just like that sun.

However, I know that for me, and I bet sometimes for you too, my relationship with God doesn't always look like that. Sometimes it's monotonous; sometimes it's distant; sometimes it's me going back and forth saying, "I know I should read my Bible, but I really don't want to." Does anyone else play that game? Sometimes my relationship with God is good, and steady, and solid even, it just doesn't dance. But I want it to dance, don't you? So how do we get to this place?

I've mentioned this before, but when Carl and I got married I was a positively terrible cook. I could make macaroni and cheese, and sandwiches, and the chances of me messing either or both up was surprisingly high.

The only thing I could make when we first got married were my grandmother's brownies, my very favorite thing to make even to this day.

I've never been a brownies from the box kind of girl; homemade is the only way to go in my mind. Gramie's brownies are a lighter brown, fluffy and dense somehow all at the same time. If you cook them just right, there's a little crisp on the top that gives way to squishy perfection I can't get enough of.

The recipe is precise, telling you exactly how to get there, exactly how to make them perfect: Melt the butter and the semi-sweet chocolate, make sure you let them cool. Beat the eggs until they're light and fluffy and then slowly (don't do this part too fast!) mix in the sugar, then add the chocolate in too. Last, but not least, fold in the flour, making sure you can still see white swirls dancing and darting through the chocolate. Don't mix the flour in fully; the swirls make it better.

It's a recipe, a path laid out for you: a dash of this, a fold of that, mix them together, and such goodness is just around the corner.

Wouldn't it be nice if there was a recipe for our relationships with God—a path to a faith that dances and sparkles like the sun on the water? In a way, I feel like there is. There's a passage in Philippians that feels like a recipe to me—a dash of this, a dash of that, mapping out our faith in such a beautiful way. It's one of my favorite passages:

> "Rejoice in the Lord always. I will say it again: Rejoice! Let your gentleness be evident to all. The Lord is near. Do not be anxious about anything, but in every situation, by prayer and petition, with thanksgiving, present your requests to God. And the peace of God, which transcends all understanding, will guard your hearts and your minds in Christ Jesus. Finally, brothers and sisters, whatever is true, whatever is noble, whatever is right, whatever is pure, whatever is lovely, whatever is admirable—if anything is excellent or praiseworthy—think about such things. Whatever you have learned or received or heard from me, or seen in me—put it into practice. And the God of peace will be with you."
>
> Philippians 4:4-9

Our relationships with God can become so stale if we let them, so religious—checking boxes and calling that good. But these words gently guide us toward a relationship with God that's fuller, and richer, and more savory. They give us small steps to take that add up to a faith that's more playful, and energetic, and tactile. They send us out on the hunt for God's goodness, sprinkled all throughout our lives, and that's how I've always experienced Him best.

Yes, God is in our churches, and our small groups, and in the time we spend with Him reading scripture. He's in those things 1000%, but He's not limited to those things. He's everywhere if we take the time to see Him. And I think taking the time to look for Him, and to find Him—especially in these excellent, praiseworthy, lovely things—is the recipe for a faith that dances.

My favorite place to see God is in real life, out in the world, traveling to other countries, or drinking a delicious cappuccino. I see God in the laughter of my best friends, and in the way my sweet husband looks into my eyes, in flowers, and sunsets, and heaping plates of pasta. God is everywhere, in everything, hiding in plain sight just waiting to be found. So let's keep our eyes peeled for the lovely, the praiseworthy, the right, and the true. Let's be on the lookout for God today.

Here's my challenge for us today: see if you can find God's goodness in five different places. They can be big things, or small ones—He's in them all. God promises us that when we seek Him, we'll find Him. So let's keep an eye out for Him today.

"Look at the nations and watch—and be utterly
amazed. For I am going to do something in your days
that you would not believe, even if you were told."

Habakkuk 1:5

It's not a sometimes thing; it's an every-time thing. Every time my
husband, Carl, and I go out to dinner, there are always two entrees
I'm torn between, and I simply cannot decide. I sometimes try to
pick one the other; I don't know who I'm fooling though. Because
after casually asking Carl what he's thinking about ordering, and
after pretending for a moment that I'm still pondering, I always
blurt out, "Do you want to get both and share?"

Lucky for me, he always says yes.

If you're not a food sharer, you'd hate going to dinner with me,
because I do this all the time. I want to choose the perfect meal.
I don't want to waste either the experience or the money. I don't
want to pick the wrong one and be stuck with regrets. So I ride the
middle. I sit on the fence. I hedge my bets. And I have to say, this
works wonderfully when it comes to eating at restaurants. It's my
favorite way to do it.

The problem is, we tend to do this fence-riding thing in other areas
of our lives, and it doesn't work out quite so well. Specifically, we
do it in our faith.

When I got back from my time studying abroad in Spain, I wanted
to incorporate Jesus and the things He'd changed and transformed
in me into my life at school, but I didn't know how. I also didn't

want to alienate myself from my old friends or give up parts of my old life that I still really liked. I wanted to take this from Christianity, while still being able to do that on the weekends. I wanted a bite of this and a bite of that.

So I sat on the fence between my old life and my new life for a good long while. I thought I was hedging my bets, keeping myself from making a mistake. I thought I was keeping the best of both worlds, but I soon realized I wasn't keeping the best of either world because I wasn't in far enough to fully experience either. Not only that, but the space between the two was really lonely. I knew something had to change.

A few months later, on the last day of my first mission trip in Costa Rica, our team was packed tightly into the chapel for one more worship session. The head missionary wrapped up the week for us and, as he talked, I thought about my place between my two worlds.

I thought about God and how I'd wanted Jesus to be my best friend so badly in the Sistine Chapel that day. I thought about the conversations I'd had with my best friends in those following months, how excited I'd been as I learned more about who God is and how He teaches us to live our lives.

Then, I remembered how hard it was to come home. I remembered how lonely I'd been feeling back at school, different from who I used to be, but also sort of the same. I remembered back to the night when I felt loneliest of all—when I tearfully accused God of abandoning me, how it felt like He'd made my life more confusing, harder, trickier, not better.

As I looked around the room at my new friends, and as I remembered all of the amazing things I'd seen God do that week, I began to wonder if maybe I'd written God off too soon. I began to consider that maybe, just maybe, He still had the full, beautiful life for me that I'd caught a glimpse of in Spain. Maybe the reason I wasn't seeing it is because I was still sitting high on the fence, because I'd only given Him a small corner of my life to work with.

I hadn't jumped all the way in. But, of course, that's not an easy thing to do—especially when you don't know what's waiting for you on the other side.

I was at Chipotle earlier this week when I started chatting with the woman behind the counter. We were comparing orders, talking about what we get every time we're there. "I always choose the same thing," she said, "Every once in awhile I consider trying something new, but I don't because I'm just not sure I'm going to like it."

I think this is how we feel about jumping in fully with God too. He's offering us something new, something better, He says, life to the full, but, in order to get it, we have to trust Him. We have to trust Him with our lives before we know how it's going to turn out, and that's scary! It really is. But it's only then that we get to truly see what He's capable of doing, both in and through our lives.

And that's the decision I was faced with that day in Costa Rica.

With the wrap-up over, worship began. The words were familiar now, and I was tucked in the small chapel, shoulder to shoulder with people who had gone from strangers to friends in ten short days. And as we began to sing, I decided I was done hedging my bets. I wanted to see what God was capable of when I gave Him not just a part of my life, but the whole thing. I wanted to see what He could do with my life when I jumped in completely. I wanted to see where He would take me.

So with my new friends tucked around me, I put my hands into the air, palms open and as everyone around me sang, I prayed a prayer that's changed everything: "I'm all in, God. I'm all in. Let's do this!"

Whether you've been a Christian forever or for thirty seconds or never in your life, I truly believe that God has an awesome plan in mind for you. I know because I've experienced it.

Life with God is wilder than the wildest roller coaster ride, and safer than your childhood bedroom. It's more thrilling than the greatest adventure, and more delicious than an Italian cappuccino—if you can even believe it.

He's just waiting for us to say yes, to open our hands and our plans and really trust Him. And when we do that, when we go all in, letting Him navigate, we'll go places that are so amazing, we wouldn't believe them even if we were told.

Have you jumped all in with God, or do you feel like you're still sitting on the fence? Do you feel like you've given Him access to every corner of your life, or are there areas you haven't let Him into yet? When we jump all in, we're able to see what God can really do in and through our lives. The things He's capable of are beyond anything we could ever ask for or imagine. So what if today was the day you opened up a new part of your life to Him? What if today was the day you decided to jump?

Acknowledgments

Life is so much better, easier, and certainly more fun when we do it together. I believe it down to my toes. I am who I am, and I'm doing the things I'm doing in the world because of the amazing women by my side and in my corner. And truly, that's never been the case more than when it comes to this devotional.

Writing this devotional was hard. It might be the hardest thing I've ever done. I've put everything I have into these pages, and truthfully, I've put more than I have into these pages because I didn't do it alone. I had my people on my team, working with me, praying for me, bringing me food, and cheering me on along the way. I quite simply could not have done it without them.

And you know what? I wouldn't have it any other way because this book doesn't just feel like a gift from me to you, it feels like a collective gift from so many women I love. It's from us to you, and I just love that. I think we can change the whole entire world when we link arms and work together as women. So I just wanted to take a few minutes to recognize the women (and a few men), who made this devotional possible. I am forever grateful.

Thank you to my dear friend (and editor!) Kacie. Thank you for believing in this book from the beginning, and for continuing to believe in it even when I couldn't on some days. Thank you for knowing my heart so well that you could help me find the words I wanted to say, and for helping me shape them into something so beautiful.

Thank you to my Mom, my most meticulous editor, who put her whole life on hold to help me make this book perfect. Not only were you the grammar queen, but you've been such a wonderful moral support—praying for me and cheering me on literally every step of the way. I cannot thank you enough.

ACKNOWLEDGMENTS

Thank you to my baby sister Kelly, whose editing insight was invaluable. But more than anything, thank you for being a cheerleader when I needed it the most. You quite literally carried me across the finish line. I never would have made it to the end without you.

Thank you to my Daddy, my hero, truly. Thank you for loving me, and encouraging me, and telling me I could do anything I set my mind to. Somewhere along the way, I started to believe you, and this book is proof!

Thank you to TahJah, and Bri, and Marri, my board of advisors, my teammates. Writing a book can be a lonely thing sometimes but, with you by my side, I knew I wasn't in it alone. This book is so much better because of you.

A big thank you to the fine people at Urban Juice here in Nashville. They say writing a book is like having a baby and, if that's the case, I had a strange and unexpected craving for kale and spinach smoothies throughout this whole process. So thank you for providing me with more green smoothies than I ever knew I would need or want. You kept me going!

Also, a big thank you to Karen for helping my sweet mama and me shuffle edits back and forth. You were such a help and such a great support during all our crazy editing. We couldn't have done it without you!

Thank you to Kelsey, Michelle, Carly, Kaitlin, Emily, Heather, Suzy, Hanna, and Kathy for being my very favorite sounding boards. I am so much better at all of this because I have you in my corner. I truly couldn't do this without you.

The world's biggest thank you to all of my dear friends, and amazing family members who show up in the pages of this devotional. You've taught me everything I know about God, and about life, and about love. You are my greatest teachers and my greatest inspiration. I wouldn't have a word to say without you.

A zillion times thank you to my sweet husband Carl for being my favorite teacher, my best friend, my biggest cheerleader, and for putting up with months of frozen pizzas for dinner as I worked to get this finished. I always tell you that you are the best gift I've ever been given and that marrying you is the smartest thing I've ever done. Not one single bit of this could happen if you weren't on my team. And a small (but mighty!) part of that is how beautiful this book is. I don't know if you're allowed to say that about your own book, but I'm going to. It's stunning, and it's because you designed it. You are the best designer I know. Thank you so much for bringing this book to life.

And the biggest thank you of all goes to God, for loving me, and redeeming me, and writing a story for my life that is truly so amazing, I never would have believed it, even if I'd been told.

Last, but certainly not least, I want to say a gigantic thank you to my wonderful launch team. I am so honored to have you on my team and in my corner. I could not have done this without you!

Thank you to...

Karen Aiello, McKenzie Alexander, Malaysia Alford, Kimberly Allred, Rachael Anacker, Ashly Andrews, Amanda Atwood, Manuela Avella, I'Esha Baber, Courtney Bales, Kelsey Diane Barber, Emily Barrus, Josephine Baykal, Bethany Beeghley, Kelsey Beggs, Sara Berry, Bailey Blair, Courtney Blankenship, Meredith Boggs, Stephanie Boggs, Bethany Boynton, Alisha Brickley, Brittany Brown, Courtney Browning, Pauleina Brunnemer, Brittany Bullard, Anna Bundy, Cassie Byrom, Callie Cagwin, Janine Carattini, Allison Carr, Abigail Carter, Camille Catapang, Cathryn Cavazos, Melissa Chaney, Kaitlynn Chase, Amanda Clark, Lauren Clements, Casady Click, Kayla Cook, Brittany Cook, Emily Copeland, Brooke Coplin, Elizabeth Cowin, Charissa Crane, Allie Crume, Shelby Crump, Meagan Davenport, Gabbie Davis, Gwen Debaun, Katie Denis, Megan Denney, Allie DeVries, Stacey Dicken, Emily Dodson, Camye Dudovitz, Whitney Engelbart, Ashlynn Eubanks, Cassidy Fernandez, Carly Fields, Chloe Finnigan, Shauna Francis, Nicole Fredlund, Olivia Frink, Chelsey Fuller, Cayleigh

Gallimore, Reychel Garren, Shawna George, Hannah Gillies, Kelsey Gipson, Annie Gray, Rachel Grayson, Kari Griffis, Jodi Grubbs, Lindsay Grzymski, Catherine Hanson, Kara Harner, Kelsey Hedspeth, Jesica Hernandez, Leighan Hernandez, Janet Heslop, Melany Hire, Tiffany Hodge, Ashley Hollister, Lindsey Hood, Lisa Hoover, Holly Hopkins, Allison Howe, Caroline Hubbard, Brooke Hunter, Erica Huntsman, Haley Jacobs, Sarah Jeffrey, Mallory Jones, Ashley Jones, Mary-Kate Kaminski, Rakenzi Kelly, Kaia Kena, Susannah Kindrick, Kaitlyn Kirksey, Christi Koons,, Lindsey Krekling, Jessica Krpejs, Joy Kuykendall, Rose Lafreniere, Elisa Lehto, Katie Lenger, Mary Lewis, Michelle Lindsay, Yolanda Limon, Molly Livingstone, Emily Long, Taylor Lowery, Ellie Ludwig, Jessica Malick, Debbie Martin, Kelly Martin, Elizabeth Matteson, Elizabeth Mayberry, Allison Melton, Kellie Metzker, Lizzie Mikita, Claire Mikita, Caitlin Milam, Heather Moore, Anna Morgan, Kristen Morris, Cassandra Naranjo, Reagan Nash, Hillary Nelson, Logan Nichols, Stephanie Niten, Heather Owen, Brittany Panus, Jordan Parsons, Nicole Grace Pastrana, Elizabeth Pea, Susan Perry, Leeann Perry, Ashley Peterson, Wendy Phillips, Jessie Pierce, Kaci Pollack, Bailey Posey, Merrilee Prill, Victoria Provost, Brooke Pugsley, Hannah Pursel, Kayla Rabalais, Hannah Ramey, Breeze Raxter, Emily Reese, Lindy Reynolds, Chantell Rice, Rhona Riley, Danielle Roberts, Madalyn Rogers, Meredith Russell, Sherri Rutherford, Jessica Rutkowski, Angela Sangalang, Kimberly Sausman, Kate Schoenherr, Kylie Scruggs, Ashley Shaw, Maddi Shea, Kristen Shealy, Bethany Sheets, Keri Simpson, Amanda Smith, Delaney Smith, Stephanie Smith, Mackenzie Smitherman, Shelby Sojka, Kelsey Sprague, Ansley St. John, Ashley Stafford, Danielle Staudte, Lauren Steele, Miranda Steward, Christina Sutton, Ashleigh Swanson, Elizabeth Tart, Jessica Taylor, Grace Taylor, Giselle Tellerin Kuipers, Andrea Tessaro, Katie Thomas, Heather Trapp, Katie Uken, Laura Van Eck, Haley Vaught, Bailey Vernon, Carmen Vigil, Emily Voigt, Ashlynn Waddill, Joanne Wagner, Jocelyn Walters, Kelsea Watkins, Kiki Weitzel, Jill White, Kaitlyn Whitlock, Mary Wilk, Megan Williams, Kelsie Witt, Maddie Witzke, Erin Wolcott, Sharon Yan, Kirstin Yates, Katelynn Young, Jane Zeman, and Kylie Zweifel!

Connect with Stephanie

Hey sweet friend,

Thank you so much for reading this devotional! I cannot tell you how much it means to me that we've gotten to spend time together over these last few months!

We've reached the end of the devotional, but the best news is that this is only the beginning. It's only the beginning for you and God, because even if you've been a Christian all your life, God is an infinite well of love, and joy, and growth, and adventure. He has so much more depth and goodness in store for you. I can't wait to see where He takes you next.

This is only the beginning for us as well because I have so many other fun things I'd love to share with you!

First and foremost, I'd love to invite you into the community my sweet readers and I have created online. You can find me writing regularly at StephanieMayWilson.com, where I write all about friendship, faith, relationships, and self-confidence. I always say that my little corner of the internet is like a girls' night at your best friends house—we're navigating life, and doing it together, and I would love to have you join us!

I also think it's high time we made our friendship official, don't you? You can find me on Instagram (@SMayWilson), and on Facebook (Facebook.com/LipstickGospel), and I would love to connect with you! Come on over and say hi!

Last, but certainly not least, there are a few more resources I would just love to share with you. I'll tell you all about them in the next few pages, so make sure to check them out!

Again, thank you so much for joining me for this devotional. It has been such an honor to get to spend time with you over the last few months.

I can't wait to connect again soon!

All my love,

Stephanie

The Lipstick Gospel Prayer Journal

HOW TO TALK TO GOD LIKE HE'S YOUR BEST FRIEND

The thing I've always found to be true about relationships is that the more time we spend together, and the more we open up to each other, the closer we feel. This is true in all of our relationships, and it's true with God too.

Whether you've known Him all your life, or are getting to know Him for the very first time, this 90-day prayer journal is a practical way of going deeper in your relationship with God. The daily prompts will help you to curl up and spend time with Him—telling Him about your life, your hopes, your dreams, and your fears—the things you find to be lovely, and hard, and really really funny.

More than ever before, we're getting to know the God who created the heavens and the earth, the God who is big and sweeping and powerful and majestic. But we're also getting to know the God who wants to become our very best friend. He's become mine, and I know He wants to become yours too.

You can pick up a copy of *The Lipstick Gospel Prayer Journal* at SMayWilsonShop.com!

The Lipstick Gospel is now available in paperback!

Inspired by a broken heart and a wicked hangover, sorority girl Stephanie May Wilson throws in the towel on the life she's been living and packs her bags for a pilgrimage across three continents. Like so many great travelers before her, she finds herself and something completely unexpected along the way. Exploding preconceived notions that Christianity is for grandmas and girls with ugly shoes, *The Lipstick Gospel* is the story of how one girl found God in heartbreak, the Sistine Chapel, and the perfect cappuccino.

Here's what a few sweet readers had to say:

"*The Lipstick Gospel* is an amazing book that draws you in from the beginning. You'll want to hug your girlfriends, travel the world, dance with a bull-fighter, and love the God she loves."

Stacy

"Her story speaks volumes to the kind of life you can have in Christ. Not a boring, vanilla-type life, but a fun, adventurous, exciting life—way more than you could ever imagine. Trust me, you'll want this book to last forever."

Lottie

Pick up a copy for yourself or for a friend at SMayWilsonShop.com!

The Real Girls Guide to Taking It All Off

A SMALL GROUP GUIDE TO CULTIVATING THE COMMUNITY YOU'VE ALWAYS WANTED

Whether you're looking to connect with old friends, to go deeper with new friends, or for the next study for your small group, our lives are so much better (and more fun!) when we have best friends to share them with, and this guide is the perfect way to get there!

Here's what one sweet reader had to say about it:

"My group and I just finished your study, *Taking It All Off*, and we absolutely loved it! Our group wasn't super close to begin with, we were all friends of friends, but now we couldn't be closer. In the study you asked questions that I would never think to ask and talking through those things together transformed our group. They transformed me! Now I have five new best friends, and I'm so grateful to this guide for making that happen. Seriously, best decision ever!"

Cara

Go to StephanieMayWilson.com/FirstChapterFree to learn more about The Real Girls Guide To Taking It All Off, and to download the first chapter for free!

Make the Most of Your Single Life

AN ONLINE COURSE
BY STEPHANIE MAY WILSON

Join Stephanie (and an amazing community of new friends!) as you transform what can feel like a season of waiting into a season of passion, purpose, and preparation.

Here's what a few sweet friends had to say about the course:

"Because of this course, I feel a million times more confident in my single life, a million times more confident in the prospect of dating, and a million times more loving toward myself and this season of life I'm in!"

Devon

"This course made me so excited to live in the here and now, and it boosted my confidence and self-esteem. I feel more empowered and confident in putting myself out there, but more than that, I feel overwhelmed by God's love and all that He is doing for me right now. I found so much joy and peace through this course. It absolutely exceeded by expectations."

Alexis

"This course is the sermon on singleness you've always wanted but have never found… helpful, applicable, relatable, and actually enjoyable. It's so worth your time and money."

Shelby

Doors to the course are only open a few times a year, so head to LoveYourSingleLife.com to find out more, and to put your name on the waiting list!

Stephanie May Wilson

is an author, blogger, speaker, and best friend who writes about the kinds of things you'd talk about at a girls' night at your best friends house: friendship, faith, relationships, and self-confidence. She says, "We're navigating life, and doing it together!"

You can join the conversation at StephanieMayWilson.com, or check out her first book, *The Lipstick Gospel*! It's her story of finding God in heartbreak, the Sistine Chapel, and the perfect cappuccino. You can also catch up with her on Instagram @smaywilson. She'd love to meet you!